ALESSANDRO SCARLATTI:

HIS LIFE AND WORKS

Scraggs Sculp

ALESSANDRO SCARLATTI:
HIS LIFE AND WORKS

BY

EDWARD J. DENT

SOMETIME FELLOW OF KING'S COLLEGE, CAMBRIDGE

New Impression
with preface and additional notes by
FRANK WALKER

LONDON
EDWARD ARNOLD (PUBLISHERS) LTD.

First published 1905
New impression 1960

MADE AND PRINTED BY OFFSET IN GREAT BRITAIN BY
WILLIAM CLOWES AND SONS, LIMITED, LONDON AND BECCLES

TO

CHARLES HARFORD LLOYD
M.A., MUS.DOC., PRECENTOR OF ETON COLLEGE

THIS BOOK

IS GRATEFULLY AND AFFECTIONATELY

DEDICATED

BY ONE OF HIS EARLIEST
ETON PUPILS

PREFATORY NOTE TO THE NEW IMPRESSION

DURING my war-time stay in Italy, whenever I met musicians and musicologists they always asked about the welfare of Professor Dent, who was, by a long way, the best known to them and most respected of our musical scholars. Often they spoke of this book. The late Alessandro Longo, who had emerged from retirement to become Director of the Naples Conservatorio in the difficult interim period, presented me with a copy of his *Symphonia* (Naples, 1924), a poem in Dantean *terza rima*. This tells of his encounter with Domenico Scarlatti, accompanied by a large and ferocious cat (of the " Cats' Fugue "), and how he was led by Domenico, as Dante was by Virgil, on a tour of the special Paradise for musicians, where all the composers of all the ages have at their service the greatest performers who ever lived. In the course of his tour, in the eleventh Canto, Longo is introduced to Domenico's father, Alessandro Scarlatti, and has pleasure in telling him :—

> *Di dì in dì la nebbia si disserra*
> *A te d'intorno, e ciò, per caso strano,*
> *Alla nebbiosa devesi Inghilterra ;*
> *Dove Eduardo Dent, un anglicano*
> *Che sì conosce l'arte antica, ed ama,*
> *Da non equivocar tra loglio e grano,*
> *Molto adoprossi a ravvivar tua fama ;*
> *Ed un suo libro d'abile scrittura*
> *I musicisti a l'opera tua richiama.*

" Eduardo Dent, un anglicano "—this amused him considerably, when I showed it to him, after the war.

I think he looked back with particular affection to this, his first book. Obviously a labour of love, it must have recalled to him his youth, and wanderings in unspoilt Italy before the age of cars and scooters, and the excitement of original research and discovery.

After more than half a century the value of the book has hardly diminished at all. The discussion of the music needs no revision. Later research, however, has brought to light some additional biographical facts beginning with the precise date and place of Scarlatti's birth. Since the photographic reproduction of the original text did not permit revision, I have dealt with the additional material in a series of notes at the end of the book. Asterisks in the margin of the text indicate topics to which the added notes refer. The appendix on the Scarlatti family, originally on page 205, has been omitted altogether. The most complete and accurate family tree is that in Ralph Kirkpatrick's *Domenico Scarlatti* (1953).

I have to thank the Editor of the *Music Review* for permission to reprint some of my " Notes on the Scarlattis ".

FRANK WALKER

AUTHOR'S PREFACE

CONSIDERING the celebrity which Alessandro Scarlatti enjoyed during his lifetime, and the important position which he occupies in the history of music, it is strange that so little attention has been paid to him. This is partly due to the fact that the modern period of careful research in matters of musical history which produced Spitta's Bach, Chrysander's Handel, Jahn's Mozart, and Thayer's Beethoven, was also marked by a decided reaction against that enthusiasm for Italian music which flourished in the days of Santini, Kiesewetter, Winterfeld, and Fétis. There are, however, signs of a revival of interest at the present day; the labours of Dr. Emil Vogel, Dr. Hugo Goldschmidt, M. Romain Rolland, Professor Kretschmar, and Sir Hubert Parry have done much for the history of the Italian music of the seventeenth century.

But Alessandro Scarlatti, though he has by no means been forgotten by them, has not been treated in any great detail; and I hope that this biography, if it does not succeed in explaining more fully his relation to the music that preceded and followed him, may at least serve as a useful foundation for future workers in the same field.

To give a list of books consulted seems superfluous; for the general history of Italian music in the seventeenth and eighteenth centuries several bibliographies have recently been printed, and for Alessandro Scarlatti there are no special authorities. Grove's *Dictionary of Music and Musicians* gives practically all the information that previous biographers have recorded. The difficulty of collecting and sifting the large mass of scattered biographical material no doubt goes far to account for the incompleteness not only of Florimo, Villarosa, and Gennaro Grossi, but also of

Burney and Hawkins; but it has been greatly lightened
by modern Italian historians of the musical drama, such
as Signor A. Ademollo (*I teatri di Roma nel secolo xvii.*,
Rome, 1888), Professor Benedetto Croce (*I teatri di
Napoli nei secoli xv.–xviii.*, Naples, 1891), Professor
Corrado Ricci (*I teatri di Bologna nei secoli xvii. e
xviii.*, Bologna, 1888), and Cav. Taddeo Wiel (*I teatri
veneziani nel secolo xviii.*, Venice, 1892), to whose labours
I am much indebted. Wherever possible, however, I
have consulted original documents, and have given exact
references to them throughout the book. 1 have also
derived valuable assistance (though less directly) from
Vernon Lee's *Studies of the Eighteenth Century in Italy*,
and Professor Corrado Ricci's *Vita Barocca* (Milan, 1904).

The catalogue will give some idea of the large number
of Scarlatti's compositions that exist in manuscript. Autographs are comparatively rare; but contemporary copies
are very numerous, made for the most part by three or
four copyists who seem to have been regularly employed
by Scarlatti, and whose work is extremely accurate. Of
modern copies the most numerous and the most important
are those made by Fortunato Santini. The originals of
many of these, either autographs or contemporary copies,
are still accessible, but for much of the church music we
are obliged to accept Santini's copies for want of anything
better, until it becomes less difficult for the foreigner and
the heretic to obtain admission to Italian ecclesiastical
libraries.[1] They are not very accurate, either in the notes
themselves or in the headings and titles, which are sometimes of great value in determining the date of a composition. Moreover, Santini, like other librarians of his
time, has a tendency to ascribe to Scarlatti any anonymous composition of his period, and to give the title of
cantata to almost any secular vocal composition. Other

---

[1] This does not apply to the Vatican or to Montecassino, where every
facility is offered for research.

modern manuscripts are comparatively rare and nearly always traceable to more authoritative originals.

The identification of libretti and of detached airs from operas has presented some difficulty. The airs seldom bear the name of the opera from which they are taken, and from 1679 to 1709 the libretti of Scarlatti's operas (and by no means only of Scarlatti's) hardly ever bear his name. We may expect to find the names of the *impresario*, the ballet-master, the scene-painter, and (less often) the poet; but it is extremely rare to find the name of the composer of the music. However, with the help of the admirably arranged collections of the libretti at Naples (R. Conservatorio di Musica), Bologna (Liceo Musicale), and Brussels (Conservatoire), together with M. Alfred Wotquenne's invaluable *Catalogue des livrets italiens du xviiᵉ siècle* (Brussels, 1901), and an alphabetical index of first lines of arias from all Scarlatti's extant operas, which I prepared myself, but which there is not room to print here, a certain amount of identification has been done ; but several hundred airs still remain that I have not been able to assign to their proper dates and places.

It only remains for me to express my sincerest thanks to the librarians of the various libraries in which I have worked, a list of which precedes the catalogue, not forgetting the much valued kindness shown to me in some libraries—notably at Florence, Bologna, and Naples—by subordinate members of the library staff. To Mr. Barclay Squire (British Museum) and M. Alfred Wotquenne (Brussels Conservatoire) I am exceptionally indebted for continued kind assistance, as well as generous contribution of important material. My thanks are also due to Dr. H. P. Allen (Oxford), Mgr. Azzocchi (*Prefetto della musica* at S. Maria Maggiore, Rome), Mgr. Bartolini (*Custode Generale d'Arcadia*, Rome), Mgr. Beccaria (Palermo), Cav. Antonio D'Ali (Trapani), Miss Dent, Col. H. A. Douglas (Rome), Mr. F. G. Edwards, Mgr. Fratta

(Ferrara), Mr. H. D. Grissell (Rome), Comm. Alessandro
Kraus (Florence), Cav. Giacomo Leo (Naples), Prof.
Alessandro Longo (Naples), Comm. Carlo Lozzi (Rome),
Comm. G. Moriconi (Rome), Miss Paget (Florence), Sir
Walter Parratt, Prof. A. Scontrino (Florence), and Dr.
Voltz (Darmstadt), for courteous assistance of various
kinds, as well as to Messrs. Breitkopf and Haertel for
kindly giving me permission to reprint (with some correc-
tions) the list of Scarlatti's operas, which appeared first
in the *Sammelband der Internationalen Musikgesellschaft*
for November 1902.

By the kindness of Mr. J. S. Shedlock, I was recently
allowed to inspect the manuscript volume of Scarlatti's
harpsichord and organ music described by him in the
Sammelband der Internationalen Musikgesellschaft for
November 1904; but the printing of this book was then
so far advanced that it was too late for me to ask permission to discuss it. For the textual criticism of this
department of Scarlatti's work it is undoubtedly the most
important and authoritative manuscript that I have seen;
nevertheless, except for the organ music, which shows
us Scarlatti in a hitherto unknown capacity, the historical
and musical value of the pieces peculiar to it would
not have much affected my account of Scarlatti as a
composer of instrumental music.

The portrait of Alessandro Scarlatti which forms the
frontispiece of this book is reproduced from the engraving
in the *Biografia degli Uomini illustri del Regno di Napoli*
(Naples 1819). This engraving seems to have been taken
from an oil painting attributed to Francesco Solimena, now
in the possession of the R. Conservatorio di Musica at
Naples, for the direct reproduction of which I regret to
say that I was unable to obtain permission. It is also the
source of various unimportant lithographed and engraved
portraits which all exhibit the mannerisms of their day
rather than fidelity to the original.

CONTENTS

CHAPTER I

ALESSANDRO SCARLATTI

ALESSANDRO SCARLATTI

CHAPTER I

EARLY YEARS; ROME, 1679-1684

"THE Renaissance of Music" is a name often given to
that change of style which spread over the art towards the
end of the sixteenth century. If we consider the movement in its initial phase only, the title is sufficiently representative of the truth. The change was essentially a
return to nature, and was intended to be a return to the
musical ideals of ancient Greece. That the new spirit
should not have dominated the art of music, even in Italy,
until the other arts had submitted to its influence for a
hundred years and more, need not surprise us. The tendencies of the Renaissance may indeed be traced dimly
even through the polyphonic music of the age of Palestrina ;
but the fact that the Church had a practical monopoly of
scientific music is sufficient to explain the lack of enterprise
in a definitely secular direction. Musicians who had been
brought up to devote their skill to the service of the Church
were not likely to be much affected by the trend of general
culture in the direction of Hellenism. Almost always
ecclesiastics themselves, their learning was naturally confined to the narrow channel of their own trade, and they
would be the less likely to attempt radical innovations
when they were in possession of an art which had just
reached a stage of technique that offered an apparently
unlimited vista of possible development. Painters and
sculptors could hardly help being influenced by the new
learning ; painting and sculpture required subjects to

A

illustrate, and the truth to nature of their representations could in most cases be judged by the eyes of all. Music, which even with all the resources of the twentieth century cannot definitely represent any visible object whatever, could hardly make an appreciable appeal to its audience in that direction at the time when one of the principal means of serious expression seems to have been the making of puns on the Guidonian syllables.

The first decisive step, therefore, was made not by the learned contrapuntists, but by a body of amateurs. The noble Florentines to whom we owe the birth of the musical Renaissance brought very little technical ability to bear on their experiments; but they brought what perhaps only noble Florentine amateurs could have brought—a pure and lofty ideal moulded by the Hellenistic influences of contemporary literature, and entirely free from ecclesiastical prejudice. Yet in studying the history of music from this point onwards, we must beware of letting ourselves be misled by the idea that the Renaissance of music followed a course exactly parallel to that of the Renaissance of the plastic arts. Peri's "Euridice" may be said to exhibit the technical ability of a Giotto applied to the expressive intention of a Botticelli; with the spread of the "new music" to Mantua, Rome, and Venice fresh influences made themselves felt, and caused the art to develop in a direction very different from that which Bardi and his friends had imagined. "Dafne" and "Euridice" were literary experiments addressed only to cultured audiences; Monteverdi and Cavalli seized on the musical and spectacular elements which they presented, and transformed a resuscitated Greek tragedy into Italian opera, a new creation full of its own natural life and energy. Freed from the restraining influence of Florentine Hellenists, encouraged either by splendour-loving courts or by a pleasure-seeking populace, to whom spectacular effect counted for a good deal more than literary elegance, this second generation of composers catered frankly for the taste of their time, and in an age notorious for extravagance in every direction were deter-

mined not to be left behind by the exponents of the sister
arts.   Indeed, so successful were their efforts that towards
the latter part of the seventeenth century music had not
only overtaken, but to some extent, outdistanced its rivals
in importance and popularity.

For the whole of the seventeenth century the history
of Italian music is the history of the opera.   Other forms
were cultivated, but to a comparatively slight extent, and
they were in almost all cases merely tributaries to the main
stream of progress.   This importance of the musical drama
accounts largely for the strange way in which Italian music
developed from "Euridice" to "Don Giovanni."   The
opera brought music into immediate contact with dramatic
poetry and the plastic arts, united for theatrical purposes
under the leadership of architecture.   We have only to
glance at the building of the age to see the sort of influences to which music was being submitted.   Florence
still preserved some remnant of her ancient traditions of
purity of style, but Venice and Rome, followed by the
smaller capitals, were rioting in all that exuberance of the
baroque which we associate with the names of Longhena
and Bernini, Guido Reni and Luca Giordano.   Some
courage is required to defend the baroque style of architecture at the present day.   It was so essentially the
expression of the pomps and vanities of its own time that
the modern spectator, unable to enter into the details of
its environment, can see nothing but the dismal wreck of
its mannerisms and affectations in its faded ceilings, its
crumbling stucco, and its mutilated marbles.   But churches
and palaces are only a small part of the life of the seventeenth century, and though to us they are its most conspicuous monuments, they are in reality not the most
representative.   The true moving spirit of the baroque
must be looked for in the social life, in the literature, the
drama, and the music of the period.   This is not the place
to treat in detail of the social history of "that strange and
savage century in which all was baroque, from its painting
to its passions, from its manners to its crimes, from its

feastings to its funerals, from its heroes to its cowards," which has recently been depicted by Professor Corrado Ricci,[1] not only with his customary learning, but also with an illuminating sense of the grotesque that throws all its characteristic lights and shadows into the sharpest possible relief.   For us the opera sums up in brief all the most typical features of the baroque.   When Venice possessed seventeen opera-houses, when Bologna was so insanely devoted to music that the despairing Cardinal Legate was driven to issue an edict (in 1686) forbidding any woman, whatever her age or condition, the nuns included, to receive instruction in music from any man, however closely he might be related to her, when Dukes of Modena and Doges of Venice were quarrelling in public over the affections of a prima donna, there can be no doubt about the opera being the most important art-form, and the most characteristic expression of the ideas of the period.

And this is only the natural result of the fact that of all art-forms the opera afforded the most ample scope for the realization of those ideas.   To the minds of most of us the baroque is represented by the typical church façade of the seventeenth century, on which the " pious orgies " of saints and angels as well as of pillars and pediments are petrified for all time in the decent convulsions of a symmetrical earthquake.   But if it offends us, the fault is less often that of the design than of the limitations imposed by the material; and we are ourselves frequently to blame for not regarding it with the necessary eye for the grotesque.   We are brought a step nearer towards the baroque ideal by such a work as Fumiani's famous ceiling in the church of S. Pantaleone at Venice.   The architect who carried out his designs in solid stone and marble was necessarily limited by the tiresome consideration that they had to be made to stand firm somehow or other.   The decorator of ceilings might freely disregard the laws of gravity; but even his advantages were slight compared with those of the theatrical scene-painter.   We

[1] *Vita Barocca.* Milan, 1904.

need only turn to the illustrations that adorn the more sumptuous libretti of the day, or, still better, to the original designs to be found in many public collections, to see what possibilities were offered by the stage to the unrestrained imagination of the architect. Paint and canvas could raise to an appearance of solidity infinite perspectives of galleries and colonnades magnificent beyond the most ambitious dreams of the Pope himself. The statues that adorned them could come to life and descend from their pedestals to take part in a ballet; and before the open-mouthed spectators had had time to weary of it, the scene could vanish, to be succeeded by another and yet another, each if possible more surprising than its predecessor in its formal eccentricity of splendour.

How important the scenery was to the baroque opera is clear also from the names of the scene-painters, among whom we often find such distinguished artists as Bibbiena and Antonio Canale; and it may be noted that their names are often given in libretti that make no mention whatever of the composer of the music. And though our imaginations may find it difficult to realize the enthusiasm which their wonderful erections aroused, yet they are sufficiently important to us to require consideration in some detail on account of their intimate connexion with the music of the period. The passion for building which had been characteristic of the best period of the Renaissance was still strong; the characteristic tendency of the baroque was the strange attempt to inspire the essential solidity and repose of architecture with the restless animation and unrestrained extravagance that marked the whole life of the century. The ideal creation would have been an architecture not only of unlimited magnificence, but alive with perpetual movement in every part, a transformation-scene that should include the whole of time and space, along with the whole range of human passions and emotions, not forgetting the antics of Arlecchino, Brighella, and the Dottor Graziano.

It is hardly necessary to point out to the modern reader

that what could never be realized for the eye might at any rate be brought considerably nearer realization for the ear. The primitive state of musical technique at the beginning of the seventeenth century naturally made it impossible at first for music to attain the same level of impressiveness as the other arts; but progress was rapid, and after a hundred years music had so far advanced as to be fully recognized as the art which most completely satisfied the needs of the time. Goethe's well-known comparison of architecture to frozen music, apt enough in his own day, though less intelligible to modern concert-goers, was still truer of the music and of the architecture that preceded him by two or three generations. While architecture, on the stage, was adopting every expedient to produce an illusive sense of motion, music, which if it cease to move, ceases to exist, was passing through a phase almost aggressively architectural in the severe symmetry of its forms. The baroque opera is, in fact, the bridge by which the artistic emotions of Italy passed finally from architecture as a chief means of expression to music, thus calling into existence the classical school of the early eighteenth century in which Haydn, Mozart, and Beethoven were to learn the first principles of the sonata and the symphony. And this early structural development of music, although, like all such movements, it was the work of many hands, owed its chief greatness to Alessandro Scarlatti. Architectural in principle with a more than Palladian severity, yet always vigorous in outline and luxuriant in decorative detail, he represents the baroque style at its best, and his working life of nearly fifty years, during which he never failed to maintain an astonishing fertility of production as well as a high standard of style, covers the extremely interesting period of transition from the earlier Renaissance of music to the decorous classicism of the eighteenth century.

* It has been generally asserted that Alessandro Scarlatti was born in 1659, at Trapani in Sicily. No record of his

birth or of his early years has yet been found, in spite of careful search in Trapani and the neighbourhood; the assertion rests solely on the evidence of an autograph score of the opera " Pompeo," said to bear the inscription, " *Musica del Signor Alessandro Scarlatti da Trapani.*" This score was seen by Fétis in the possession of Gaspare Selvaggi,[1] but, like many other manuscripts described by him, it is not to be found now. Selvaggi's collection of music was bought by the Marquis of Northampton, and presented by him to the British Museum in 1847; but the score of " Pompeo" is not there. There is a score of " Pompeo" (the only one known) in the Fétis collection, now in the Royal Library at Brussels; but it is not autograph, and it does not mention the composer's birthplace. In the records of the Arcadian Academy at Rome, Scarlatti is described as a native of Palermo, but neither the original manuscript list of members nor those subsequently printed can be relied upon for absolute accuracy any more than the *Biographie Universelle des Musiciens.* That he was a Sicilian is quite certain, as will be seen later; and the year of his birth (1658 or 1659) is deduced from the statement on his tombstone that he died on October 24, 1725, at the age of sixty-six.

Of his parentage nothing whatever is known. In order to account for the absence of a baptismal register at Trapani, it has been ingeniously suggested that his father must have been a soldier, in which case he would have been baptized in the chapel of the fortress, of which no records were kept. But it seems easier to suppose that he was born elsewhere. The name Scarlatti is not Sicilian at all, but Tuscan. If he was of Sicilian origin, his real name was probably *Sgarlata* or *Scarlata*, both fairly common in Sicily then and now; and his name is spelled *Scarlati* in the archives at Naples and in Conforto's Diary.

[1] Florimo also professed to have seen it, and gives the inscription as " *Pompeo del Cav. Alessandro Scarlatti di Trapani.*" As "Pompeo" was composed in 1683, and Scarlatti does not appear to have received the title of *Cavaliere* before 1716, Florimo's statement hardly deserves very much confidence.

On the other hand, those libretti that mention his name invariably print it, as he invariably signed it himself, *Scarlatti.* It is conceivable that he came of a Tuscan stock ; but this is a mere conjecture. It may be noted that he hardly ever set to music words in the dialect of Naples ; his one comic opera is all in Italian, though composed after a long residence in Naples, for a theatre which for some years had made a speciality of comic operas in Neapolitan. Moreover, his early life appears to have been spent mostly in Northern Italy.

Before 1679 we have no definite information about him. Various statements have been made with regard to his teachers, but none are supported by trustworthy evidence. The tradition which finds most credence is that he was a pupil of Carissimi, and it probably represents the truth, though it must not be forgotten that Carissimi died at an advanced age when Scarlatti was only fifteen. That he should have been a pupil of Giovanni Salvatore and Francesco Provenzale at Naples was a natural conjecture for those biographers who believed Naples to have been his birthplace. But there is no reason to suppose that he had any connexion with Naples before 1684 ; indeed it will be shown later that he was regarded as a stranger there when he received his appointment as Maestro di Cappella. Besides, the musical life of Naples was at this period so far behind that of Rome and Northern Italy that it is inconceivable that Scarlatti should have found opportunities there for developing his talents as he did. The first operatic performance in Naples seems to have been that of Monteverdi's " Nerone," given in 1651 by the *Febi Armonici*, a company of Venetian singers who continued their representations of Venetian operas until Naples was able to start a school of its own under the lead of Francesco Provenzale. His " Teseo" appeared in 1658, and his last opera, " Lo Schiavo di sua Moglie," in 1671 ; but both this and " La Stellidaura Vendicata " (1670), the only operas of his that remain, show him to have been far inferior to his Venetian and Roman contemporaries.

The early compositions of Alessandro Scarlatti point clearly to the influence of the Roman master Carissimi, and to that of Cavalli, Cesti, and Legrenzi, who may legitimately be classed as Venetians. He was also much influenced by Stradella, whose work seems to have been done mostly in Rome and Northern Italy. If we look at any of the contemporary manuscript collections that include early chamber-cantatas by Scarlatti, we shall be sure to find him in Stradella's company, along with other north Italian composers, such as Alessandro Melani, Perti, Gasparini, and Pier Simone Agostini. And no sooner had he made a success in Rome with his first opera, "Gli Equivoci nel Sembiante," than his work was immediately in demand at Bologna and Modena, besides smaller places in Northern Italy, probably including the private theatre of the Contarini family at Piazzola near Venice.

It is impossible to arrive at the exact chronology of Scarlatti's early Roman works. Writing to Ferdinand de' Medici in 1705, he says that he has composed eighty-eight operas in less than twenty-three years;[1] but of those eighty-eight only thirty-five have survived, and not all of them complete. This would place his first opera soon after 1682, when he was twenty-three years old; but there is no doubt that "Gli Equivoci" was produced as far back as 1679. It is indeed possible that "Gli Equivoci" was not his first opera; it is, however, the earliest that has survived, and seems to have been the first that brought him fame.

In any case we may be fairly certain that some of the chamber-cantatas date from still earlier years, and these are of such importance as to call for treatment in some detail. The immense popularity of the chamber-cantata during the whole of the seventeenth and the early part of the eighteenth century is a phenomenon for which musical historians seem to have had some difficulty in accounting. Even Sir Hubert Parry[2] finds it "a strange puzzle that a

---

[1] Not "thirty-three," as erroneously printed by Puliti.
[2] "Oxford History of Music," vol. iii. p. 393.

form of art which is so undeniably long-winded should have been so popular." But the puzzle is not quite so strange when we consider the remarks which immediately follow. "It would appear to have been the main staple of domestic vocal music for many generations, and it is certainly creditable to the taste of the prosperous classes that a branch of art which had such distinguished qualities should have been so much in demand; for the standard of style, notwithstanding obvious defects, is always high." It may seem ridiculous at the present day to maintain that music which is acknowledged to be good is therefore sure to be popular; but we must remember that music in the seventeenth century occupied a different position to that which it occupies in the twentieth. The music of the people in seventeenth-century Italy is practically unknown to us; the music that has survived has been preserved in the libraries of princes and nobles, or in those of churches. Students of seventeenth-century Italian music know how rare it is to find more than a single manuscript copy of any given composition; and we may safely assume that the chamber-cantata was cultivated only by those who were ready to bring serious enthusiasm to bear on any music that they could get. That the *cantata a voce sola* should have been the favourite musical form is by no means strange. To understand the music of the seventeenth century, we must bear in mind, above all things, that the supreme executive artist of the time was the singer. Not only was the technique of vocalization by far the most advanced, but a very much higher intellectual standard was expected and attained than modern composers even hope for. Justly indignant if a singer presume to embellish Wagner or Brahms with extemporary graces, we find it inconceivable that Scarlatti and his contemporaries should have expected such additions as a matter of course; and we can hardly realize that in elaborating his written melodies in performance with such exquisite ornaments as Geminiani records, Corelli was only following the example of the great singers of his generation. Before Corelli and his

school had shown that from a purely musical point of view
the violin could do as much as the voice and a good deal
more, there could have been no instrumental competition
against the singers. The *cembalo* had no sustaining power;
the large organ, besides being unwieldy, was confined to
the churches, and the resources of the small regals and
organi di legno were very limited; of wind instruments the
trumpet alone had an advanced technique, but its imperfect
scale necessarily caused it to take a subordinate position.
The voice was the only instrument for which chamber-
music of a really advanced type could be written; it was the
only instrument which combined a finished technique with
the greatest variety of beautiful tone-colour, and which in
the majority of cases was governed by minds of a high
order of intelligence. Besides, the spirit of the Renaissance had not yet died out, and the ancient Greek principle,
that the function of music is to express the words of a poet,
was still fresh in the minds of composers.

U nder these circumstances it need not surprise us to
find that at the end of the seventeenth century the
chamber-cantata was at the climax of its excellence and
popularity among serious lovers of music in Italy; indeed,
it is to the seventeenth century what the violin-sonata
is to the nineteenth. Alessandro Scarlatti is at once its
greatest and its most fertile exponent. His extant cantatas number over five hundred, and every phase of his
artistic development is reflected in them. They are of
very special importance, because they always represent
the composer in earnest. Some are dull, but not one
is trivial or vulgar; many are of great beauty, and the
majority of them are deeply interesting as studies in
composition.

The earliest dated cantata belongs to 1688, but there
are many which are undoubtedly some ten or twelve years
earlier. At this time the cantata had not received a
sharply defined form. It was originally narrative; Vincenzo Galilei's setting of the story of Conte Ugolino is
the first example of the style, although according to

Burney the term *cantata* was first used by Benedetto Ferrari in 1638. But the lyrical element very soon came in, and by Scarlatti's time it was the more important part of the composition. Still there is nearly always a pretence at a narrative, or else the poem takes the form of a dramatic monologue put into the mouth of some classical personage. Some of Scarlatti's early cantatas, such as " Il Germanico " (" *Già di trionfi onusto* ") and " Il Coriolano " (" *La fortuna di Roma* "), are little more than lectures on Roman history set to recitative with an occasional aria. On the other hand, we get a few in which four or five arias or *ariosi* succeed each other directly, with only a short recitative at the beginning or end. This irregularity of form is one of the distinguishing characteristics of Scarlatti's early cantatas : by about 1690, or even earlier, he had adopted a regular alternation of recitative and formal aria from which he very rarely diverged. To this early period also belong airs in binary forms, airs on a ground bass, and all airs, in whatever form, that have two stanzas ; and there are other characteristics of the early style that are easily recognized.

The cantata " *Augellin sospendi i vanni* " is a good specimen of this period. It opens with a little air of two stanzas in ¾ time in C minor ; this modulates first to G minor, then by a sequence to B flat major and B flat minor, and returns to C minor by a repetition of the two previous phrases in G minor and C minor respectively, ending with a *codetta*. The melody is decidedly awkward and angular, with frequent imitations between the voice and the bass. The recitative which follows soon drops into an *arioso* in ¾ time, and here the struggle with technical difficulties is very obvious. The composer is unable to get a clear idea of a key, and hovers undecidedly between tonic and dominant, repeating his stiff little phrase first in C minor and G minor, then in G minor and D minor, and finally returning to C minor only to end at once in G minor. Next comes what he definitely marks as " *aria* "—two stanzas in C minor on a ground bass. Another recitative

follows, again dropping into *arioso* with the same sort of
angular imitations, this time dividing the key between
tonic and subdominant. After this the first aria, "*Augellin
sospendi*," is repeated : then, after a recitative, comes another "*aria*" of two stanzas in B flat in a still more curious
form. It begins with a short section in common time,
evolved bar by bar with some difficulty, which runs on
into a longer section in $\frac{3}{4}$; the first part of this is on a
ground bass, ending in the dominant, after which the
figure is abandoned, and a new one, more freely treated,
takes its place. Finally, after a recitative leading to
another awkward *arioso*, the first air is again repeated,
and the cantata ends with a little contrapuntal *ritornello*
for two violins and bass.[1]

Scarlatti's want of fluency in the early cantatas is
very curious, the more so since in his later works his
supply of melody is inexhaustible. It must, of course,
be remembered that at this time the vocabulary of monodic
music was very limited. It was left for Scarlatti himself to
invent many of those conventional turns of phrase which
became the common property of later composers. The
ground bass was no doubt considered a valuable aid
to composition. The history of the form is more complex
than is generally imagined. As used by the seventeenth
century Italians in vocal music it has very little in common
with the *chaconnes* and *passecailles* of Bach and Handel.
Probably the instrumental movements of Monteverdi, built
up on sequentially recurring figures,[2] are the real ancestors
of the ground basses of Legrenzi and Scarlatti. The
chaconne is simply a set of variations, each clearly defined,
though forming a continuous movement ; Legrenzi and
Scarlatti, on the other hand, often conceal the symmetry
of their foundations by arranging their superstructure

---

[1] In the autograph at Berlin the *ritornello* has been sketched first for two
violins, viola and bass. No other manuscript has this movement, and the
violins are not employed at all before.

[2] For a full analysis of these see "*Die Instrumentalstücke des Orfeo*," by
Dr. Alfred Heuss (*Sammelband der Internationalen Musikgesellschaft*, Jahrgang iv. 2).

on different rhythmical principles.   It is obvious that
such basses as these—

taken from early works of Scarlatti, could not be treated
in the spirit of a *chaconne*, still less so when the bass
is seldom repeated more than twice consecutively in
the same key. Thus the bass in Ex. 1 is given out
four times in the tonic, twice in the dominant, twice in
the relative major, and finally three times in the tonic.
The first statement of it is introductory, the third is
due to the habitual repetition of the first vocal phrase,
and the last forms a coda.   The treatment of Ex. 3 is
more elaborate.   After a single introductory statement
by the *continuo* alone, the bass is given out twice in
the tonic and twice in the dominant ; two entries in the
relative major form a strongly contrasting second section,

after which it is heard not twice but eight times in the
tonic, the first four corresponding to the four entries
in tonic and dominant, the next two forming a vocal
coda and the last two a *ritornello* for the strings. The
scheme may be represented shortly thus—

    B. Introduction.
    B B F♯ F♯. First section ending in dominant.
    D D. Contrasting second section.
    B B B B. First section ending in tonic.
    B B. Vocal coda.
    B B. Instrumental *ritornello*.

That by itself, disregarding the voice part, is a very
neat piece of ternary form on a small scale, and it is
clear that both these examples are akin not so much
to the variation type as to Monteverdi's instrumental
movements, of which the following bass

Ex. 6.   Monteverdi, "Orfeo."

shows clearly the typical structure. It will be noted
too that the basses quoted have a very distinctive
individuality; indeed Ex. 5 is derived directly from the
initial vocal phrase—"*Chi non sa che sia dolore.*" This
feature of Scarlatti's early work is noteworthy, because
it helps to explain the origin of what is the most important
factor in all modern music, from Scarlatti to the present
day, namely, thematic development. Scarlatti seems to
have discarded the ground bass soon after he went to
Naples, and with good reason. In his early years, when
a good phrase was a rarity to be made the most of,
he saw that more could be done with it by placing it
in the bass than by giving it to the voice alone; but
as soon as he acquired a greater fluency of inspiration,
the ground bass became a hindrance rather than a help

to composition. Besides, it subordinated the voice to
the instruments, a state of things at all times undesirable
(being detrimental to the highest effects, both musical
and dramatic), and especially so in an age when instrumental technique was very immature. He therefore
abandoned it in favour of thematic development, which
is exhibited to advantage in all his chamber-music, and
to a less extent in his work for the stage.

The influence of Carissimi and Cavalli is apparent
in his early recitative and also in his contrapuntal sense
of harmony. If his arias are sometimes awkward, his
recitative is generally most expressive from the very
outset, as will be seen from the following illustration, from
one of his earliest cantatas.

Ex. 7.   Cantata, "*Lagrime dolorose.*"

La-grime do - - - - - lo - ro-se, dagl'oc-chi

miei ve - ni - te,   ve - ni - te, ve - ni - te,   con dop-pio

fiume ad in - on-dar - - - - - - - mi il se-no,

His *coloratura* is for the most part restrained, thoroughly
vocal and in good taste. He never commits such extravagances as are found in the cantatas of Stradella, who

often gives the voice figures obviously derived from the *cembalo*, such as this from " L'Ariana "—

Ex. 8.   Stradella, " L'Ariana."

E   sog - get - ta al   mio   fu - ror......

Scarlatti shows a very keen sense of harmony as a means to dramatic expression, and it is interesting to watch the development of this sense in his later work. The feeling for harmonic expression remains, but the methods employed undergo a considerable modification. In his early work he still adopts the attitude of his predecessors, whose harmonic combinations resulted from the contrapuntal movement of parts. Another example from

B

Stradella will show a progression which was now common property :—

Ex. 9.

Se dol-ce è'l suo lan-gui-re,   se vi-ta è'l suo mo-ri-re, si, si, si, si, ch'io sem-pre sof-fri-rò.

Scarlatti uses it at first like every one else, and sometimes goes a good deal farther in the same direction. The early motet for two sopranos, "*Vexilla Regis*," has a characteristic example :—

Ex. 10.

ful - get   cru -
Vex-il-la,   vex-il-la Re-gis pro-de-unt, ful-get cru-cis, cru-
- cis, ful-get cru-cis mys-te - - ri-um,
- - cis, ful-get cru-cis mys-te - - ri - um,

and it appears in an even more curious form in the cantata

"*Lagrime dolorose*," the second time rendered additionally harsh by inversion of the parts.

These asperities are for the most part confined to the chamber-cantatas. In opera they were not appropriate, and since opera was for the next twenty years the field in which Scarlatti did most work, they soon disappear from his music entirely. They are, however, not without their interest. It is in connection with them and with the recitatives that we must consider the early *ariosi*, which often present harmonic treatment of great dramatic value. The *arioso* is most frequent in the early cantatas. In the very earliest it is singularly awkward, but the composer soon finds a surer footing, and the next few years bring us many beautiful specimens, such as the following :—

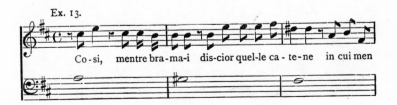

This example illustrates several characteristics : the broad sweeping line of the melody, the co-ordinate arrangement of phrases, as well as the keen sense of contrast between the major and minor modes. That eternal difficulty of the student of musical aesthetics, the melancholy effect of the minor mode, will probably have some light thrown upon it when it is investigated from a historical point of view. Scarlatti affords important material for such investigation, being probably the first composer who sharply defined the emotional difference which all later composers have almost invariably adopted.

It is these *ariosi*, more than the arias themselves, which foreshadow the style of Scarlatti's maturity. The arias in the early cantatas are for the most part long and straggling, and in curious forms, which, like the ground bass, he abandoned later. Although ternary form is as old as Monteverdi, it was a long time before composers realized the subtler applications of its principle. In the cantatas of Luigi Rossi, Carissimi, Stradella, and Scarlatti we may find the separate movements arranged in the scheme of a rondo, either obviously, as in Scarlatti's "*Augellin sospendi i vanni*," or disguised, as is often the case with Rossi, by the recurrence, not of the same movement, but of a movement of the same character, an exact parallel in key and time, sometimes even built upon an identical bass. Scarlatti's motet, "*Vexilla Regis*," furnishes a specimen of this. But within a single movement the alternation of subjects is rare. There are comparatively few airs which conform even to the simplest ternary type (A B A) ; those that are more organized are in binary forms, in which different subjects may be sharply defined, but do not alternate. The formula $A_1B_2B_1$ is a convenient representation of the type, the letters representing subjects and the figures keys. Variations, such as $A_1A_2B_2B_1$ and $A_1B_2B_1C_2C_1$, are derived from the first. The curious thing is that the types $A_1B_2A_1B_1$ and $A_1B_2A_2B_1$ are conspicuously rare. Probably the natural desire for alternation was felt to be satisfied by the immediate repetition of the whole scheme sung to a second stanza of the poetry. This is the more likely, since the second stanza disappears more or less simultaneously with the air in binary form. Ternary form also admitted of greater musical expansion, which would have been too long-winded if each air were sung twice. This long-windedness is often seen in Stradella, who carries repetition of phrase to excess, and rarely uses ternary forms.

Scarlatti's early devotion to the opera is undoubtedly an important factor in his development. The chamber style, as has been shown, admitted and even encouraged a certain diffuseness, but the necessity of stage effect forced him to be concise, and to pack his material into small and clearly organized forms. Moreover the large number of airs required for a single opera stimulated his invention, and taught him to economize material. We shall see later that it also led him to write a great deal that had no permanent value ; but the practice and facility so gained were doubtless of great importance to him, and also to his followers, who turned his musical commonplaces to good account.

Opera was being carried on in Rome with some difficulty. The first Roman opera-house had been opened in 1671, before which year operas had been given frequently, but only in private houses. This theatre, at the Tor di Nona, had been built by a certain Count D'Alibert before 1660, and he now obtained a concession from Pope Clement X. that whenever musical entertainments were allowed to be given, open to the public on payment, they were to take place only in this building. The count was a Frenchman in attendance on Queen Christina of Sweden, who had made Rome her residence after her abdication and conversion to the Catholic faith. A woman of strong independent character, thoroughly religious, yet tolerating no interference even from the Pope himself, she was a liberal patron of literature and art, and her original personality exerted its influence as much here as in the world of politics. Her profession of Catholicism at Innsbruck in

1655 was celebrated with the performance of an opera by Bernardo Pasquini, who afterwards became her Maestro di Cappella, and when in Rome she was an enthusiastic supporter of the musical drama. But in 1676 Clement X. was succeeded by Innocent XI., who immediately began to introduce reforms and economies of all kinds. Of his political quarrels with the queen we are not concerned here; but he did not confine his innovations to politics. The opera was the object of his special aversion, and he issued a decree absolutely forbidding all public performances with a charge for admission. He even tried to suppress private and gratuitous performances, by forbidding those who had sung in theatres to sing in churches, and by refusing to allow women to appear on the stage at all. The decree, however, was naturally circumvented, and things appear to have gone on much the same as before, except that the female parts were always taken by *castrati*. In 1677 this came to the queen's ears, and with characteristic impetuosity she sent word to the Pope that she much regretted having allowed Count D'Alibert to make use of the concession granted to him by Clement X., and that in future she should feel it her duty to burn down the theatre if operas were still given before a paying public. But her severity does not seem to have lasted long, for in 1678 she was interceding with his Holiness for Don Benedetto Pamphili, who was in disgrace for having secured the services of the Pope's own singers for a performance in which they appeared in female costume. To any one who reads the libretti of these operas, Innocent XI. seems to have been unnecessarily prudish, but even if authors and actors were blameless the audiences certainly were not.[1]

Scarlatti's first known opera, "L'Errore Innocente ovvero Gli Equivoci nel Sembiante," was produced privately at the Collegio Clementino on February 8, 1679. The libretto was by the Abbé Contini—"*un tale architetto*

---

[1] See the *Avvisi di Roma* quoted by Ademollo (*I Teatri di Roma nel Secolo XVII.*), and the same writer's articles in *L'Opinione*, Rome, January 1882. Casanova's memoirs also throw a curious light on the subject.

Contini," as he is called in the *Avvisi di Roma.* The
young composer was evidently in high favour with Christina, judging from the *Avvisi.* " Her Majesty, who was
so much pleased on Sunday by Contini's comedy, that she
desired to hear it at the Collegio Clementino, desired to
hear it these last two evenings also ; and since the Pope's
Swiss guard, who were keeping the door from the tumult
of the people, would not admit the lackeys of Cardinal
Colonna, who was in attendance on her Majesty, his
Eminence ordered them to enter, which they did, with
many blows to the Swiss guard. It is commonly known
that the composer of the music of the said comedy, a
Sicilian, is in very bad odour with the Court of the Vicar
on account of the secret marriage of his sister with an
ecclesiastic. But the Queen sent one of her own carriages
to fetch him, that he might play in the orchestra, even
when the Cardinal Vicar was himself in attendance on her
Majesty."

"Gli Equivoci nel Sembiante" is on quite a small scale,
as was suitable to a private performance. It is a very
innocent little drama, containing four characters only.
Clori is in love with *Eurillo* and *Eurillo* with *Clori;* but
the unexpected arrival of *Armindo, Eurillo's* exact
"double," produces confusion, further complicated by the
jealousy of *Lisetta,* and it is only after three acts of sighs
and recriminations that matters are cleared up. There is
not much scope for variety, though the distribution of
voices (two sopranos and two tenors) was decidedly unusual at a time when the *castrato* reigned supreme ; but
Scarlatti at least provided a good many pretty little airs,
and even attempted character-drawing to an extent which
he himself seldom equalled for some time afterwards.
Clori and *Lisetta* are as distinct as *Agathe* and *Aennchen*
in " Der Freischütz " ; indeed *Clori* is an even more insipid
ingénue than the heroine of Kind's drama, and *Lisetta* can
only be described as a spiteful little cat.

The airs are never very remarkable, though always
pleasant. One recognizes the individual Scarlatti style at

once, especially in melodies of a curious half pathetic, half playful type, which for a long time remained very characteristic of him. Perhaps the contemporary hearer did not feel them to be as pathetic as we do, for it cannot be doubted that the prevalence of minor keys in the music of this time was the result of modal survivals rather than of melancholy temperaments. The best numbers are the little duet in Act I., "*Si, si, ti voglio amar*," which combines clever characterization with great neatness of form ; *Eurillo's* air, "*Se ho d'amar*," a pleasing example of the typical Scarlatti style, as is also the air for *Armindo*, "*Cara semplicità*" in Act III., and *Clori's* beautiful melody, "*Dormi pur e sogni intanto*." The third act has also an air for *Clori*, "*Vaghi rivi*," which although binary and in two stanzas has florid *coloratura* and elaborate string parts that seem to forecast the style of the next century.

"Gli Equivoci" was followed in 1680 by "L'Honestà negli Amori." The opera is interesting from the glimpse which it gives of the composer's personality. The libretto of "Gli Equivoci," like many libretti of Scarlatti's operas, makes no mention whatever of the composer of the music ; that of "L'Honestà" is, however, unusually full of information. The *Avviso al Lettore* informs us that "the music is the composition of Signor Alessandro Scarlatti, called the Sicilian, Maestro di Cappella to the Queen of Sweden, a *virtuoso* who at other times has deserved your applause, and for whose praise it will suffice to say that in the springtime of his years he has begun where many of his profession would be proud to end."[1]

But there is a more curious allusion to Scarlatti in the opera itself. In the third act there is a scene for the two comic characters, *Bacucco*, an old servant, and *Saldino*, a page, in which they comment on the events of the preceding scenes, *Bacucco* saying that it is a tragedy rather than a

---

[1] "*La compositione della Musica è del Sig. Alessandro Scarlatti, detto il Siciliano, Maestro di Cappella della Regina di Svetia, Virtuoso, che altre volte hà meritato i tuoi applausi, per lode del quale basterà il dire, che nella Primavera della sua età hà cominciato, dove molti della sua professione si pregiarebbero di finire.*"

comedy that they are acting. *Saldino* takes up the word
comedia, and adds "'tis a Sicilian has set it to music";
Bacucco continues—

> "Ah yes, 'tis that young fellow—softly now—
> This is the same that wrote a year ago
> That opera which is going everywhere.
> The songs are charming, new, of sundry kinds;
> They tell me he has brought
> From the far end of Christendom itself
> A whole sack full of airs."[1]

From this it is clear that "Gli Equivoci" was regarded
as a great success, and that the composer was a very
young man, the evidence of the tombstone as to the year
of his birth being thus corroborated. It also seems to
imply that "Gli Equivoci" was his first opera, and indeed
the first work of his to bring him into public notice.

"L'Honestà" is a good deal stronger than "Gli
Equivoci." It is on a larger scale, being of the type
described as *opera semi-seria*. It has several airs on a
ground bass, the best of which is *Elisa's* "*Io per gioco vi
mirai*," analysed earlier in this chapter (Ex. 3), and another very interesting air in a form derived from the ground
bass—"*Scogli voi che v'indurate*." It is accompanied by
the strings in five real parts from beginning to end except for
a single bar's rest—a most unusual style of treatment. The
gloomy opening phrase (see Ex.
14 opposite) is repeated at once
in the relative major, but with
a different bass figure (Ex. 15)
and modified so as to end in C sharp minor. The cadence

Ex. 15.

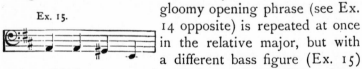

[1] "*Saldino.* E in musica l'ha posta un Siciliano.
Bacucco. Ah sì, quel Giovinotto; oh piano, piano,
Questo è quel, che compose un anno fà
Quell' opera che tanto intorno và.
Son le canzone belle, nove e varie;
Mi dicon, che hà portato
Sin dal confin della Christianità
Un sacco pieno d' Arie."

Scarlatti omitted these lines in setting the libretto to music.

is no sooner made than the music modulates at once to D
major, with a repetition of the same vocal subject on the new
bass figure, ending in F sharp minor, the tonic.   Here a new
subject appears, more or less derived from the first, modulating strangely to E minor; and it is immediately repeated
a tone lower, to end in the tonic by an audacious change
of key.   The little coda finishes the movement neatly.
The construction of this last section presents an interesting parallel to the opening of Brahms' violin sonata in
A major, where an analogous device is used.

Ex. 16.

Per - der la vi - ta,   per - der la vi - ta

e non po - ter,...........   e non po - ter mo - ri -

- - re...........   Per - der la vi - ta   e non po-

- ter,........   e non po - ter mo-ri - - re.........

e non po - ter   mo - ri - - - re...........

Apart from the tragic feeling of the song and its strange sense of oppression, of groping in darkness, the structure is very noteworthy. In regular ternary forms Scarlatti is almost always sure of his key at this time; but in his airs on a ground he modulates on different principles and covers a wider area. Here, working on the lines of a ground but not observing it strictly, he seems to have lost his way and only extricated himself by sudden modulations, as beautiful as they were unexpected.

Of Scarlatti's characteristic charm and delicacy of treatment no better example could be given than the little duet, "*Dite amanti*," perfect in finish, with a wistful expression that culminates just before the *Da Capo* in the following beautiful phrase:—

Ex. 17.

ELISA. S'è tor - men - to per - che pia - ce, s'è pia - cer, s'è pia -

"Pompeo" (1683) was probably Scarlatti's first attempt at *opera seria*. It contains a few good airs, but on the whole it is stiff and tedious. *Arioso* is for the most part avoided, though it would have relieved the monotony of the recitative, the composer not yet having developed that fine declamatory style which served as a model to all succeeding generations. The libretto is poor. The librettists of this period are, as a rule, either ignored or ridiculed by modern critics, and their contemporaries speak little better of them. Quadrio,[1] although he devotes considerable space to them, and finds some worthy of high praise, begins his chapter with a good description of their style :—

"He who would justly describe what a Musical Drama is, should say that it is a strange work made up of Poetry and Music, in which the Poet and the Composer, each alternately the slave of the other, wear out their brains to make a bad Opera ; but in which the superior is servant to the inferior, and in which the Poet occupies the position of a Fiddler that plays for Dancing. . . . Wherefore truly never did Poetry give her name to absurdities more ridiculous or more unendurable than these ; nor could any person of sense tolerate their improprieties, if he were not enchanted by the Musicians, the proof of which is sufficiently seen in the fact that in most cases the recollection of such compositions perishes with their sound."

Nevertheless some of the libretti were at least adequate for their purpose, either in the pastoral or the heroic style. "Pompeo" aims at the heroic ; but in the second act it lapses into a stupid intrigue of mistaken identity in the

---

[1] *Della Storia e della Ragione d' ogni Poesia*, vol. iii. p. 434.

dark, which is not even amusing as farce. The best movements are *Sesto's* charming airs, "*Non mi curo della vita*" and "*Da quegli occhi luminosi*"; the well-known "*O cessate di piagarmi*"; and a very interesting study in expression, "*Tormentosa gelosia*," sung by the half-civilized king *Mitridate*, whose passionate jealousy is well suggested by the straining syncopations.

Ex. 18.

Tor - men- to - sa ge - lo - si - a......

These three operas—"Gli Equivoci nel Sembiante," "L'Honestà negli Amori," and "Pompeo"—are all that remain to represent Scarlatti's first period of dramatic composition. But although it has not been possible hitherto to identify any other libretti set to music by Scarlatti before he left Rome in 1684, there can be hardly any doubt that he produced several other operas about this time. There is an enormous quantity of single arias extant which certainly belong to this period, mostly in the libraries of the Conservatoires of Paris and Naples, and in the British Museum (Harleian MSS.). There is also a collection of "Thirty-six Ariettas" by Scarlatti, printed in London towards the beginning of the eighteenth century, all of which are in his early style, some being identified as belonging to operas already known.

The strongest influences in Scarlatti at this period are those of Legrenzi and Stradella, each in rather different directions. From Legrenzi Scarlatti gets his dancing dactylic melodies, and many other characteristic turns of phrase; even more important than these is his conciseness and clearness of form. Here Legrenzi offers a great contrast to Stradella, who even in his operas is conspicuously wanting in this respect. He is by no means without a sense of form, but he applies it almost entirely to the detailed development of small figures, neglecting the larger outlines; and the result is that nearly all his airs are interminably straggling. Yet he had certain characteristics which Legrenzi had not, and which Scarlatti was quick to seize. It is from Stradella that Scarlatti gets his characteristic charm of melody, though he soon surpassed his predecessor. Stradella's best melodies are often very beautiful, and full of that sunny tenderness of expression which is very typical of Scarlatti ; but they are always so extremely simple that a whole opera in this style strikes the reader as almost childishly naïve, all the more owing to the composer's habit of stating nearly every phrase twice in succession, if not oftener. Scarlatti gets rid of much of this repetition, thus simplifying the organization of his tunes, and also shows a greater fertility of invention as well as a deeper poetic feeling in the melodic themes themselves. Stradella is also greatly superior to Legrenzi in the movement of his basses. Legrenzi, though he made frequent use of the ground bass, seldom shows much character in this most important part of his music. His basses are at all times quite uninteresting. Stradella seldom uses the ground bass ; but his basses are generally full of life and individuality, and here his passion for the development of small figures shows to the greatest possible advantage. He seems to have been altogether more of an instrumental composer than Legrenzi, using his violins and trumpets very effectively, though, of course, not at all in a modern spirit. His feeling for bass movement shows itself again in his recitatives, which are often founded on thoroughly logical successions of chords, besides being as a rule well declaimed. Indeed the general style of his operatic recitatives is rather different to Legrenzi's, and seems to have served as Scarlatti's model ; though here, as in everything else, the younger composer soon improved upon it. This improvement, however, can hardly be said to have taken place altogether until after Scarlatti left Rome. His early operas show the germs of his great genius, but they also show the immaturity of youth ; and considered as a whole, Stradella's " Floridoro " is a much better opera than any of Scarlatti's first three.

The strong influence of both Stradella and Legrenzi on the young Scarlatti suggests that in his earlier years he may have had some connection with Modena. The Biblioteca Estense, which is peculiarly rich in manuscripts of Stradella's works, also possesses many of Scarlatti's early compositions, including the autograph parts of the motet " *Vexilla Regis*," as well as two operas of Legrenzi, which were performed at the court theatre. Information about Stradella's life is so scanty that it can be at best no more than a plausible conjecture that the two composers may have met under the protection of Duke Francis II.; it is equally possible that Rome may have offered similar opportunities. But in any case the direct influence of Stradella, like that of Legrenzi, though strong at first, did not last very long. Scarlatti's own individuality matured rapidly, and with the transference of his sphere of activity to Naples a new phase began which led to a change of style that is of considerable importance in the history of his artistic development.

CHAPTER II

NAPLES, 1684-1702

NAPLES had already made the acquaintance of Scarlatti's music with "Gli Equivoci" in 1680, and in February 1684 "Pompeo" was performed at the Royal Palace. The libretto describes Scarlatti as Maestro di Cappella to Queen Christina, but it was his last appearance in that capacity, for in the same month his services were secured to the Court of Naples.[1]   On February 17, 1684, he was appointed Maestro di Cappella on the retirement of Pietro Andrea Ziani, and on the same day his brother Francesco was appointed a violinist of the royal chapel. The career of Francesco Scarlatti is even harder to trace than that of Alessandro, and such details of it as have been recorded may conveniently be given here.   His stipend from the royal chapel, like his brother's, was paid him for a year only, and the next we hear of him is that in 1699 his oratorio " Agnus Occisus ab Origine Mundi " was performed at the Vatican.   In 1715 he turned up in Vienna, and applied for the post of Vice-Kapellmeister. Fux was favourably impressed with him — "*Ich finde diesen Supplicanten wegen seiner virtù vnd sonst beywoneten gutten Aigenschafften sehr tauglich,*" he reported to the Emperor ; Francesco, however, did not get the appointment, although he urged that his sympathies with Austria had lost him his post as Maestro di Cappella at Palermo after twenty-six years' service.[2]   This, however, was possibly an invention on his part ; the archives at Palermo make no mention of him, and Mongitore's diary expressly

[1] Naples, R. Archivio di Stato : *Scrivania di Razione e Ruota de' Conti,* vol. iii. fol. 82 *verso.*

[2] L. von Köchel, *J. J. Fux, Hofcompositor und Hofkapellmeister.* Vienna, 1872, p. 378.

names one Giuseppe Dia as Maestro di Cappella there in
1703. He then seems to have returned to Naples, as he
was on the staff of the royal chapel in 1719; but he
was not there long, as he gave a concert in London on
September 1, 1720, "the greatest part of his own composition." He advertised himself as "brother to the famous
Allessandro [*sic*] Scarlatti," and no doubt was encouraged
by the presence of Domenico in London for the production of "Narciso" at the Haymarket in 1719. He is
supposed to have resided later at Venice.

The circumstances under which the two Scarlattis
received their appointments were peculiar. The Neapolitan diarist, Domenico Conforto, tells the story thus:

"At the beginning of November [1684] the Viceroy
deprived of their offices and disgraced the Secretary of
Justice, by name Don Giovanni de Leone, Don Emma-
nuel . . . , [*sic*] the chamberlain, who was also Governor
of Pozzuoli, and a favourite page, for holding close and
illicit intercourse with certain actresses, one of whom was
called the Scarlati [*sic*], whose brother was by this Viceroy
made Maestro di Cappella of the Palace, though there
competed other *virtuosi* who were of this country. For
they had formed a triumvirate to dispose as they pleased
of such posts and offices as were to be distributed, getting
them filled by those who offered and gave them the best
price, and doing other unlawful acts to make money and to
please their —— actresses (*gradire alle loro Puttane
Commedianti*), and this without the knowledge of the
Viceroy, who, being made aware of everything, deprived
them, as has been said, of their offices and disgraced them;
and he had orders given to the Scarlati and her companions
that they should either leave this city or else go into a
convent; and in obedience to this order they entered the
convent of S. Antoniello, near the Vicaria."[1]

We have already seen what sort of a reputation Anna
Maria Scarlatti had at Rome in 1679. In the following
year she was singing in Venice at the Teatro S. Giovanni

---

[1] *Giornali del Sig. Domenico Conforto* (MS. in the Bibl. Nazionale, Naples).

Crisostomo,[1] and in the same company was Giovanni Francesco Grossi, called Siface, who sang the part of *Mitridate*
in her brother's opera, "Pompeo," at Naples. The Spanish
Viceroy, Don Gasparo d'Haro y Guzman, was only adding
hypocrisy to his other vices when he vented his righteous
indignation on the protectors of "La Scarlati" and her
friends.   All over Italy, Muratori tells us,[2] opera in the
most sumptuous style was the fashionable entertainment
of the day.   The courts of Modena and Mantua vied with
each other in the extravagance of their productions and
in the acquisition of the most celebrated singers, for whom,
by a strange irony, *virtuoso* and *virtuosa* became the recognized title.   The court of Naples, at this time more than
ever the "city of pleasures," though it had not yet attracted
composers of any great distinction, had at any rate as great
a reputation as any for its liberal appreciation of professional "virtue."   It was the fashion to have opera-singers
as mistresses, and the Viceroy set the example on the scale
that became his position.[3]

The exact history of the affair can only be conjectured.
We may be fairly certain that Anna Maria Scarlatti depended less upon her musical ability than on her personal
attractions as a means of livelihood.   She could not have
been singing in opera at Rome in 1679, as no women
were allowed to appear on the stage.   Her part in " Il
Ratto delle Sabine" at Venice was only a small one, and
there is no record of her having sung in any other opera.
Even in her brother's "Pompeo" she did not take part,
unless it were in the chorus or the ballet.   And it is significant that when given her choice either of leaving Naples
or of entering a convent there, she preferred the latter
alternative, probably having little chance of obtaining a
serious musical engagement elsewhere.

There can, however, be no doubt that " Pompeo " was

---

[1] In " Il Ratto delle Sabine," of Pietro Simone Agostini.   (A. Wotquenne,
Catalogue des livrets italiens du XVIIe siècle.)

[2] *Annali d' Italia, anno* 1690.

[3] Benedetto Croce, *I teatri di Napoli nei secoli XV.-XVIII.*   Naples, 1891.

a great success at Naples, and that its success was largely due to the singing of Giovanni Francesco Grossi. He was the most celebrated singer of his time, and had probably had plenty of experience of Scarlatti's style when singing in Rome under the protection of Queen Christina. He was in the service of the Duke of Modena, but much in demand everywhere else, in spite of his rather capricious manners. For us he has a special interest, as having been sent by the duke to his sister Mary of Modena, wife of James II. He was only five months in England (January 18 to June 16, 1687), and suffered considerably from the climate; but he had time to acquire some considerable celebrity there, and may very likely have helped to introduce Scarlatti's music to English audiences.

Don Gasparo d'Haro y Guzman made every effort to retain Siface for the opera at Naples. He made him write to the Duke of Modena, and wrote to the duke himself as well, begging him to allow Siface to stay, both letters being dated from Naples on February 19, two days after the appointment of the two Scarlattis. How far the Viceroy approved of the appointment cannot be said ; probably he was personally inclined towards it, in view of the success of "Pompeo," and was carefully persuaded to ratify it by the "triumvirate" of whom Conforto tells us, in spite of the dissatisfaction which seems to have arisen, according to Conforto, from the post being given to one who was not a Neapolitan. In any case Anna Maria Scarlatti deserves to be remembered, since, had it not been for her, Alessandro might not have remained at Naples to be for eighteen years the leading composer of operas there. And these eighteen years, though they do not represent the best period of Scarlatti's production, are of the greatest importance for his own career and for the history of music generally, since the encouragement that he received at Naples, in spite of obvious disadvantages, enabled him to develop his style steadily in one direction in a way that he could never have done under other circumstances.

It was probably on the strength of this appointment that Alessandro Scarlatti married a certain Antonia Anzalone, by whom he had three children, of whom Giuseppe Domenico, born October 26, 1685,[1] was the eldest. He apparently received no stipend after February 1685, but he stayed on in Naples and retained his title until 1702, hardly a year passing in which he did not compose at least two operas, most of which were produced either at the royal palace or at the royal theatre of S. Bartolomeo.

We can hardly be surprised that, under such circumstances, he soon took to modelling his work on fixed patterns, from which he hardly ever departed. But the system had its advantages as well as its drawbacks. It limited the composer's sphere of action, but it gave him leisure to develop this style to the utmost within the limits imposed. Thus this period, which, more than any other, marks the first step to the final decadence of old-fashioned Italian opera, is of the greatest importance in the history of pure music, and it is mainly from this point of view that it will be treated in this chapter.

It is not easy for the modern reader to form a clear conception of what an operatic performance was like at this time. The modern romantic opera, to say nothing of the modern music-drama, seems to have nothing tangible in common with the opera of Scarlatti. The

---

[1] *Parocchia di S. Liboria della Carità* (*Chiesa di Montesanto*), fol. 65 :

Die p.mo 9mbre 1685. Io sud.o curato (D. Gius.e Sorrentino) ho batt.o uno figliuolo nato a 26 del caduto figlio del Sig.r Alessandro Scarlati e Sig.a Antonia Anzalone coniugi hebbe nome Gius.e Dom.co fu tenuto al sacro fonte dalla Sig.ra D. Eleonora del Carpio Principessa di Colobrano, e dal Sig.r D. Domenico Martio Carafa Duca di Maddaloni.

Fol. 97. Catarina Eleonora Emilia 29 9.bre 1690 f.a di Alessandro e Antonia Scarlati Padrini D. Marino Caracciolo P.pe di Avellino e D. Eleonora Cardines P.ssa di Colobrano come proc.ce della Sig.ra D. Emilia Carafa Duchessa di Maddaloni.

Fol. 107. A 12 Maggio 1692 Carlo Francesco Giacomo figlio del Sig.r Alessandro Scarlati et la Signora Antonia Ansalone [*sic*] coniugi, nato a 5 d.o fu battezzato p̃ me D. Nicola Cuoci sacrista et economo li Padrini li Sig.ri Ecc.mi D. Nicola Gaetano p̃ procura in nome del Sig.re D. Carlo Caracciolo Duca d' Ayrola, et la Sig.ra D. Aurora Sanseverino.

descendants of Scarlatti's operas move now in somewhat
humble circles, but they still keep their original title—
melodrama. The persecuted heroine, the splendid hero,
the heavy father, the adventuress, and even the comic
lovers, familiar to us, if no longer on the boards of the
Adelphi, at least in the pages of Mr. Jerome, were all
stock characters at the *"Real Teatro di S. Bartolomeo."*
The details of the plot may vary, but there is hardly any
variation in the characters, and none whatever in the love-
making which is their one and only occupation.   The
author may cite Aulus Gellius and Polydore Vergil in the
most learned manner in the *avviso al lettore*, but once the
curtain is up history retires into the background, and for
three acts we do nothing but watch the progress of
interminable love intrigues between personages whose
very existence is often no more than one of the poet's
"accidenti verissimi."   The scenery too, as has been
already pointed out, was a most important part of the
entertainment, there being generally three if not four
separate scenes in each act, each no doubt of a most elaborate kind, judging from the designs that remain ; and
many operas included some sort of transformation-scene.

An outline of "L'Olimpia Vendicata" will serve to
illustrate the type.   When the curtain rises, *Olimpia*, a
princess of Holland, is discovered alone on a desert island
in the Spanish main, where she has been left by her
faithless lover *Bireno*, prince of Zealand.   She is immediately taken prisoner by *Araspe*, a pirate chief, to whose
inquiries she answers that her name is *Ersilla*.   The scene
now changes to the court of Spain.   The king *Oberto*
wishes to marry his sister, the princess *Alinda*, to *Osmiro*,
prince of somewhere else (his country is not named) ;
Alinda, however, refuses, preferring a stranger who has
just arrived in the guise of a pilgrim.   At this juncture
Araspe appears, having been cast ashore by a convenient
storm, and *Ersilla-Olimpia* is given to *Alinda* as a slave,
Oberto himself immediately falling in love with her.   This
ends the first act.   In Act II. *Alinda* receives a letter

from the pilgrim, revealing himself to be *Bireno* in disguise and professing his love for her. It being apparently one of *"Ersilla's"* duties to read *Alinda's* love-letters aloud to her, and write the answers at her dictation, *Olimpia* is thus made aware of the situation, and determines to avenge herself. *Bireno* sees her and recognizes her. He attempts to explain his rather awkward position ; she cuts short his apologies and protests that she is not *Olimpia* but *Ersilla*. Believing himself to have been mistaken, he proposes to elope with *Alinda*, who says she will give him an answer by letter. She dictates a refusal to *Olimpia*, but immediately tears it up, and the act ends with her again refusing *Osmiro*. In Act III. *Olimpia* tells *Bireno* that *Alinda* loves *Osmiro*, and invites him to surprise them together and kill his rival. *Bireno* comes at the appointed hour, and *Olimpia* prepares him supper. As she has drugged the wine he falls asleep, and she is just on the point of murdering him, when she is prevented by *Alinda*. She then reveals herself and tells the story of her desertion ; *Bireno* is cast into prison, *Olimpia* marries *Oberto*, and *Alinda* consoles herself with *Osmiro*.

It is obvious that the complication of the plot leaves very little opportunity for the study of character. Whether the *dramatis personae* are princes and princesses of mediaeval Holland or of ancient Greece, they act and talk and sing in precisely the same way, just as they no doubt wore the same sort of costumes in front of the same sort of scenery ; indeed everything, including the turgid language of the libretti, to which no translation could do justice, belongs to no other age than the last twenty years of the seventeenth century.

Scarlatti was not by temperament a reformer or an iconoclast. He took things as he found them, and did the best that could be done on the lines of his predecessors. The libretti of his day offered him any quantity of heroic sentiments, which he set to a dignified recitative, as well as straightforward obvious emotions, which he could express in a neat aria at the end of each scene. He soon found that the best type of aria for his purpose was the ternary form. It satisfied the natural aesthetic need of contrast and recognition in the clearest possible way, and the *Da Capo* gave the singer a favourable opportunity of exhibiting his skill in extemporizing variations, as was expected of him by both audience and composer. Writing every air (and each opera would contain some fifty or sixty) in the same form, Scarlatti attained a wonderful mastery over his material, and besides displaying an infinite variety of style within the given limits, he gradually developed the form to a very high degree of emotional and structural organization. Outside the aria, there was hardly any formal music in the opera. There was the overture, the evolution of which will be discussed in detail later on, and there were occasional dances and marches. The marches and pageant music are all written by Scarlatti himself, but the ballets are frequently absent from the score. From the indications given in the libretti they seem to have been almost always of a comic nature, and sometimes they are directly associated with the comic characters. It seems probable that they were not regarded as an integral part of the opera, and that the ballet music, like the ballet-master, was generally imported from France.

The descriptive symphonies which are so important in the earlier Venetian operas find no place in Scarlatti. Musical scene-painting is really a modern growth. In " Der Freischütz" and " Der Fliegende Holländer" the orchestra is used to stimulate emotions which the stage carpenter cannot awaken. The music throws our nerves into a state of abnormal excitement, in which our own imagination can easily complete the illusion which the scenery has suggested. The emotional aspect of land-scape is essentially a characteristic of the nineteenth century, and in connection with this we must also take into account that owing to altered circumstances of theatrical management, scenic arrangements in Weber's and Wagner's days were not so elaborate as in the seven-teenth century, when opera was the plaything of princes.

In Scarlatti's time the theatrical architect was technically far ahead of the dramatic composer, whose work was confined to the objective expression of personal and individual emotion. The subjective expression, or rather suggestion, of the collective emotions of the audience is a different thing, and is certainly not older than Gluck. It is very easy to think that it existed already in Peri, Monteverdi, and Cavalli, but we must beware of letting our modern romanticism run away with us. It is not reasonable to suppose that because Monteverdi or Purcell happened accidentally on a device, be it structural or harmonic, that to our ears is characteristic of Wagner or Tchaikovsky, they or their audiences necessarily attached the same emotional impression to it that we do. In studying the dramatic music of the first half of the seventeenth century we must always remember that, however anxious composers might be in theory to get away from polyphony, vocal or instrumental, they were obliged to fall back upon it in practice, because it was a material which they were accustomed to handling, and which their audiences would understand without effort. There is no direct connection between the choruses and descriptive symphonies of Monteverdi and those of Weber, except by the circuitous route that traverses the stony asperities of French opera. The chorus and the descriptive symphony disappear simultaneously from Italian opera as soon as composers had acquired sufficient mastery over the new style to put all they wanted into the solo parts, and it was only when instrumental technique progressed in advance of vocal technique that the orchestra began to be used for independent dramatic effects. Scarlatti's work covers exactly the period when concerted instrumental music was beginning to be recognized as a possible rival to the voice, and it is interesting to trace the gradual development of instrumental music in the work of a composer whose natural sympathies were all with the singers, but who was quick to take advantage of any other means that facilitated the expression of his thought.

There are many places in Scarlatti's operas where the recitative is interrupted for an appreciable time by some sort of action, such as the wrestling match and the lottery extraction in "Olimpia Vendicata," and numberless duels and battles, or by an elaborate change of scene such as takes place in "Massimo Puppieno." But Scarlatti never seems to think it necessary to fill up this gap with descriptive instrumental music, unless we suppose that he extemporized it himself at the *cembalo*. That is conceivable, for we do sometimes find a battle scene accompanied by a direction for a trumpet fanfare, which is very rarely written out in full. But he more probably realized that such music was impracticable, owing to the great difficulty of making it synchronize exactly with the action on the stage, and also owing to the noise that would be made by the energetic movements of combatants or scene-shifters, to say nothing of the buzz of conversation among the audience. But if the stage be quiet, and it be desirable to produce some sort of illusion of mystery, he is ready with his band. Thus in "Massimo Puppieno," when *Massimino* the African king, after fighting outside, staggers in mortally wounded to die on the stage, the few bars played by the strings must have invested the action with a simple dignity that would lift the audience for a moment into a higher emotional plane.

Ex. 19.

The great advantage of music of this kind is that it falsifies our sense of time. The *Intermezzo* in "Cavalleria Rusticana" takes some three or four minutes in performance. Suppose that in "Cavalleria Rusticana" there

were no *intermezzo*, the curtain falling between the two
scenes; the break would be intolerable.   The drama is so
exciting that we want to go straight on; yet a certain
amount of time must elapse while the people are supposed
to be in church.   We cannot really wait all that time,
whether the curtain be up or down; and if there was a
long silence, and no fall of the curtain, the audience would
resume their talk—if indeed they had ever interrupted
it—and lose their interest.   But by putting in the *intermezzo* our attention is held; we are able to keep up the
religious feeling of the previous scene, and at the end we
are quite willing to believe that thirty minutes have
elapsed instead of three.   Another example of the same
thing occurs in " Fidelio," where *Florestan* falls asleep after
his solo, and the orchestra makes us forget how short an
interval actually elapses before *Rocco* and *Leonora* enter.
Scarlatti's " Olimpia Vendicata " is interesting as showing
us the first germs of this idea in a way that makes it
impossible to mistake the principle which guided him.
When the curtain rises, *Olimpia* is discovered asleep on
her desert island, and speaks a few unconscious words
before she awakes.[1]

[1] The original has two flats in the signature; but it is evidently a copyist's
error, since the E flat is always marked as an accidental wherever it is
required.

As soon as she awakes, the violins leave off, and she soliloquizes in *recitativo secco*. The example quoted is more an *arioso* than a recitative; but in the third act the device is employed again, when *Bireno* falls asleep after having been drugged by *Olimpia*; and here we have an unmistakable *recitativo stromentato*, the earliest (1686) that I have been able to find.

Ex. 21.

BIRENO (Alto).

Quanto,   quanto tar-da-te pi-gri mo-men-ti, oh Di-o!

Two Violins, Viola, and Continuo.

Ma qual pos-sen-te o - bli - o   le pu - pil - le m'ingombra?

Por - ta - mi o son - no in om - bra   fra i tuoi fan - tas - mi al -

- men l'i - do - lo mi - o.   (s'addormenta).

Nevertheless, accompanied recitative is rare in these Neapolitan operas, and it is not until the last years of Scarlatti's life that it becomes the rule to have at least one example in each opera. One reason for its sparse employment is that it would have been far more tedious than *recitativo secco*, since it necessarily was sung slower, and took a still longer time owing to the pauses for the instrumental phrases. It could hardly ever be employed except in very impassioned soliloquies.

The disappearance of the chorus has been viewed by historians with unnecessary regret. Like the descriptive symphony, it was a survival of the polyphonic period, and it was all the better that it should die down and be absorbed into the soil only to push up again later with new vitality. The elaborate choruses of the earlier Roman operas [1] are not really dramatic at all : the chorus is merely a background, not a factor in the development of the plot. Scarlatti, in confining his chorus to short exclamations—shouts of "*evviva*" or "*mora il tiranno*"—such as a crowd might really utter, is much more dramatic than if he made them sing long polyphonic movements. The choral finale was a device that had to wait many years for its development. The choral finales of the earlier operas were traditional survivals of the madrigals sung as *intermezzi* at the dramatic performances of the previous century ; and Arteaga points out that when it became customary to have a different scene for each act, it was dramatically absurd that the same chorus should always be there. Besides, as he says, by clearing away the chorus, the composer was able to get variety by ending his acts with a solo or a duet. The customary "*coro*" at the end of an opera, which was often sung by the principals only, must not be regarded as a step towards the "concerted finale" of Mozart. Scarlatti nearly always treats it in the most perfunctory way possible. "Gli Equivoci" ends with five bars of quartet—just the words, "*Oh nozze fortunate*,

---

[1] *E.g.* the scene representing a fair in the opera of Vergilio Mazzocchi and Marco Marazzoli, "Chi soffre, speri."

oh lieto giorno!" "L'Honestà" ends with an air for the heroine; "Clearco in Negroponte" with a recitative. "Olimpia Vendicata" ends with a quartet of some length; but it has no dramatic importance, nor is it developed even to a purely musical climax. It is to the final scenes of the first two acts that we must look for the first tendencies towards a dramatic *ensemble*.

The invention of the concerted finale is generally ascribed to Logroscino. Logroscino certainly treated it with a sense of humour peculiarly his own; but it had been often used by Leo and Vinci several years before. It was only in comic opera that the form could receive any vigour of treatment, for in *opera seria* it was regarded as a gross impropriety that one personage should interrupt another. A duet was only possible when the characters taking part in it were supposed to be in harmony of sentiment. But Scarlatti does not seem to have accepted this convention entirely. The concerted movements of his later operas will be discussed in detail in a subsequent chapter: here it need only be said that though he had a very much more vivid feeling for *ensemble* than his immediate successors in serious opera, he hardly ever places a serious *ensemble* at the end of an act.

The reason of this is simple. Comic opera, as a separate form, of the type of Leo and Logroscino, had not yet come into being, and the serious opera or *dramma per musica* still kept up its *parti buffe*. Scarlatti is the last composer with whom the comic characters are essential to the opera itself. But although they have their part in the development of the play they are already sufficiently conventionalized to be given a regular scene to themselves in each act.[1] This scene comes at the end of the first two acts, and just before the end of the third. The finale therefore of the first two acts was in their hands, and this accounts for the history of its development.

It is not necessary to trace here the history of the

---

[1] In some operas, *e.g.* "La Caduta dei Decemviri," the comic characters have two scenes in each act.

comic characters from the traditional comedy of masks through Vecchi and Banchieri to the Roman and Venetian operas of the seventeenth century. In Scarlatti's early operas they are generally an old woman and a page ; but the old man is also found. The *soubrette* was impossible in the early Roman operas, because women were not allowed to appear on the stage. The tragic female parts were sung by *castrati*, and from all accounts it was fairly satisfactory; but a *soubrette's* part could obviously be taken only by a woman.

The old woman was, of course, always sung by a tenor. She is generally the heroine's nurse—sometimes a lady-in-waiting, in which character her grotesque humour and her invariably very outspoken desire for matrimony must have been startlingly incongruous. But Italian audiences seem to have enjoyed a touch of the grotesque at the most tragic moments, perhaps realizing that the tragedy was thus made all the more true to real life. So in " Il Figlio delle Selve," when *Teramene*, the dethroned king in disguise, asks for news of his queen *Arsinda*, who is supposed to have been drowned, though really wandering about disguised as a man, *Gobrina*, her former maid-of-honour, replies—

> " *Fu detto, e mi rincresce,*
> *Che andasse a far da cena à più d'un pesce.*"

This juxtaposition of serious and grotesque is by no means confined to the opera of the period. The *Ferragosto* of Zappi and Crescimbeni, to which reference will be made later, is a good example of its literary treatment. In painting we can trace it back as far as Paolo Veronese, and it reaches its height in Tiepolo. The frescoes of the Palazzo Labia show exactly the operatic arrangement—a large serious composition in the centre, with popular types in narrow panels at either side, so designed as to be yet continuous with the main picture ; and in the frescoes

---

[1] " It was said, and I regret it, that she went to make a supper for more than one fish."

from the life of Abraham in the archbishop's palace at Udine we may see a perfect parallel to Scarlatti's grotesque old women and pert little pages in the figures of Sarah, attired as a fine lady of the seventeenth century, her toothless mouth convulsed with hideous laughter, and the very debonair young angel who hitches up his gaily-patterned skirt and appears to be almost as much amused at the situation as she is.

The most amusing of Scarlatti's old women is *Filocla*, in "Clearco." There is no other comic character in the opera, and she flits across the stage at odd times, absurd under all circumstances. At the end of the second act *Asteria*, the heroine, has an air in which she invokes the "horrid spectres of Cocytus"; *Filocla* immediately follows with a parody of it, after which there is an elaborate comic ballet. A pavilion rises from a trap during the aria, and *Filocla*, believing it to be occupied by a young man on whom she has fixed her affections, "goes to open the pavilion, from which comes forth a phantom, and *Filocla* wishing to escape from one of the wings, there appears a Moor, and the same thing follows at the others [*i.e.* she tries to escape at each exit in turn, and on each occasion another Moor appears]. Finally, she hides in the pavilion, whence she peeps out, while the said Moors dance with the phantom. *Filocla*, after the dance is finished, thinks that they have gone away, and comes out. The phantom, who is hidden, takes hold of her by her dress; she tries to escape, leaves her dress behind, and runs away. The phantom follows her." There is not a note of music to all this, nor to the ballet at the end of the first act, which is indicated in the stage directions.

At Naples there were no restrictions on female singers, but the *soubrette* does not appear for some time. The usual types are the old man and the old woman, bass and tenor respectively. In "La Caduta de' Decemviri" (1697) the old nurse *Servilia* is a soprano, but the first real *soubrette* appears to be *Lesbina* in "Odoardo" (1700). In "La Caduta de' Decemviri" the comic characters are very pro-

minent, and are both closely concerned with the abduction
of *Virginia*. *Flacco*, the servant of *Appio*, who is rather
like *Leporello*, has an amusing air in Act I. with a *colascione*,
which he thrums at intervals during the recitative. The
instrument was a kind of lute with two strings tuned a
fifth apart, and being popular in South Italy, often appears
in later comic operas. Scarlatti gives it a characteristic
figure :—

Ex. 22.

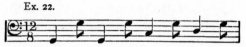

There is a good scene in Act III., where *Flacco*, disguised as a woman, is discovered asleep by *Servilia*. The
song which he sings before falling asleep is a very clever
study of a yawn.

Ex. 23.

mor - to di son - no.

As a contrast to this, there is the duet "*Non ti voglio*," in "Tiberio imperatore d'Oriente" (1702), with a page of breathless "patter" worthy of Sullivan.

Ex. 24.

Per te piango, per te peno, M'esce l'a-ni-ma dal seno, Per te manco, per te

mo-ro, Non ho pa-ce nè ri-sto-ro, Gio-ia ca-ra, vi-ta mi-a,

The close connection of the *parti buffe* with the ballet may be seen in "Odoardo," where a duet between *Lesbina* and *Adolfo* is continually interrupted by a troop of crippled beggars. On the exit of *Lesbina* and *Adolfo* the cripples dance to a rather stupid little tune in ⅜ time, after which *Lesbina* returns dressed as an old beggar woman, and the dance is repeated, *Lesbina* refusing to give the others anything. *Adolfo* returns and sings a *ciacona*, which is a lively movement in ⅜ on a free ground bass, after surprising the cripples in their dance and giving them a beating. Even if they are not associated with a regular ballet, the comic characters often dance themselves, as in "Tito Sempronio Gracco."

There being never more than two comic characters in a serious opera, it is obvious that the nearest Scarlatti

could get to a concerted finale was a duet. But in these
duets there is never any dramatic development. In the
finales of Mozart the drama is still in progress ; the
situation at the end is not what it was at the beginning.
In the finales of Leo and Logroscino, which are in one
movement only, this was hardly possible, yet we can
see that they were dimly working towards it. But in
Scarlatti's comic duets we must be content to find the
tendency indicated only by a conflict of interests. His
characters quarrel, but he does not go so far as to
let either win. This conflict of interests may easily be
illustrated by contrasting a serious duet such as this
from " Eraclea "—

Ex. 25.

with a duet such as this from " La Teodora Augusta,"
which is one of the earliest of its kind—

Ex. 26.

ten - di, da me che pre - ten - di, Sap - pia - mo-lo, dì, sap - pia - mo-lo,

dì.

Va det - to co-sì, va det - to co - sì, hai ra-gio - ne, fal -

Oh tu vuoi ch'io ti can - ti la sol - fa, ti can - ti la

- done, for - ci - na!

sol - fa, mar - col - fa, Ga - bri - na!

Se t'ar - ri - vo, se t'ar -

mar - col - fa, Ga - bri-na! mar-col-fa,

- ri - vo ti vuò far tonni - na, ti vuò far ton - ni-na,fal-do-ne,for-ci - na! fal -

6

Ga-bri-na! marcol-fa,Ga-bri-na! marcol-fa,Ga - bri-na!

- do-ne, for-ci - na! fal-do-ne,forci - na!

(*segue Ritornello*).

The comic duet is made up of short vigorous phrases tossed from one voice to another, which would lend themselves to thematic development on a larger scale, while the serious duet is really no more than a simple aria divided between two voices. Still, the division of a single melody between various voices has a charm of its own, and in this same opera, "Eraclea," there is a very interesting septet, which is so obviously conceived as a single melody, not a combination of melodies, that the copyist has saved space by trying to write out all the voice parts on one stave. He has, however, mutilated the music in so doing, and I give it here in score, emending the obvious errors.

There is nothing in any previous opera of Scarlatti's that in the least leads up to this. It was hardly the sort of thing to please a Neapolitan audience, except by its novelty, and the composer did not repeat the experiment until nearly twenty years later. We cannot regard it as being a direct ancestor of the concerted finale, but it was at any rate an interesting contribution to the technique of *ensemble* writing.

It was during this period of Scarlatti's activity that he definitely settled the form of the Italian overture. During the seventeenth century the opera overture had been gradually developed and extended, mainly by the Venetians ; but the struggle between counterpoint and harmony was still undecided by the time that Scarlatti began his career. If the use of free imitation in a fugal style was a convenient aid to the composition of vocal chamber music, it was still more so in writing for the orchestra alone. It was natural, therefore, that when composers began to write quick movements as introductions to operas they should make use of contrapuntal forms. But the Italians soon found that it was quite sufficient to start a movement contrapuntally and then abandon counterpoint as soon as all the voices had entered. It is easy to sneer at them, as Gounod has been sneered at, for "setting out with a pompous fugue exposition and discarding counterpoint at the moment when its difficulties begin." But in dramatic music, where a parade of learning is out of place, and a composer is bound to do his best to get the maximum of effective contrast with the minimum of labour, Cavalli did quite right to remember that the fewer the parts are in a contrapuntal movement, the more "contrapuntal" it will sound, and that when all the instruments are playing their loudest together, plain harmonic successions will produce the most imposing result. With Cavalli and his immediate followers there is no regular plan for the connexion of different movements in an overture. The fragmentary slow movements still survived, but the scheme of the overture as a whole was not clearly organized. The tendency, if any, was to the French form, though the *fugato* between two slow movements, as written by Cavalli and Agostini, is still far removed in spirit from the pompous Lullian type.[1]

---

[1] For a more detailed treatment of the subject see "Die Venetianischen Opern-Sinfonien," by Dr. Alfred Heuss, in the *Sammelband der Internationalen Musikgesellschaft*, Jahrg. iv. 3.

Scarlatti's early overtures are still experimental. "Gli Equivoci" has a slow introduction, not stiffly rhythmical, like Lulli's, but built up of organ-like suspensions in the regular Italian manner, followed by a quick movement in ¾ time in a rough ternary form somewhat obscured by its vagueness of tonality ; after this comes a "*balletto*." This final dance movement is the essential characteristic of all Scarlatti's opera overtures from "Gli Equivoci" to "Griselda." It appears in various forms—minuet, march or gigue—and occurs in some of the oratorio overtures as well, though in these it generally wears the more sober guise of an allemande. The distinguishing features of the movement are its clear division into two parts, each repeated, and its vigorously rhythmical character.

The *balletto*, which occurs several times in Scarlatti's early works, is a dance of quite definite character, as this example from "Gli Equivoci" will show—

Ex. 28.

Its characteristic feature is the "double knock" at the beginning, and the fact of this being the first type of dance tune selected by Scarlatti to conclude his overtures, shows how much importance he attached to the insertion in this place of a sharply rhythmic movement.

"Pompeo" begins with a *grave* of fifteen bars in a definitely binary form, followed by two dance movements, a *balletto* and a *corrente*, though neither is expressly so called. "La Rosmene" (1688) exhibits a similar form. This type of overture is found also in some of the early chamber cantatas with instrumental accompaniment; in these a solid *allegro* in the grand manner would have been out of place. The oratorio "Agar et Ismaele" (1683) brings us nearer to the "Italian overture" type. It begins with a *grave* in a very clearly binary form $(A_1A_2B_2B_1)$; then comes a *presto* in the Venetian style, starting contrapuntally, but continuing on a harmonic basis. A *largo*, which is purely transitional, leads into a square-cut movement in two repeated sections, followed by a curious little coda in a different *tempo*. This type of coda never occurs in the opera overtures, but in most of the oratorios and serenatas there is some sort of attempt to make the overture run straight on into the work itself. It is not so much a tail-piece to what precedes as an introduction to what follows, and seems to have been designed to provide a new nervous stimulus to the audience to make up for the loss of the one which they would have received in the theatre on the rising of the curtain. We find much the same form in "La Rosaura" (1690), an analysis of which is given in the "Oxford History of Music," vol. iii. Two serenatas of 1696 ("Genio di Partenope" and "Venere, Adone, Amore") give us a quick movement in clear binary form, both preceded by an introduction of slow suspensions and followed by a dance movement; in the second this is separated from the *presto* by fifteen bars of *tremolo* passing through various chromatic chords from the relative minor to the tonic. This overture marks the transition to the new style. The first example of it is the overture written about 1696 for the revival of "Dal Male il Bene." The slow introduction drops out altogether, the overture beginning at once with a quick movement in no very definite form, though more or less ternary as regards key distribution. A *grave* of eight bars leads from the relative minor to its dominant through various suspensions, and the overture ends with a minuet in two repeated sections. From this date the overture form is fixed, and hardly ever varies. The first movement gradually develops into a more organized structure; the second fluctuates between a mere chromatic transition passage and a definite slow movement; the third exhibits all varieties of rhythm—but the main idea remains the same. It took some time, however, to arrive at a clear alternating binary form ($A_1B_2A_1B_1$) in the first movement. In "La Caduta de' Decemviri" Scarlatti still retains the old-fashioned arrangement $A_1A_2B_2B_1$, in which the subjects do not alternate. "Il Prigioniero Fortunato"[1] provides no more than a series of antiphonal trumpet flourishes; the opportunity for colour effects provided by the use of four trumpets seems to have distracted the composer's attention. In "Eraclea" there is more definite organization, though the type is more that of a rondo. The first subject is given out by the trumpets—

and immediately repeated by the flutes and oboes, the trumpets continuing an independent part, from which we may infer that the two groups balanced in tone, though we certainly should not expect them to do so now if playing *forte*. This is followed by a second subject—

after which the first reappears in the violins, in its original key. The second subject is then developed in various keys, as far as the trumpets will permit, and finally the first subject reappears imitated at half a bar's distance by flutes and oboes in unison, violins, and trumpets in turn,

---

[1] Extracts are to be found in Grove's *Dictionary of Music and Musicians*, vol. iii. p. 620.

ending with two and a half bars of coda on the tonic and dominant. The whole movement occupies only twenty bars, and is a very neat piece of construction.

These extracts from "Eraclea" will also show the change that was taking place in Scarlatti's melodic style. Dealing always with conventional passions, his melodies get conventionalized, and his operatic style gradually diverges farther and farther from the intimate intellectuality of his chamber-music. "La Rosaura," of which two acts have been reprinted by the *Gesellschaft für Musikforschung*, is very characteristic of the composer at his best, representing a slightly earlier style, and one that approaches more nearly to that of the chamber-music. It was performed both at Rome and Naples in 1690, but though there is no definite evidence of date, it is almost certain that it was originally written for Rome for private festivities on the occasion of two marriages in the Ottoboni family. It is eminently suited for a private performance, being on the same sort of small scale and in the same quiet pastoral manner as "Gli Equivoci nel Sembiante." It seems to have been revived later, as the only two complete manuscripts of the score show considerable differences, especially in the third act, which possibly was one reason why the recent reprint did not include more than the first two. "La Statira," composed in the same year, is a very fine example of the grand manner.[1] The libretto, by Cardinal Ottoboni, is very typically baroque, but is on the whole interesting, and presents several good situations. Scarlatti seems to have treated it with more care than usual, and has drawn his characters very clearly. Not only are the principal figures well distinguished—the youthful and magnanimous *Alessandro*, *Statira* magnificent in despair, but also the minor personages — *Oronte*, cherishing a secret passion which at times breaks out savagely ; *Campaspe*, worldly and frivolous, yet attractive in her way ; *Perinto*, the boy of inexhaustible cheerfulness ; *Demetrio*, the rough but kind-hearted old soldier; and *Apelle*, the rather languishing painter

---

[1] An extract is printed in the "Oxford History of Music," vol. iii., p. 385.

—all are quite clearly individualized. There are no comic scenes ; *Perinto* is the only approach to a *parte buffa*, and he has very little to do ; but all through there runs a little vein of humour, as in the libretto of Scarlatti's later opera " Tigrane," which rather seems to suggest that the author, in the true spirit of the baroque, caught the grotesque aspect of his own creations. The airs are for the most part strikingly good, and the opera is also very interesting from its employment of *recitativo stromentato*. As we have already seen, the device had been used by Scarlatti before,[1] but in " La Statira" it is employed with great dramatic effect, both on the first rising of the curtain, when *Oronte* is discovered on guard with the Persian army in the moonlight, and later in the introduction to his fine air " *Re trafitto* " (" *Crudo cielo, empio fato* "), in which Scarlatti makes use of a more vigorous and broken style of accompaniment than he had hitherto attempted. The whole opera has that sense of brilliant effect that characterizes the gorgeous frescoes with which the school of Guido Reni decorated the palaces of Rome or Bologna.

" Pirro e Demetrio " (1694) is perhaps the best of the earlier Neapolitan operas. Its airs show us Scarlatti in his first maturity, after he had definitely shaken off the traditions of Stradella and Legrenzi, and begun to develop a style that may be considered as really his own. The opera had a great success, and even reached England ; it was performed in London in an English version in 1708, and no doubt contributed much to the popularization of Italian opera in this country. Unfortunately it was the only one of Scarlatti's operas that was ever given in London as a whole. With the advent of Italian singers came the custom of " polyglot opera," which has survived down to our own time, though we have for the most part got rid of the "*pasticcio*" as the favourite type of operatic

---

[1] In the reprint of " La Rosaura " published by the *Gesellschaft für Musik-forschung*, Professor Eitner stated that the *recitativo stromentato* in Act III. was the earliest known. It cannot, however, be even anterior to that in " La Statira," as it is found only in the manuscript representing a later revival of the opera.

entertainment. Some of the airs in "Pirro e Demetrio" are well known still—"*Rugiadose, odorose,*" and "*Ben ti sta, traditor,*" both reprinted fairly recently, are typical examples of Scarlatti's style during this period.

But with "La Caduta dei Decemviri" (1697) and "Il Prigioniero fortunato" (1698) there appears a new element. Here Scarlatti either languishes to cloying airs in $\frac{12}{8}$ time, all charming, and all exactly alike,[1] or else stamps across the boards to music of that straightforward, square-cut character that one would naturally describe as "Handelian." They remind one of nothing so much as Sullivan's famous parody in "Princess Ida." Needless to say, the style did not originate with Handel, and judging from Handel's early Italian compositions, it does not seem likely that Handel got it altogether from Scarlatti. Its inventor was probably Giovanni Bononcini, of whom it is very characteristic. His opera, "Il Trionfo di Camilla," performed at Naples in 1697, is full of vigorous, incisive rhythms of this type; and some readers will perhaps recollect the once very popular airs in a similar style, "*L'esperto nocchiero*" and "*Vado ben spesso,*" both from his opera "Astarto."[2] It was the kind of tune to which even a viceregal foot could quite easily beat time, and no doubt Scarlatti received an intimation from high quarters that he would do well to apply his talents in that direction. He did, and between 1697 and 1702 provided the viceroy with as much rubbish as the most exalted patron of the fine arts could desire to encourage. Nothing could be more tedious than to wade through such operas as "Odoardo," "Tiberio Imperatore d' Oriente," and the first version of "Tito Sempronio Gracco." They were evidently written in a great hurry, with the thinnest possible scoring, and seldom contain anything worth remembering except now and then

---

[1] "*Povera Pellegrina*" (from "Il Prigioniero fortunato"), reprinted in *Les Gloires de l'Italie*, is an easily accessible example.

[2] "*Vado ben spesso*" has sometimes been erroneously ascribed to Salvator Rosa. "Il Trionfo di Camilla" is attributed in M. Wotquenne's catalogue of libretti to M. A. Bononcini; but a score at Münster, dated 1697 (Naples, Teatro S. Bartolomeo), bears the name of his brother.

E

a comic scene of some humour. They seem, however, to
have been successful, as many airs have survived in manuscript ; still we may note that whereas of the earlier operas
we often find complete scores, sometimes written out in
the most beautiful handwritings, and elaborately bound,
these later Neapolitan operas are hardly ever to be found
complete. Of most of them we possess only collections of
airs, without any recitatives to connect them with an intelligible story, except in the comic scenes ; often the
instrumental parts are omitted with the exception of the
bass, and the handwriting is that of the ordinary copyist
of the music-trade. " Eraclea " is the best and the most
characteristic of the type ; " Laodicea e Berenice " (1701)
seems also to have been a great favourite, no doubt on
account of the jerkily pompous style of most of its airs.

Not only at the theatres of the palace and of S. Bartolomeo was Scarlatti's work in demand, but also for the
celebration of court functions and the entertainments of
the nobility. On these occasions the form taken by the
music was the Serenata, a dramatic cantata for from two
to five singers accompanied by the orchestra. As in the
operas, the chorus hardly ever appears at all. The usual
serenata consists simply of a number of airs and duets
strung together on a flimsy thread of recitative. The
subjects are pastoral or mythological ; but, as with the
operas, the subjects are of little importance. Arcadian
love-making at the beginning, versified politics at the
end—one could scarcely imagine anything less inspiring.
Conforto has many very vivid descriptions of the kind of
entertainment for which it was evidently the proper thing
to secure the services of the royal Maestro di Cappella,
and the following account, though it certainly tells us little
about the actual music, gives us a characteristic glimpse
of the social surroundings in which Scarlatti was obliged
to work :—

" There is no lack of change to be seen in this city, the
vanity and folly of both the nobles and the people having
reached its highest ; nor do they care if they reduce

themselves to poverty to satisfy their tastes. Scipione Giavo . . . [obliteration in MS.] posthumous son of Scipione . . . [obliteration in MS.] not wishing to do less than his elder brother, who wasted all his inheritance (and that a very rich one) in vain extravagance (wherefore he is reduced to living in some straitness on nothing but the dowry of his wife, daughter of Captain Peppo Pepe), determined that he too would ape the other's ways ; wherefore, having obtained at great expense from the Count Palatine of the Rhine, Duke of Neuburg, the title of Marquis of Landskron, of which he took possession at the Palace in order to enter the Chamber of Nobles, he, to this same end, gave an entertainment, lasting several days, in a house of his near the fountain of Mont' Oliveto, in the most sumptuous style, inviting ladies and gentlemen of the first rank, and spending indeed some thousands of ducats. Among other things, on Monday of last week, the eighth of this month [October 1691], he held at his house a most lively assembly, with the choicest music, consisting of ten instruments and four of the best voices of this city, directed by the Maestro di Cappella, Alessandro Scarlati [*sic*] ; and to the large crowd of titled persons, gentlemen, and ladies that attended, he caused to be offered continuously an unspeakable quantity of meats and drinks of all kinds, with various fruits both fresh and candied, as he did also for the large number of servants in attendance on them. His palace was all most nobly decorated, and all lit with wax torches as far as the court-yard ; the sideboard consisted of two long tables of silver fairly and symmetrically disposed, and there was visible in the distance a most beautiful fountain, also of silver, which for seven continuous hours spouted perfumed water, about which fluttered a large number of live birds. There was also a pavilion of crimson damask, under which were fourteen superb *trionfi*[1] of fruit both fresh and candied, as well as other curious inventions. The which entertain-

---

[1] A *trionfo* was an erection in sugar, &c., rather after the manner of a modern wedding-cake.

ment lasted some time after midnight, the ladies and
gentlemen, according to their usual habit, after having
filled their bellies and their bosoms with sweetmeats,[1] and
having had every pleasure of sight, taste, and hearing,
not failing to scoff and make a mock of the solemn folly
of the last new marquis."

Evidently the music was quite the least important
feature of these entertainments, and private persons merely
imitated the extravagances of the Spanish court. Yet,
considering the occasions for which they were written,
Scarlatti's earlier Neapolitan serenatas are fairly good.
The most charming of all his youthful works in this form,
"Diana ed Endimione," was probably written before he
left Rome, as it is in the careful manner of his earliest
operas, with airs on the smallest possible scale, and accompaniments finished with a delicacy for which he had
no time at Naples. The best of the Neapolitan serenatas
is one composed in 1696 for the birthday of the viceroy's
wife, in which she is saluted by three allegorical represen-
tatives of Naples, the *Genius of Parthenope*, the *Delight
of Mergellina*, and the *Glory of Sebeto*.[2] Here Scarlatti
seizes such advantages as the form presented. Not being
represented on the stage, there was more scope for purely
musical treatment, and the composer could approximate
more nearly to the chamber style ; at the same time the
very best singers were available. The result is something
half-way between the chamber and the stage, and this
particular example contains some very good music, the
most attractive number being an air, "*Venticelli lenti, lenti*,"
accompanied by the *concerto grosso* and two *concertini*, one
at a distance, producing the effect of two sets of echoes.
The final air, "*Godi e spera*," in which the *Gloria del*

---

[1] "*Doppio d'haversi empito il ventre et il seno di canditi*"—Conforto seems
to mean either that they stuffed sweetmeats into the bosoms of their dresses to
take home with them, or perhaps more probably that, being greedy and in a
hurry, they spilt half of what they tried to eat.

[2] The Mergellina (the extreme part of the Riviera di Chiaja, before the
ascent towards Posillipo) and the river Sebeto are the western and eastern
boundaries of the city.

Sebeto expresses the hope that the viceroy's wife will shortly give birth to a son and heir, is also extremely beautiful.

Indeed, in writing music of this kind Scarlatti seems to have been less quickly influenced by the style of Bononcini than in the opera. Even the serenata, " Clori, Dorino, Amore," composed for the visit of Philip V. of Spain to Naples in 1702, and sung while the king was at supper, though it contains nothing very striking, is still good on the whole. It is not until we reach " Il Giardino d' Amore " that we find Scarlatti descending to positive vulgarity. The date of this serenata cannot be definitely fixed, nor can we be certain whether it was written for Rome or Naples; but it is more probably Neapolitan, owing to the inclusion of an air with a florid violin solo, which also occurs in " Laodicea e Berenice," produced at Naples in 1701.

But although the chamber style still afforded Scarlatti an opportunity of writing serious music, as will be shown in the next chapter, yet Naples was becoming more and more irksome to him. He was probably in financial difficulties, since in February 1699 he had written to complain of his stipend being four months in arrear, adding that he was urgently in need of payment owing to the large family which he had to support.[1] He no doubt earned a certain amount by his operas and serenatas, but we may be sure that the kind of patrons whose reckless extravagance Conforto describes were not very likely to have been regular in payment of their debts. The political disturbances of the kingdom of Naples may very well have been an additional reason for his deciding to leave the capital and find a home elsewhere. The struggles for the Spanish succession had been troubling the peace of Europe for some little time, and in 1703 the Austrian

---

[1] Naples, R. Archivio di Stato, *Mandati dei Vicerè*, vol. 313, fol. 138. From the registers of the church of Montesanto, quoted on page 38, it would appear that his "*numerosa famiglia*" consisted of three children only : but perhaps others had been born to him, and baptized elsewhere.

claimant, the Archduke Charles, formally assumed the title of King of Spain as Charles III.   On May 5, 1705, he was proclaimed king at Madrid, and on July 7, 1707, Count Daun marched into Naples at the head of the Austrian troops, being appointed viceroy very soon afterwards ; not, however, for long, as in July 1708 he was sent to Piedmont on active service, and was succeeded by Cardinal Grimani, a Venetian.   We shall see later how favourable a reception Scarlatti obtained when he yielded to the cardinal's persuasions, and returned in 1709 ; it therefore seems reasonable to connect his departure from Naples in some way with politics, although there is no means of knowing whether he himself took any active part in them.

CHAPTER III

On January 9, 1702, Scarlatti applied for ten months' leave of absence on full stipend for himself and his son Domenico. It can hardly surprise us that this was not granted; nevertheless, on June 14, he succeeded in obtaining leave for himself and his son to go to Florence for four months.[1] At Florence he was under the protection of Ferdinand III., son of the Grand Duke of Tuscany, and though he never held any regular appointment under him, as far as we know, he was employed by him to write operas for several years. The prince was keenly devoted to music, and if we may to some extent trust the flattering letters that he received from various musicians, he possessed some considerable skill in the art himself.

He appears to have been a good performer on the harpsichord, and some interesting instruments still survive that were made for him by Bartolomeo Cristofori, the inventor of the pianoforte. Fired with enthusiasm after a state visit to Venice in 1687, then, as we have seen, the most celebrated city in Italy for operas, he built a theatre at his villa of Pratolino, not far from Florence, and started a series of operatic performances there. He also gave his protection to the opera-houses of Florence, Pisa, and Leghorn, and probably of other Tuscan towns as well. He took the most detailed personal interest in the performances, selecting the librettists himself, and giving the most minute directions to the composers as to the style in which he wished them to be set to music, a great part of his voluminous correspondence being still preserved in the Archivio Mediceo at Florence.

[1] Naples, R. Archivio di Stato, *Mandati dei Vicerè*, vol. 317, fol. 80 verso, and vol. 318, fol. 60.

Scarlatti's early connection with Ferdinand is not easy to determine. Probably his first appearance on the Tuscan stage was in 1688, when "Pompeo" was given at Leghorn. The same year, however, he produced " Il Figlio delle Selve " at Florence in the Teatro della Pergola, rebuilt at the prince's direction and newly opened on the occasion of his wedding. This was not a new opera, having been given at Rome in 1687, and possibly earlier. It is a "*favola boscareccia*," and, though rather absurd, contains some good music, in a style that points to a fairly early date of composition. Another opera, of which the title is not known, came out at Pratolino in 1690, and in 1698 " L' Anacreonte Tiranno," which had appeared in Naples nine years before. But although these first operas of Scarlatti performed at Pratolino were not entirely new, they were probably much rewritten. The sixteen airs which survive of the version of " Flavio Cuniberto " given at Pratolino, are not to be found in either score or libretti representing earlier performances ; indeed, the manuscript describes the opera as "*nuovamente posta in musica.*" It was probably for this performance that Scarlatti went to Florence in 1702. Once safely out of Naples, he had no intention of returning. He appears to have stayed on at Florence for the production of " Arminio " in the following year, but he probably found that Ferdinand was not inclined to give him a permanent appointment, as he went to Rome at the end of the year. He nevertheless continued to write operas for Pratolino, and during the next few years carried on a considerable correspondence with the prince, evidently in the hope of obtaining some more satisfactory position than he held in Rome.

On the recommendation of Cardinal Pietro Ottoboni, Archpriest of S. Maria Maggiore (*Basilica Liberiana*) at Rome, the chapter of that church had on December 31, 1703, appointed him assistant Maestro di Cappella to Antonio Foggia.[1] The appointment cannot have been a

---

[1] Archives of S. Maria Maggiore. This is the only occasion on which Scarlatti's name occurs there.

very lucrative one compared to that which he had held at
Naples, at least if his salary had been paid him, and the
subordinate position in a purely ecclesiastical establish-
ment must have been additionally irksome to him.   Naples
indeed seems still to have held out some hope of his returning, as his post there was not officially declared vacant
until October 25, 1704.[1]

How unsatisfactory both places were to him may be
seen from his letters to Ferdinand de' Medici.   He writes
to him from Rome on May 30, 1705, presenting his son
Domenico, whom he has sent on a musical tour with
Nicolino, the singer :—

"I have removed him [Domenico] by force from
Naples, where his talent had room indeed, but it was not
the sort of talent for that place (*dove benchè avesse luogo il
suo talento, non era talento per quel luogo*).   I send him
away from Rome also, since Rome has no roof to shelter
Music, that lives here in beggary." [2]

Writing again (July 18, 1705) about his opera, "Lucio
Manlio," which was to be produced at Pratolino, he
says :—

"May your Royal Highness deign to regard the opera
as your vassal ; and as a wandering maiden who, with no
home to shelter her from the mocking blows of fortune,
kneels at the feet of your Royal Highness, and invokes
as a suppliant the mighty shield of your high protection
and assistance, as in a safe harbour where she may rest
without having to fear the violence of the tempest." [3]

This flowery language appears to mean that neither in
Naples nor in Rome could Scarlatti find an opera-house to
produce his works ; and this was very probably the case,
owing to political disturbances at Naples, and at Rome
owing to clerical hostility.   Pope Innocent XI., as we
have seen, did all he could to suppress operatic performances, although they were carried on with some success

[1] Naples, R. Archivio di Stato, *Mandati dei Vicerè*, vol. 319, fol. 20.
[2] Archivio Mediceo, *Filza* 5891, No. 502.
[3] Ibid., *Filza* 5903, No. 165.

by various noble *impresari* under the pretence of private
entertainments.   The short pontificate of Alexander VIII.
(Ottoboni), who, being a Venetian, was known as *Papa
Pantalone*, as his Milanese predecessor was called *Papa
Minga*,[1] was more favourable to opera, especially as his
great-nephew Pietro, whom he raised to the purple in
1690, cherished ambitions as a dramatic composer.   The
young cardinal's opera, "Colombo," which was performed
at Rome in 1692, was not very successful—an amusing
satire on it is quoted by M. Wotquenne in his catalogue
of Italian libretti—but he was certainly a sincere and
enthusiastic lover of music, and will always be remembered
gratefully in the history of the art for the generous encouragement which he gave to Corelli, Alessandro and
Domenico Scarlatti, Handel, and many other musicians.
Alessandro's friendly relations with him probably dated
from 1690, when he set his libretto of "La Statira" and
also composed "La Rosaura" for festivities at the French
Embassy in honour of the marriages of Marco Ottoboni
with Tarquinia Colonna and of Urbano Barberini with
Cornelia Ottoboni.   Conforto also tells us that when the
cardinal and his father, Prince Antonio Ottoboni, a general
of the papal army, came to Naples in 1694, almost the
first thing they did was to go and hear the opera at
S. Bartolomeo, the opera being Scarlatti's "Pirro e
Demetrio."   It is not until 1707 that we have definite
evidence of Scarlatti's being his Maestro di Cappella,[2]
but he probably received the appointment immediately
on his return to Rome in 1703 or 1704.   The cardinal
seems to have had a considerable connexion with the
French government, as he became *Protettore della Corona
di Francia* at the papal court in 1710, contrary to the
will of the Venetian Senate, who for this offence struck
his name off the list of the Venetian nobility and deprived
him of his patrimony; and ¯it may have been partly
through his interest that Lulli's "Armida" was per-

---

[1] *Minga* is a Milanese form of the negative.
[2] He is so described in the libretto of "Mitridate Eupatore."

formed at Rome in Italian in 1690. Innocent XII., who became Pope in 1691, was not favourable to opera, but encouraged oratorio; and Alessandro Scarlatti, though principally occupied at Naples, composed a Christmas Oratorio for him in 1695. There were also a few opera performances during his reign, including Scarlatti's " La Teodora Augusta" (1693) and his "Gerone Tiranno di Siracusa" (1694), which does not appear to have been very successful. But in 1697 the Pope ordered the destruction of the Tordinona theatre on grounds of public morality—the wits of Rome quoting the psalm, "*Manus tuae fecerunt me et sic repente praecipitas me*"—since the same theatre had been almost entirely rebuilt earlier in his reign. The performances were also forbidden at the Teatro Capranica, which was the property of Count D'Alibert, who had built it at considerable expense. Even after the death of Innocent XII. things were little better, there being no performances of operas that year on account of public mourning. During the next two years (1701 and 1702) there were some private performances, but in 1703 the earthquake again put a stop to opera, and no records of further operatic productions in Rome are forthcoming until 1709, when the Queen of Poland (Marie Casimir) took Domenico Scarlatti into her service.

Under such circumstances Alessandro, as long as he remained in Rome, was inevitably reduced to confining his talents to the chamber and the church. Fortunately Cardinal Ottoboni was as devoted to chamber-music as to the opera, and it was at his weekly music meetings that Scarlatti's cantatas were in the greatest demand. An exceptionally large number of them date from this period, beginning indeed as early as 1701, and it is interesting to see that while Scarlatti was obliged to write his operas down to the level of the taste of the Neapolitan court, he found in the chamber-music an outlet for the truer utterances of his genius. At Rome these were better appreciated, and the more genuinely musical atmosphere of the place, as well as the influence of such musicians as Corelli and Francischiello the violoncellist soon made itself apparent in the steady improvement of his work from both the poetical and the technical point of view.

The charming cantata "*Sarei troppo felice*" is one of the most interesting of those written before he left Naples.[1] It is rather more elaborate in form than most, and shows the way in which Scarlatti was constantly using the cantata as a field for experiment. It begins with a very characteristic *arioso*,

Ex. 31.

---

[1] The autograph bears the date 30 April 1702.

the main idea of which is repeated several times in the
course of the cantata.   These repetitions come at the close
of the recitatives, and are all much curtailed except the
final one, which forms the conclusion of the cantata.
Here Scarlatti treats the theme at greater length.   I quote
the recitative in its entirety, so that the scheme of key-
relationship may be understood.   The preceding aria is in
G minor.

-ce - ro   in - ca - te-ni il pen - sier, se v'è ca - te-na c'human pen-

-sie-ro in-ca-te-nar si van-ti ;   io per me la de - sio, ma non la spero.

a tempo.

Sa - rei trop-po fe - li - ce, trop-po fe - li - ce,

s'io po - tes - si dar leg - ge   al   mio pen - sie - ro,

s'io po - tes - si dar leg-ge, Sa - rei trop-po fe - li - ce trop - po fe -

- li - ce, s'io po - tes-si dar leg - ge,   s'io po - tes - si dar

leg-ge al mio pen-sie-ro, al mio pen-sie-ro.

The modulation through the dominant to the super-tonic, as soon as the theme "*Sarei troppo felice*" returns, is unexpected, the hearer being accustomed to the invariable return of the theme in its original form. But the variation is welcome, as is the alteration in the voice part, and the return to F major is made all the more striking by being deferred and brought in at a melodic climax. The simple and natural use of a sequence and a deceptive cadence in the last five bars shows Scarlatti's easy mastery of musical rhetoric, and still more so does the final fragment of recitative which makes a characteristic coda. These five notes are of course historically a survival of the original narrative idea of the chamber cantata, when it was usual to end with a recitative, the arias being considered as merely incidental. But here, following the *arioso*, they give an interesting illustration of the aesthetic ideas of the period. The *arioso* forms a complete whole in a quite modern spirit, but it wants a little coda of some sort to round it off. All composers since Schumann and many before him would have given this coda to the accom-paniment; we feel that the voice part has come to its proper end, and if anything more has to be said, it must be said differently. Scarlatti evidently felt exactly the same: but for him the *cembalo* was not the right medium for the expression of such ideas as Schumann puts into his codas for the pianoforte. The voice alone is both adequate and available, and he gets over the difficulty of the vitally necessary differentiation of style by the use of recitative, and that in a conspicuously conventional formula.

Attention has been drawn to the sequence and the deceptive cadence. We are so accustomed to these devices in Bach and Handel that it may be hard to realize how gradual is their adoption by Scarlatti. But it should be observed that both of them, together with various other rhetorical devices, receive their full value only when used in conjunction with modern tonality. We have already seen in Scarlatti's early work how the influence of the modes was still comparatively strong in Italy after German and English composers had almost entirely shaken it off. The more rapid progress of Germany and England in this direction is due mainly to the healthy influence of the Reformation and the consequent increase of serious interest in the squarely rhythmical tunes of the people. Northern composers, too, have always had more sense of harmony than of melody, and it will easily be seen how the study of harmony, in connexion with simple rhythmical tunes like German chorales, led to the concise organization of harmonic principles on a sharply defined rhythmic basis. The air from a wedding cantata of Pachelbel, quoted in the "Oxford History of Music," vol. iii. p. 441, is a convenient illustration of this. It is to some extent under Italian influence ; but it is thoroughly German in the forcible logic of its harmonic progressions taken in conjunction with its straightforward obviousness of rhythm. The blunt directness of its style could never have been acquired by composers who, both during their early training and in later life, were obliged, owing to the traditions of the Catholic Church, to devote themselves to elaborate contrapuntal studies on the pulseless and drawling rhythms of the ecclesiastical *canto fermo*, that like

> "the serpent sly
> Insinuating, wove with Gordian twine
> His braided train, and of his fatal guile
> Gave proof unheeded."

It was only when both composers and audiences were absolutely certain of the principle of tonic relations that even the easy modulation to the subdominant could be employed with a sense of security as a necessary balance to the influence of the dominant, to say nothing of modulation to keys more remote.

Returning to the cantata "*Sarei troppo felice*," the arias offer interesting material for the study of structural development. The first, in B flat, is in a developed binary form, with no *Da Capo*. This is quite exceptional in the cantatas of this period, and indeed the structure of the whole cantata is abnormal; but its variety of forms and the beauty of its material make it useful for analysis here. The words of the air consist of four short lines :—

> " *Tal se premo sentiero odorato,*
> *Dura spina che punge il mio core*
> *Va dicendo ; costante dolore*
> *Non vien meno fra i vezzi del prato.*"

The normal practice is to divide such a stanza in half, setting the third and fourth lines as a second section, after which the first two are repeated. In this case, however, such treatment was impossible, owing to the sense not following the metre ; and the same thing has happened in the second aria, thus compelling Scarlatti to abandon the *Da Capo* form in both cases. This is no doubt the reason why he has seized on the poet's repetition of the line "*Sarei troppo felice s'io potessi dar legge al mio pensiero*" in the recitatives, and extended it into an *arioso* of sufficient musical importance to make up by its return for the want of the *Da Capo* in the first two arias. The third aria suits the conventional plan admirably, and the ternary form is therefore adopted : but the fact that the poet has supplied two stanzas has again guided the composer to a particular treatment of structural details. As in almost all cases, the first two lines are sung twice to form the first section. Now, if a composer sets the same words twice over in one continuous section of a composition, he may treat them, roughly speaking, in three different ways. Excluding the case in which the music is exactly repeated, under which circumstances

F

the composer cannot really be said to have set the words twice, he may make his second setting correspond to the first in rhythm, but not in melody; he may make it correspond in both melody and rhythm, varying only in key, or he may make it definitely contrast in rhythm as well as in melody and tonality. In the aria before us, Scarlatti adopts the third plan. It is obvious that if, in the formula ABA, A can be represented as $a_1b_2a_2b_1$, or some such group, the repetition will be intolerable when the original formula ABA is itself immediately repeated in its entirety. If A is to be heard four times, we can afford to put more material into it, and make its organization more subtle. Scarlatti therefore utilizes the *continuo* as a means of unification. Its introduction

Ex. 33.

is made up of two figures, which accompany the first and second statements of the words respectively,

Ex. 34 (*a*).

Il pen - sie - ro è un prato a - me - no ove i sen - si

Ex. 34 (*b*).

Il pen - siero è un prato a - me - no ove i sen - si

both being developed a little beyond the quotations given.
The second phrase naturally is made to end in G minor,
and, as usual, a little coda follows.   The vocal material is
new, but the bass is not :—

Ex. 35.

han - no   han - - - - - -

- - no il con - fi - - ne

and the *continuo* adds yet another coda on the same subject
after the voice leaves off.   The form cannot in any way be
classed as a ground-bass, but there is a certain analogy with
the air *"Io per gioco vi mirai"* analysed in Chapter I.   The
second section (B) must be studied in connexion with the
first.   Just as there were three types for section A, so for
section B we may apply much the same system of classifi-
cation.   B may be as complete a contrast to A as possible
both in melody and rhythm (its tonality is always contrasting as a matter of course) ; it may reproduce A more or
less in rhythm or melody, or both ; or it may combine both
schemes, as it does here.   As a whole, it forms a complete
contrast : in detail it is almost entirely made up of fragments
of A worked up into something like a regular modern
"development section."   This is complicated ; but the
complication is justified because the poet's two stanzas
cause the whole movement to be heard twice.

Let us now turn back to the first aria—*"Tal se premo."*
Here there is only one stanza, and no *Da Capo.*   Scarlatti

can therefore treat his words at rather greater length, and in this way is better able to organize the aria in such a way as to combine elaboration with lucidity.

Ex. 36.

-to. Tal se pre-mo sen-tie-ro o-do-ra-to, du-ra spi-na che punge il mio co-re va di-cen-do, co-stan-te, co-stan-te do-lo-re non vien meno, non vien meno fra i vez - - - - - zi del pra - to.

fra i vez - - - - zi del pra -

to.

I have quoted the aria at length in order that the variety of detail and the relation of the parts may be fully appreciated. The four lines of verse are cut up into six groups of words, each of which is quite sharply defined, though together they form a melodious whole of singular beauty. Lines one and four provide what we may call definite first and second subjects of strongly contrasting character, and the subsidiary figures taken from lines three and four are useful for purposes of modulation, and not without an individuality of their own. The ingenuity of the construction is further enhanced by the vocal coda derived from the second subject, and the instrumental coda derived from the first but modified so as to ballast the whole aria with a powerful subdominant influence. At the same time it should be noted, in connexion with what has been said about the use of the subdominant and modern tonality, that the aria contains no example whatever of a deceptive cadence.

The second aria is less important. It is shorter than the first, but is definitely organized in a scheme based on the formula AABB. The first strain A ends on the dominant; the second starts again on the tonic, and does not modulate. The first strain B is in the relative minor; the second, which is rather extended, starts in the

supertonic minor and returns to the tonic. There are
short vocal and instrumental codas. Here again the music
is unified by a single characteristic figure in the *continuo*
which runs all through against both subjects. This time it
is more definitely instrumental:—

Ex. 37.
a tempo giusto.

and we frequently find in the cantatas of this period basses
that seem to demand imperatively the assistance of a
violoncello. It was always customary to play the *continuo*
on violoncello and *cembalo :* but in the earlier cantatas there
is nothing distinctively instrumental about the basses.
Later, Scarlatti acquired the reputation of writing exceptionally difficult violoncello parts, and it is to the
influence of Francischiello, a virtuoso whose playing,
as well as Scarlatti's accompaniment of him, excited
Geminiani's enthusiastic admiration at Naples, that we
may safely ascribe such development of instrumental style
as is apparent in the following examples.

Ex. 38.

Parte il piè ma resta il co - re, che più

dar - ti, oh Dio ! oh Dio ! non so.

Ex. 39.

The refinement of violin technique in Corelli's time was due to the desire to emulate the example of the singers, and no doubt the violoncello felt the same influence. But as early as 1702 the influence of the instrumentalists was beginning to react in the converse direction, as we see from the following extracts.

Ex. 40.

Here we can still say that the influence is for good ; the figure is as apt to the voice as to the violoncello. This development of instrumental style is important also in its relation to structure.   The arias in almost every cantata begin with an introduction for the *continuo* alone.   In most of the earlier cantatas and in some of the later ones this introduction is derived from the opening vocal phrase, and an audience would no doubt watch with interest to see how the accompanist would treat as a bass what in the majority of cases seems more adapted to harmonization from below. But when in the later cantatas the voice is accompanied on its entry by a contrasting and clearly individualized instrumental figure, it is this figure that forms the introduction, and it often becomes easy for the composer to use it throughout, independently of the formal scheme of the voice-part.   In theory a mere figure of accompaniment, it gains additional thematic importance in practice from the fact that the whole is conceived in two-part harmony;[1] the examples already given, as well as those to follow, will sufficiently illustrate its value as a structural element.

On April 26, 1706, Corelli, Alessandro Scarlatti, and Bernardo Pasquini (then organist of S. Maria Maggiore) were admitted members of the Arcadian Academy under the pastoral names of *Arcimelo, Terpandro*, and *Protico*.[2]

---

[1] The bass would, of course, be harmonized on the *cembalo*, but its thin metallic sound would give the chords a jingling elusiveness that we can hardly realize on a modern pianoforte.   For us it is better to treat the accompaniment polyphonically, but not in more than three parts ; and indeed Scarlatti's own polyphony is so complete that it is often difficult enough to add a single part in a worthy style.

[2] The entry in the original MS. catalogue runs as follows :—

> *Ragunanza LXXX*
>   *Chiamata Generale*
> *Al x° di Targelione stante l'anno I° del Olimp. DCXXI ab A.J. Olimp. IV. An. IV. giorno lieto*
>   *Furono surrogati*

<table>
<tr><td>✠
M</td><td>| Terpandro |</td><td>990.
Politeio—dalle Camp^e presso</td></tr>
</table>

> la Terra di Politeia in Acaia
> Alessandro Scarlatti Palermitano
> Insigne Maestro di Musica.

Crescimbeni gives us picturesque glimpses of their musical performances in his curiously "precious" records of the early Arcadian meetings. We see them on one occasion taking part in a concert at the house of *Metaureo*—Abate Domenico Riviera.[1] It was arranged by Scarlatti, and there was a considerable band of strings and wind. First came a *Sinfonia* of Corelli ; then two cantatas of Pasquini to words by Gian Battista Felice Zappi (*Tirsi*). After this came a duet by Scarlatti, also to words by Zappi, followed by an instrumental piece of some sort. Scarlatti was at the harpsichord, but managed at the same time to observe that Zappi was in process of thinking out a new poem. He begged Zappi to produce it ; Zappi agreed to do so on condition that Scarlatti set it to music at once. Scarlatti assented, and "no sooner had *Tirsi* finished his recital than *Terpandro*, with a truly stupendous promptness, began to transcribe the verses recited, with the music thereto ; and when these had been sung, the souls of those present received of them so great delight, that they not only obliged the singer to repeat the song again and again, but also urged both poet and musician to display their skill afresh." After some pressing, Zappi and Scarlatti repeated their impromptu performance, and "meanwhile every one was astonished to see how two such excellent Masters, the one of poetry and the other of music, did contend ; and their contention was so close that scarce had the one finished repeating the last line of the new air than the other ended the last stave of his music."

Prince Ruspoli was another great Arcadian and patron of Scarlatti. For him were written some of the serenatas, a form of composition for which Scarlatti was much in request at Rome. They were probably sung at entertainments, as at Naples, rarely as serenades beneath a lady's window, though there are a few solo cantatas with some direction indicating the latter purpose. In such cases there is nearly always some characteristic style of treatment, as in the cantata "*Hor che di Febo ascosi*" for soprano and two

[1] Crescimbeni, *Arcadia*, Lib. vii. Prosa v.

violins, the last movement of which is irregular in form, with a curious ending that makes the voice and violins vanish like ghosts into the starry distance.

Ex. 42.

The larger serenatas have little intrinsic interest, though there are a few good numbers, such as " *Sento un' aura* " from " Endimione e Cintia." But they sometimes have overtures in curious experimental forms, and the treatment of the instruments has peculiarities. The orchestra is often divided into *concerto grosso* and *concertino*, which in the operas is unusual.   It is moreover in these serenatas that the influence of Corelli is most apparent.   To what extent Scarlatti and Corelli were personal friends it is difficult to say. According to Burney, whose information, coming from Geminiani, ought to be trustworthy, Scarlatti had no very great opinion of Corelli as a composer, though he admired his playing and his direction of the orchestra.   It can hardly be doubted that Corelli did quite as much for orchestral playing as for solo playing or composition. How great his reputation as a leader was is seen from the quaint description of him in the *Ferragosto* of Zappi and Crescimbeni :—

> " *Or vedi lui, ch' al Coro almo gentile*
> *Sovrasta, e par la destra armi di penne ?*
> *Egli è a se solo, e a null' altro simile.*
> *Degli Angelici Spirti ei già sostenne*
> *Le melodie ; poscia a beare il suolo,*
> *Lasciò il celeste Coro, e a noi sen venne ;*
> *E seco trasse dal suo chiaro Polo*
> *L' unisonanza non più in Terra udita ;*
> *Onde crediam cento stromenti un solo.*" [1]

To his influence we may safely attribute the development of that definitely orchestral style which made its appearance in Scarlatti's operas after his second return to Rome ; and however little Scarlatti may have professed to admire his compositions, he at any rate did not disdain to imitate them.   Indeed the lilt of Corelli's gigues seized him like a St. Vitus' dance, and turns up everywhere, sometimes in the most unexpected places.

Geminiani's well-known story (recorded by Burney) of Corelli's break-down in a composition of Scarlatti's at Naples

[1] " Seest thou that gentle soul that leads the quire,
Bearing as 'twere a feather in his hand ?
Like to none other but himself alone,
Once of the angels' holy songs he bore
The tuneful burden ; then to bless the earth,
Left the celestial quire and came to us ;
And with him brought from his bright heavenly home
That pure concent ne'er heard on earth before,
By which a hundred instruments seem one."

is hard to understand. Corelli, as we know, was never a great executant, but Scarlatti is hardly likely to have written difficult passages for him after being so much under his influence. Indeed in the whole of Scarlatti's extant works there is only one passage of violin music which seems intended for a display of virtuosity—the introduction to the air " *Ti rendo ancor la palma*" in " Laodicea e Berenice." Fétis supposed it to have been written for Corelli ; but as " Laodicea" came out at Naples in 1701, and Corelli never visited Naples till about 1708, this does not seem very plausible. The passage is not at all in Corelli's style, and goes a good deal higher than he was accustomed to, besides including a trying passage across two strings in a high position ; but it is curious that Scarlatti should have transplanted the entire air, solo and all, into the serenata " Il Giardino d' Amore," especially as it was quite contrary to his custom to dish up a composition a second time.

It was hardly possible for a composer to live in Rome, especially under the patronage of a cardinal, without writing a certain amount of music for the church. It was still the tradition to write masses "*alla Palestrina*," and Scarlatti accordingly produced the " Missa Clementina I." in 1703, and in 1706 a mass for Cardinal Ottoboni. The first is well written and contains many canons, but although, judging from the number of copies to be found, it seems to have excited the admiration of professional contrapuntists, like the Mass in F, which is all in canon, it is extremely dry. Of the ecstatic feeling of Palestrina there is not the least trace. The Ottoboni Mass[1] is rather better ; it has a sense of modern tonality and a certain amount of feeling. But Scarlatti was not by nature a church-composer, least of all at this period of his life.

---

[1] The autograph is in the Vatican library. It is a huge folio, with the music not in score but in separate parts so arranged that all the singers could sing from the same book, the notes being very large. The whole manuscript is so beautiful a specimen of musical caligraphy that one could hardly believe it to be the autograph of a great composer were it not for the words "*propria manu scripsit Alexander Scarlattus*" on the title-page. It is unfortunately in a very bad state, the ink having eaten through the paper so that the pages are literally dropping to pieces.

In his motets and oratorios he is often picturesque and
sometimes quite beautiful; but he is too classical in spirit,
too much of a poet, to write such music as is usually considered to be devotional. Of the early oratorios "Agar
et Ismaele" (1683) is the best; like the early operas, it
is carefully written, with great attention to poetic expression. "Il Martirio di S. Teodosia" (1685) is of interest
only for the fine fugal chorus which concludes it. Apparently, however, it was not to the taste of the audience,
as nothing of the kind occurs in the later oratorios.

The *Concerti Sacri* published by Étienne Roger at
Amsterdam probably date from somewhere about 1700.
These are a series of ten motets for from one to four voices,
accompanied by two violins and *continuo*. They consist
mostly of *Da Capo* airs and recitatives, with an occasional
arioso or ground-bass; there is little four-part writing.
The style is generally florid, and suggests the gay
decorations of the Italian Jesuit churches. Sometimes
it is positively ludicrous in its baroque brilliance; and
when one comes across a passage like this—

Ex. 43.

Alto.

qui tri-bu-it   mi-hi in-tellec -   -   -   tum

Violins.

Continuo.

intellec - - - - - - - - -

it is hard to believe that there was not a malicious intention in the choice of such peculiarly grotesque *fioriture*. Yet along with these oddities there is much that is genuinely beautiful—the peaceful duet, "*O fluida vita*," the melodious *pastorale*, "*O nimis clara lux*," the happy grace of "*Rorate coeli*," as well as the bold harmonies and passionate earnestness of "*Infirmata vulnerata*."

With such music as this to be heard in the churches, it is small wonder that Benedict XIV. was obliged to order that the consecrated elements should be kept in a side chapel, because the congregations habitually turned their backs on the high altar to listen to the singers placed in the western gallery![1]

The papal taste, however, does not seem to have been too severe, at any rate in Scarlatti's time. He produced several oratorios and sacred cantatas while in Rome, mostly for performance at the Vatican, but there is very little serious music in them. They are generally either dull or frivolous. " Il Sedecia " contains a beautiful duet,

---

[1] Grétry, *Mémoires*.

"*Col tuo velo*,"[1] but the greater part of the oratorio is extremely tedious, and it is curious that it should have been so much admired as the number of extant copies, both contemporary and modern, would seem to attest. The Annunciation Oratorio is rather better ; the air "*Verginella fortunata*," in which the angel delivers his message, is pure and dignified in style, and the Virgin has a very beautiful air, "*Stesa a piè del tronco amaro*," in which she contemplates her future sorrows with a fine expression of exalted feeling. The work is also interesting from a curious arrangement of the introductory *Sinfonia* which recalls Mendelssohn's " Elijah " ; indeed, the displacement of the movements is made from an analogous motive. The overture begins with an *allegro* of fifteen bars in G minor ending in the dominant ; this is immediately followed by the Virgin's air, " Sommo Dio," which is in a calm and serious style. The rest of the overture is then played ; a short passage of slow-moving suspensions and an *allegro* in binary form, not a definite dance-movement, but, as is usual in the oratorios, strongly rhythmical, and fulfilling the same aesthetic purpose. This movement, however, is not in the key of the first, but in F major, and is at once followed by the angel's air in the same key ; Scarlatti seems to have wished to effect a compromise between the conventional overture-form and a descriptive symphony suggesting the angel's arrival.

As a rule the libretti of the oratorios are not very inspiring. They read like inferior opera-books, and indeed, except that the operas are in three acts and the oratorios in two, the only difference is in the absence of professedly comic characters, and of the formal statement in which the author protests that the words *Fato*, *Dio*, *Deità*, &c., are only *scherzi poetici* and imply nothing contrary to the Catholic Faith. Indeed, when in the *Ferragosto* of Zappi and Crescimbeni *Alfesibeo* can thus

---

[1] Published (not without some touching up) in Carl Banck's " *Duette Alter Meister*."

explain to *Tirsi* the shaven polls and hairless faces of the
papal singers—

> " *Servono al sommo Pan quei, che vedesti*
> *Senza le chiome, e son cantor' del tempio,*
> *Adorni di pensier saggi e modesti,*" [1]

it seems almost curious that an analogous protest was not
required for the oratorios from the point of view of
Olympus.

Scarlatti, as usual, makes the best of a bad job.
" Humanità e Lucifero " is rubbish from beginning to end,
but in the " Rosary " oratorio he probably delighted his
audience by giving *Penitence* an air—" *Starò nel mio*
boschetto qual dolce rosignuolo "—accompanied by two
violas and a nightingale, the latter being treated in the
toy-symphony style, at the player's discretion ; and the
Assumption oratorio ends with a duet for the heavenly
Bride and Bridegroom, the fascinating grace of which
could only be paralleled in the frescoes of Correggio.

Ex. 45.

[1] " They serve great Pan whom here thou dost behold
With hair and beard close shorn ; chaste are their thoughts
And wise, for in the temple rites they sing."

Christmas was a season at which oratorios were customary, and Scarlatti shows us some interesting examples of the traditional pastoral style. Besides a very attractive solo cantata, "*Oh di Betlemme altera*" (words by Prince Antonio Ottoboni), there is a duet for two shepherds —Arcadian, needless to say—and a formal oratorio, in which Abraham, Isaiah, Jeremiah, Daniel, and Ezechiel prophesy the birth of the Messiah in a series of charming airs, the cheerfulness of which is somewhat tempered by the "*lacrimoso Profeta*" Jeremiah. The other three prophets remonstrate with some curtness in *recitativo secco*, but to no purpose, until finally Daniel draws their attention to the hymns of the angels and shepherds at the manger. The air is singularly beautiful, and interesting as the prototype of the "pastoral symphonies" of Handel and Bach.

gl'an-gio-li van can-tan - do,   gl'an-gio-li van can -

-tan - do e i pas - to - rel - li.

Compositions of this kind were always performed at the Vatican on Christmas Eve after vespers, before the Pope and the cardinals sat down to a banquet decorated with *trionfi*, representing the Nativity.[1] Corelli's once very popular Pastoral Concerto was, no doubt, composed for a similar occasion. The question has been much discussed as to whether the Pastoral Symphony in "The Messiah" is an original composition of Handel's or not, and I believe that the word "*Pifa*" with which he headed it has been sometimes accepted as definite proof of its being an actual folk-tune. It seems much more reasonable to consider the movement simply as an imitation of the traditional style. To recover the precise melodies of the *zampognari* of Handel's Roman days is impossible; most probably they played then as they do now, tuneless melodies, picturesque enough in rhythm and colour to make the passing stranger stop and listen for a moment,

[1] Adami, *Osservazioni per ben regolare il Coro dei Cantori della Cappella Pontificia.* Rome, 1711.

but not sufficiently definite in character for a composer to utilize without modification. The variety in similarity displayed by the numerous specimens in Scarlatti's works should be enough to prove that they were not derived from any one particular traditional tune. The most we can say of Handel's Pastoral Symphony is that it was very probably modelled on this particular air of Scarlatti, certainly the most attractive of all his pastoral movements.

Rome was not Scarlatti's only field of activity at this period. His dramatic talent found scope at Pratolino, though it may be doubted whether his work there was entirely satisfactory to him. An "Arminio" was performed at Pratolino in 1703, but there is not sufficient evidence to identify it with Scarlatti's opera of that name given at Naples in 1714. But it is fairly certain that "Turno Aricino" was the drama of Stampiglia which Scarlatti's letters prove him to have set to music in 1704, although for the later revival at Rome it must have been almost entirely composed afresh. There can be no doubt as to "Lucio Manlio l'Imperioso" (1705) and "Il Gran Tamerlano" (1706). The music to all four operas, except fragments of the revised version of "Turno Aricino," has entirely disappeared, a loss the more to be regretted since Scarlatti evidently took a great deal of trouble over both the last two, and seems to have considered them as the best that he had produced up to that time.

His correspondence with Ferdinand throws an interesting light on his ideas and his methods. The opera performances at Pratolino took place in September; accordingly Ferdinand sends Scarlatti the first act of Silvio Stampiglia's drama, "Lucio Manlio," on June 9, 1705, Scarlatti acknowledges the receipt of it on June 13, with his usual compliments, and a fortnight later sends Ferdinand the music. "I have paid more attention," he writes, "to the mixed character of the audience, than to the natural impulses of my own insipid pen, precisely as the author of the drama seems to desire ; and perhaps the music will be able to give more pleasure to those who like to take home with them some tune that they can easily remember, and that all can sing." A year before he had assured Ferdinand of his efforts to be "pleasant and tuneful, rather than learned"; but the prince seems to have been rather hard to please.

"Lucio Manlio" was finished on July 18, having taken only five weeks to write. "I humbly lay at the feet of your Royal Highness," he writes, "the third act of 'Lucio Manlio' set to music, which ends the opera, but not my most feeble labours, the which, in blind obedience to the revered directions of your Royal Highness, I am ready to resume with untiring devotion; to rewrite the whole from the beginning in such a way as may best satisfy whatever commands the high and mighty clemency of your Royal Highness shall deign to impose upon me; for which sole reason (as is indeed my unforgotten duty as well as the highest honour and glory that I could ever desire), I have changed the style of my most feeble pen; yet have I not been able to do so to the extent of abandoning entirely that character which it has by nature. This pen, however, overshadowed by a new spirit, has been able, with a felicity that I seldom have obtained, to render me so fertile (especially in composing this third act), that when I thought to let the fruit ripen by giving it more time, I saw the work completed with rapidity and without opposition from my imagination, accustomed though it be to blame my pen's ideas.[1] Nevertheless, I have set it before myself in judgment dispassionately, and have diligently examined it with regard to the style that the author of the words desired, and which he has repeatedly informed me to be the amiable will of your Royal Highness; and I think that in this third act at any rate, if not in the whole opera, I have found means to fulfil the revered com-

---

[1] "*Questa [penna] però obumbrata da nuovo spirito, hà potuto con felicità, rare volte ottenuta, rendermi una tal fecondità di specie nel vestire questo terz' atto, che quando credevo di maturarne il parto, coll' impiego di maggior tempo, l'ho veduto posto in luce con velocità, e senza opposizione della fantasia, avvezza in me ad accusarne le idee.*"

mand that was laid upon me. Nevertheless, I may have deceived myself; perhaps from the vehemence of my desire to fulfil it in that form which should best succeed in meeting with that most gracious compassion which the noble and heroic mind of your Royal Highness has deigned to grant me, if only from excess of the inimitable clemency which there occupies its rightful throne. Having complete confidence in the same, I take the liberty of offering, in the semblance of a holocaust, a brief epitome of my intentions in composing the music of this opera, although as regards the two preceding acts, I can say little, not having them by me; although I have given precise instructions with all possible clearness to the author of the words : saying that where the music is marked *grave*, I do not mean it to be melancholy ; where marked *andante*, not fast, but with a feeling of melody. Where *allegro*, not at a headlong rate ; where *allegrissimo*, not in such a style as to drive the singer to despair, or to drown the words. Where *andante lento*, in a style that should not be pathetic, but rather tender and charming, so as not to lose the sense of melody ; and in all these airs there should be no melancholy.[1] I have always made it my aim, in composing for the theatre, to make the first act resemble a child that takes its first steps but feebly ; the second a youth that walks erect and sure ; and the third should be like a young man, swift and strong, bold of undertaking and successful in all that he undertakes. This I have done in 'Lucio Manlio,' an opera which completes the number of eighty-eight dramatic works composed in less than twenty-three years, and to which I should have wished to give a crown as being the queen of all the others. If I have not had the ability to make it such, I have at least been bold enough to attempt to do so."[2]

[1] " *Dove è segnato grave, non intendo malenconico ; dove andante, non presto, ma arioso. Dove allegro, non precipitoso ; dove allegro, tale che non affanni il Cantante, nè affoghi la parole. Dove andante lento, in forma, che esclude il patetico, mà sia un amoroso vago, che non perda l'arioso ; ed in tutte le arie nessuna malenconica.*"

[2] Archivio Mediceo, *Filza* 5903, No. 165.

This lengthy letter, of which the rest has already been quoted earlier in this chapter, is of interest as showing us something of Scarlatti's methods. He seems to imply that composition was almost a mechanical process for him, and that the function of the imagination was not to direct but to criticize. And indeed the process, strange as it may seem to a generation that has not yet been able to shake off the false sentiment of the romantic movement, was yet legitimate and natural enough to a composer who belongs to the severest period of classicism, when beauty and purity of style were still considered as more important than originality and violence of expression.

The directions given as to style, as well as several passages in other letters, show that Scarlatti was anything but indifferent as to the proper interpretation of his music. I have been careful to give the original Italian as well as a translation, since it is difficult to find adequate equivalents in English for some of Scarlatti's expressions. The composer's meaning becomes rather clearer if we remember the extent to which singers were accustomed to vary the melody of an air. Audiences of Scarlatti's day must have been sufficiently familiar with this habit to be able, perhaps half unconsciously, to decipher the original melody under the variations of the singer, or at any rate to form an idea of the principles of its construction that would suffice to give them a logical understanding of the performance. It is however obvious that a singer who was not a good musician might not merely extemporize bad variations, but might even so far ignore the original melody as to entirely stultify the faculty of the audience for the appreciation of musical form. Thus the word *arioso*, which we now use conveniently and not illogically to denote a kind of music between recitative and air, was used by Scarlatti not as the title of a form, but as a direction to the singer to be careful to preserve the melodic sense in music which at first sight might seem to demand the declamatory style of recitative; and it was equally natural that he should use it in a case where a singer might have been tempted to take too many liberties with the time or to indulge in an excess of extemporary *coloratura*. His insistence on avoiding the "*patetico*" and "*malenconico*" shows us that even the age of *bel canto* was not free from singers who made a speciality of the tearful and mawkish style.

"Lucio Manlio" was Scarlatti's eighty-eighth opera: "Il Gran Tamerlano," which was written for Pratolino the following year, he describes in a letter as his ninetieth. What was the eighty-ninth, and for what theatre was it written? No trace of it is to be found, unless we suppose Scarlatti to have counted as an opera the few airs which he added to a pasticcio called "La Pastorella," composed by Cesarini, Giannino (Giovanni del Violone?), and Bononcini, that was represented by marionettes—the real singers singing behind the scenes—at the Palazzo Venezia in 1705.

"Il Gran Tamerlano" seems to have given Scarlatti some trouble. The part of *Rossane*, composed originally for a contralto who had sung the previous year, had to be rewritten for Signora Tilla, who was a soprano; and in spite of all efforts, "Lucio Manlio" appears to have been too serious, as Ferdinand wrote to Scarlatti on April 2, 1706: "I shall be very much pleased if you will make the music [of 'Il Gran Tamerlano'] rather more easy, and noble in style; and if, in such places as is permissible, you will make it rather more cheerful."[1] Scarlatti was very much pleased with the libretto (by G. A. Salvi). "I have read the third act of 'Tamerlano' and find it all that it ought to be, and an excellent end to its admirable beginning and continuation, the proof of which is that in the whole course of this beautiful work I find the plot so strong, so charming, so new and so spirited, that the strength and quality of the recitative (in which the scenic action is represented) prevents me from wishing for the airs, as is generally the case."[2] The opera was finished

---

[1] Archivio Mediceo, *Filza* 5903, No. 497.
[2] Ibid., *Filza* 5903, No. 208.

in six weeks, and Ferdinand seems to have been satisfied with it, graciously considering it quite unnecessary that Scarlatti should make any further alterations. It apparently had a *finale* of some special interest, as Scarlatti acknowledges having received Ferdinand's instructions on this point through Salvi; and the prince especially mentions that the finale has given him satisfaction. "Tamerlano" was performed at Pratolino in September 1706. Whether Scarlatti directed the production himself is doubtful. He was very busy in Rome during that year with various compositions, and he would hardly have insisted so minutely on details of style in his correspondence if he had been able to superintend the rehearsals in person.

Certainly, however, the most interesting work of this period is the opera "Mitridate Eupatore," written for Venice and produced at the Teatro S. Giovanni Crisostomo in 1707. It was followed by a second opera, "Il Trionfo della Libertà," in the same year. Both are entirely different from anything that Scarlatti had done before, being five-act dramas with ballets, but without comic characters. The poet, Count Girolamo Frigimelica Roberti, was evidently a man of considerable literary ability. He shows a close familiarity with Greek tragedy, and imitates its methods freely; he also has a strong dramatic instinct and an eye for effective situations. Unfortunately, he is too anxious to point the political moral, and often spoils good work by being didactic; and the reader soon realizes that dramatic instinct is not the same thing as theatrical experience. Roberti, like Scarlatti's first librettist Contini, was an architect as well as a poet, best known to us as the designer of the Villa Pisani at Strà, between Padua and Venice; and indeed we may see in the opera the same intention of severe grandeur, and the same effect of frigid immensity that characterize the palace.

The main idea of the plot is borrowed from the "Electra" of Euripides. *Stratonica*, wife of *Mitridate*, king of Pontus, has murdered her husband and raised her paramour *Farnace* to the throne.   Her son *Mitridate Eupatore*, the rightful heir, has disappeared, and his sister *Laodice* has been married to a shepherd to get her out of the way.   At the beginning of the opera *Stratonica* and *Farnace*, fearing the return of *Eupatore*, offer a reward for his head.   Two strangers undertake to bring it ; needless to say one of the two is *Eupatore* in disguise, and the other is his wife *Issicratea* in male attire.   The brother and sister have a recognition-scene in the classical manner, and the opera ends with the death of *Farnace* and *Eupatore's* return to his kingdom.

Scarlatti seems to have done his best to produce a masterpiece worthy of the glorious traditions of Venetian opera.   The style of "Eraclea" is not altogether abandoned, but the airs are mostly broader and more dignified, besides having more material put into them.   The characterization too is very good.   *Eupatore* himself is perhaps a rather conventional *primo uomo*, but the tyrant *Farnace*, cynical and cowardly, is well drawn.   Still finer creations are the two women.   *Stratonica* is an eighteenth-century *Ortrud*—the political woman, ready to commit any crime to gratify her ambition.   *Laodice*, however, is far removed from the type of *Elsa* or any other namby-pamby heroine of early German romanticism ; hers is the classic grandeur of *Leonora, Donna Anna,* and *Iphigénie.*   It is curious that in this opera, perhaps the finest that Scarlatti ever wrote, there should be no love scenes.   The most passionate emotional outburst is that of *Laodice*, when she laments the supposed death of her beloved brother.   No love-song of Scarlatti's, beautiful as his love-songs often are, can rival the intense sincerity with which he has painted a sister's affection ; is it too fantastic to suppose that we have here a touch of autobiography, and that he remembered Anna Maria in the convent of Sant' Antoniello at Naples—Anna Maria, who, nearly thirty years ago, was singing on the stage of this very theatre ?

The fourth act, in which this occurs, opens with a solemn march, during which the procession starts that is to carry *Eupatore's* head to the usurpers.   Two muted

trumpets and drums lead off, echoed by two trumpets[1] and
drums from the ship at the back of the stage :—

after which the strings effect modulations to the dominant
and the relative minor, ending with a few bars of coda in a
brisker *tempo*.   Handel seems to have remembered this
when he wrote " Saul," for if he did not actually hear it
performed, he may very likely have seen the score, being
thrown much with the Scarlattis at this time.

Laodice enters.   She takes the funeral urn from
Eupatore's reluctant hands, and pours out her lamenta-
tions on it in a magnificent recitative, too long to quote
here entire.

[1] It is hardly conceivable that the " *Trombe marine*," as they are called in
the score, were the stringed instruments of that name, although the parts might
have been played on them.   The instrument was almost entirely obsolete in
1707, and at the height of its popularity was practically confined to Germany
and France.

gra - do, Per cu - ra, per e - tà per a - mor, Fi - glio!

Ex. 49.

O va - na spe - me! o rot - ta fe - de! o bre - ve,

lu - sin - ghie - ra, fu - nes - ta, em - pia al - le - grez - za! Da chi più

cer - co ai - u - to, o più con - for - to? o in cie - lo o in ma - re o in ter - ra,

o neg - li ab - bis - si? Ahi! ahi! Mi - tri - da - te è mor - to!

Segue l'Aria.

The air "*Cara tomba del mio diletto*" which follows
is worthy of J. S. Bach at his best.   The accompaniment
of plain repeated chords for the strings is of course not in
his style, but it is very masterly—always subordinate to
the voice, yet full of feeling in the fragment of violin solo,
and the numberless suspensions which add poignance to
the sweeping phrases of the melody.   The *ritornello*, with
its broad arpeggio figure climbing from agony to agony
and then sinking down suddenly to an unutterable despair,
makes a frame well worthy of the picture.

tom - ba   del mio di - let - - - - to

The recognition takes place directly after this, and brother and sister join in a duet that strangely expresses their half-frightened joy; but after a good scene between *Laodice* and *Stratonica* the act loses in interest. The last act is most disappointing; Scarlatti makes nothing of the fine dramatic situation where *Eupatore* presents *Stratonica* with the head, not of her son, but of her lover. Still, although "*Cara tomba*" stands head and shoulders above all the rest, and indeed above any other air in any other opera of Scarlatti, "Mitridate Eupatore" contains a great many very fine movements, in spite of its inequalities. But it appears to have been rather beyond the appreciation of the audience, for his second Venetian opera, "Il Trionfo della Libertà," as far as we can judge from the fragments that remain, was far inferior to its splendid predecessor.

CHAPTER IV

It can hardly be doubted that Scarlatti went himself to
Venice to direct his operas; it was the general custom for
composers to preside at the harpsichord, at any rate for a
first production, and Scarlatti is not likely to have been
absent on so important an occasion as this. If further
evidence be needed, there is the cantata in Venetian dialect
"*Dove xestu, cor mio?*" which he is not likely to have
written anywhere else. He probably remained at Venice
up to the end of the Carnival, or perhaps not so long. We
hear of him next at Urbino, and it is not unlikely that he
went there from Venice by way of Ferrara. Two *Misereres*
for five voices and strings were copied by Santini at
Ferrara in 1824, apparently from the library of the cathedral. One is dated 1705, and another copy by Santini of
the same composition is dated 1714. The latter date is
quite a possible one as far as the music itself is concerned,
but Scarlatti seems to have been firmly established at
Naples then; 1705 is an equally unlikely date, as his
correspondence with Ferdinand de' Medici shows him to
have been at Rome during Lent of that year. It is only in
1707 that there is a decided probability of his having
passed through Ferrara. No trace, however, of the
original manuscript is now to be found in the library of
the cathedral, and it is not even mentioned in a catalogue
of the eighteenth century. Why he should have visited
Urbino is not very clear, though as the reigning Pope
(Giovanni Francesco Albani) was a native of Urbino, at
that time no longer an independent duchy but incorporated
with the Papal States, there may have been some special
reason for Scarlatti's remaining there from April to Sep-

tember.   The length of his stay at Urbino is proved by a
manuscript of the beautiful duet-cantata " *Questo silenzio
ombroso* " dated " *In   Urbino*, 17 7bre 1707." Another
charming duet-cantata, "*Ahi che sarà di me*," was written
on September 2, no doubt for the same singers.

Scarlatti seems to have been in financial difficulties
again, as far as can be deduced from his correspondence
with Ferdinand.   He wrote to the prince from Urbino in
April, sending his good wishes for Easter and hinting
obscurely at misfortunes of some kind.   The etiquette of
the day apparently considered it indecent to allude frankly
to money matters in corresponding with royalty ; but we
gather that he was without occupation and unable to support
his family.[1]   Ferdinand, however, must have been convinced
by this time that Scarlatti's operatic style was too learned
for the autumn diversions of Pratolino, and had no intention
of appointing him permanently as Maestro di Cappella.
Indeed he was now entirely taken up with Perti, who wrote
the next four operas for Pratolino, and who, to judge from
his epistolary style, was more inclined to write music according to Ferdinand's taste and less given to long-winded
explanations.   Ferdinand's answer to Scarlatti, written on
April 23 from Florence, is conventionally polite, but not
encouraging ; he contents himself with saying that he
is sure that Scarlatti will always meet with the due reward
of his merit, and that he may count upon his sympathy and
his prayers.

Scarlatti was probably back at Rome for Christmas,
since it was for this occasion that he wrote the first of his
two masses in A with orchestral accompaniment.   The
work is interesting as being one of the earliest of its kind ;
but it is very evidently a first attempt in a new style and
not altogether successful.   The second, which will be discussed later on, is very much better.

Few works can be ascribed to 1708.   Of the opera
" L'Humanità nelle Fere," which was probably a revival
of an earlier work under a new title, the music is lost,

[1] Archivio Mediceo, *Filza* 5903, No. 287.

as is also that of the Passion Oratorio, unless some lucky chance brings it to light at the Biblioteca Casanatense in Rome; as not infrequently happens, the catalogue names it, but the manuscript is not to be found. Otherwise the work is represented only by the libretto and by a score at Dresden attributed to Scarlatti, but which from the style seems rather to be an original work of Scarlatti very much altered and expanded by a later hand, probably Hasse's. Four cantatas and the motet "*Adorna thalamum*" are the only other known compositions of this year.

Scarlatti was still in correspondence with Ferdinand de' Medici, and possibly the prince had changed his mind and was thinking of getting Scarlatti back again, as he apparently sent him money both in April and October 1708. Scarlatti outdoes himself in fulsome adulation, but we may suspect him of having had an ironic intention (trusting no doubt to Ferdinand's being too vain to see the point of his sneer) when he wrote of the prince's "having wished to give me a token of satisfaction for the most feeble services that I have rendered with various musical compositions, which your Royal Highness has been pleased to choose rather from mine than from those of many other composers, much better than myself, any one of whom could be a master to me."[1] And again in October he writes: "The more I enjoy the benefits of your Royal Highness' generosity, the more I am confounded by the sense of my own unworthiness, and I do not know how I may give proof to your Royal Highness of the gratitude of my heart for such great and lasting kindness. Silence, respectful and profound, shall best speak for me, accompanied by the most feeble though incessant prayers of myself and my family."[2] It was evidently not worth while sending Ferdinand serenatas and madrigals by way of polite attentions, as he had done in previous years. The correspondence ended with this letter: Ferdinand remained faithful to Perti

[1] Archivio Mediceo, *Filza* 5904, No. 40.
[2] Ibid., *Filza* 5904, No. 143.

until in 1711 his last lingering illness put a final stop to the operatic performances at Pratolino.

According to Baini[1] Scarlatti resigned his post at S. Maria Maggiore in 1709, having succeeded Antonio Foggia as principal Maestro in May 1707. But it seems more probable that he left Rome towards the end of 1708, since the *Gazzetta di Napoli,* mentioning his opera " Teodosio " produced at the Teatro S. Bartolomeo on January 28, 1709, says that he " was persuaded by His Eminence during the last few months to return here from Rome to the service of this royal chapel." His Eminence was of course Cardinal Vincenzo Grimani, then Austrian Viceroy of Naples.

Scarlatti's precise position at the Neapolitan court is a little difficult to determine. After the leave of absence granted him in 1702 had expired without his returning, a certain Gaetano Veneziano was appointed to the vacant post on October 25, 1704.[2] Gaetano Veneziano was succeeded on December 5, 1707, by Francesco Mancini.[3] On December 1, 1708, Cardinal Grimani ordered that Alessandro Scarlatti, having been obliged to give up his post after nearly twenty years' service, should again be admitted to the service of the royal chapel to act as deputy first organist in the absence or illness of other musicians.[4]

It was only natural that Scarlatti should feel such favours as humiliating ; and he probably refused to accept them, since on January 9, 1709, the cardinal gave instructions that Scarlatti should be restored to his original office of Maestro di Cappella, and that his stipend should be increased from thirty to forty-two ducats a month (about £84 a year), Mancini being consoled with the title of Vice-Maestro, and being allowed to retain his original stipend of thirty ducats a month (about £60 a year), with the duty

---

[1] *Memorie storico-critiche della vita e delle opere di Giovanni Pierluigi da Palestrina.* Rome, 1828.

[2] Naples, R. Archivio di Stato, *Mandati dei Vicerè,* vol. 319, fol. 20.

[3] Ibid., *Mandati dei Vicerè,* vol. 322, fol. 16.

Ibid., *Mandati dei Vicerè,* vol. 324, fol. 28 *verso.*

of acting as Scarlatti's deputy in his absence or illness, and the right of eventually succeeding to his post.[1]

Scarlatti certainly returned to Naples, and seems to have been well received by the court, since in addition to "Teodosio" (the music of which has disappeared) he produced an oratorio for the feast of St. Joseph, "Il Trionfo del Valore" (also lost), at the palace; in May appeared the opera "L'Amor Volubile e Tiranno," and on August 28 a cantata for four voices for the birthday of the queen— Elizabeth, wife of Charles III. But it seems doubtful whether he was definitely reinstated as Maestro di Cappella, or at any rate whether he accepted the position, since in 1713 (May 27) the new viceroy, Count Daun, repeated the orders given by the late Cardinal Grimani on December 1, 1708, and January 9, 1709, with regard to Scarlatti's reinstatement and increase of salary.[2] This time he must have accepted the post definitely, since on July 22, 1713, the viceroy allowed him an additional five ducats a month for the servant whose duty it was to call the musicians of the chapel together for the ceremonies in which they took part.

It is possible that Scarlatti did not establish himself definitely at Naples. He is described as *Maestro della Real Cappella* in the libretto of "L'Amor Volubile e Tiranno" (1707) and "La Principessa Fedele" (1710), but during the next three years he does not seem to have written anything for Naples. In 1712 he produced "Il Ciro" at Rome, having composed it in the previous autumn, and in 1713 his oratorio "S. Filippo Neri" was performed at Foligno, whether for the first time may be doubted. But the confirmation of his appointment by Count Daun seems to have been definite, and for the next few years, at any rate, Scarlatti remained at Naples.

"L'Amor Volubile e Tiranno" is a retrogression towards the style of "Eraclea"; no doubt Scarlatti thought that Neapolitan taste would be no better now than it was ten years before. But with "La Principessa Fedele" he enters

---

[1] Naples, R. Archivio di Stato, *Mandati dei Vicerè*, vol. 324, fol. 39-40.
[2] Ibid., *Mandati di Vicere*, vol. 331, fol. 1 *verso* and 2.

definitely upon the new phase to which "Mitridate" looked forward. None of the operas of this period rise to the height of "Mitridate," but they show a continuous progress in technical development. One of the most noticeable features is the treatment of accompaniments. In the early operas the *cembalo* is almost always the principal accompanying instrument, the violins being used only in occasional airs, and then as a rule only for colour effects, like the trumpets ; it is very rarely indeed that they support the main burden of the harmony. But as violin-playing improved Scarlatti made more use of the strings, sometimes even trying experiments in dividing them. These, however, are less modern than would appear at first sight ; for the object of Scarlatti's division of the violins into four parts is not to get four-part harmony from them, but to obtain two orchestras which play antiphonally, as for instance in *Appio's* air, "*Ma il mio ben che fa, dov è ?*" in the first act of "La Caduta dei Decemviri." In most of the airs in "Eraclea" and the other operas of this time we find the strings accompanying all through, as well as the *cembalo*. The noise must often have been consider-able, but it perhaps suited the cast-iron style of the tunes. In "Mitridate," however, there is a tendency to get rid of the *cembalo*, and during this further period it becomes Scarlatti's frequent practice to accompany the voice with violins, violas, and violoncellos alone—sometimes, indeed, without violoncellos, or even violas—letting the *cembalo* and double-basses enter in the *ritornelli* only.

The airs, too, contain much more material than before. Then, the only contrast was between the first part and the second, and that a slight one at the best; now, by en-larging the scheme, Scarlatti gets quite strongly contrasted material into both parts, as well as a sharp contrast between the parts themselves. The theatrical style of the third period is still kept up, and considerably developed, but though his work has gained in vigour and incisiveness of expression, it has lost much of its old tenderness and charm. He uses *coloratura* very freely—sometimes, it

must be admitted, in rather doubtful taste, but generally
with a keen sense of dramatic effect.   Two examples from
" La Principessa Fedele" will illustrate his methods.

The first is in the vigorous style, and calls down
the vengeance of heaven in a most spirited manner :—

Ex. 51.

lam - po ful - mi - ne e sa - et - te ca - der - an ....

.... sul tra - di - tor, sul tra - di - tor.

Coloratura employed in this way has a dramatic value
which no declamation, to however elaborate an accompaniment, can equal.   Such a triumphant rush of rapid notes
can only produce its proper effect when sung.   The modern
plan of giving the *coloratura* to the orchestra and declamation to the voice makes us almost always feel that
the singer is battling against the instruments instead of
leading them.

The second example shows a different use of *coloratura*,
less obvious, but none the less beautiful.   The "faithful
princess" *Cunegonda*, disguised as a boy, is asked to sing,
to soothe the sleep of the Sultan *Aladino*, and complies
with a quiet little ditty, which she says was composed by
a lover in prison.   It is in the style of Scarlatti's early
Neapolitan period, and contains little *coloratura* beyond
delicate flourish which marks a cadence in the second
section ; but at the end of the first part there is a wonderful long, lulling passage of great decorative beauty—

Ex. 52.
CUNEGONDA (*Alto*).

spe - ra, spe - ra, ch'avrai pres - to, presto, pres - to tua bel -

which is not *virtuoso* music at all, and was most probably
sung *pianissimo* in a tender, dreamy style. The idea is carried
out by the recitative in which she tells the story of the song,
quite in the manner of a chamber-cantata.   But it is rare
to find such luxuriant *coloratura* used in this way ; for
later composers it was not showy enough, though there is
just a touch of it in Leo's "S. Elena al Calvario."   We
shall find a truer parallel in the *Choralvorspiele* for the
organ of Buxtehude and J. S. Bach.

"Il Ciro," begun in October 1711, and produced in
Rome for the Carnival of 1712, is notable for its ballets.
Whether they are all Scarlatti's cannot be said, since the
autograph score has been much altered for a later revival.
But some are undoubtedly his, being in his own handwriting.   They are for the most part curious little scraps
of music, so short, even with the repeats, that the dance
could hardly have got well started before it was all over.
The dances of Furies at the end of Act II. are typical of
the style.

Such quaint little movements are in themselves sufficient proof that the ballet in Italian opera was still regarded as necessarily grotesque. The heading of the second "*presto in menuet*" is curious. There are plenty of minuets in Scarlatti's operas, and it is clear that they must have been danced much quicker than the "*menuet de la cour*" as we know it in "Don Giovanni." Indeed Rousseau in his dictionary tells us that the minuet was always danced faster on the stage. But we can hardly conceive Ex. 54 being played as fast as the other minuets seem to require, although its rhythms do not seem very suitable to the stately movements of the classical dance. It must, however, be borne in mind that in Scarlatti's day there was always less difference between fast and slow *tempi* than there is now. We have already seen how he protests against an extreme interpretation of his *tempo*-marks, although he wishes careful attention to be paid to them. As M. Saint-

Saëns has said in his preface to Rameau's *Pièces de Clavecin*, "*Jusqu'au milieu du siècle dernier le degré de vitesse ou de lenteur, si important à notre époque, n'avait probablement pas la même importance qu' aujourd'hui; d'ailleurs, la distance entre les mouvements extrêmes était assez faible. Tous les mouvements devaient être compris entre ce que nous appelons actuellement l'Allegro moderato et l'Andante.*" He might have added that we shall always get nearer to the spirit of the older composers when we translate their directions quite literally, instead of giving them the conventional values which the same words bear in modern music. Another specimen from "Il Ciro" shows how indifferent Scarlatti was to the exact regulation of pace that modern composers require. It is a dance or march of priests, accompanying *Elcino* (i.e. *Ciro* in disguise) in the performance of a sacrifice to Apollo. The same music serves both as *ritornello* and dance, "at whatever pace may be necessary."

Ex. 55.

Coro di Sacerdoti che portano vittime per Sacrificio accompagnando ELCINO *con ballo, suono, e canto.*

Ritor^{lo} e ballo insieme, a tempo che sarà necess^o, o grave, o allegro a piacere.

Con oubuoè all' unis. de' Violini se così piacerà.

Although called "*ballo*," it can hardly have been anything less stately than a march.   It is followed by a hymn,
sung by *Elcino* and repeated in chorus, which seems to
anticipate the similar scenes in "Alceste," "Iphigénie en
Tauride," and "Die Zauberflöte."

"Tigrane" (1715) is the most famous of all Scarlatti's
operas, and though no doubt it owes much of its dictionary
reputation to its being his hundred and sixth work for the
stage, it certainly is the best representative of this particular
period.   It has the great advantage of a clear and well-
designed plot, which in addition to its regular *parti buffe*
has a vein of subtle humour running all through ; *Tomiri*
makes fun of her lovers as she plays off one against the
other, and her rival *Meroe* in the disguise of a gipsy
fortune-teller makes fun of everybody.   But from a musical
point of view the opera is not equal to its reputation.   It
produces a general impression of brilliance and magnificence ; but examples of really deep feeling or exalted
musical beauty are rare.   This is characteristic of the
whole of this period.   The characters are striking, the
music is striking ; variety of expression, brilliant *coloratura*
and melodic beauty contribute to make everything as

showy and effective as possible; but there is no getting
away from the utter unreality of the whole business. The
outrageous incongruities of the comic scenes are a positive
relief; crazy as their characters are, they are very much
more human and natural than the heroes and heroines
of the conventional tragedy.

The comic scenes of "Tigrane" are distinctly good,
and are also notable as being among the very few where
dialect is employed; not Neapolitan, however, but
Bolognese, and that only for a few sentences, mixed with
the absurd Latin of *Orcone* as a *Dottor Graziano*, and
Dorilla's still more absurd attempts at German.[1] The
final scene of Act I. deserves mention, as it shows a
certain sense of musical parody in the use of pompous
recitativo stromentato for comic purposes. In the previous
scene *Meroe* has arranged a simulated evocation of her own
ghost for *Tigrane*, who believes her dead; the part of the
wizard is played by her servant *Orcone*. During the
serious interview between *Tigrane* and the supposed ghost
of *Meroe*, he has gone to sleep, but wakes up after they
are gone and is discovered by *Dorilla*. She of course sees
through his disguise, and wishing to have some fun with
him, requests him to raise her a ghost; he somewhat
reluctantly proceeds to perform an incantation, stammering
with fear lest it should really take effect. The stammering
is a rather trite form of humour, but contrasted with the
solemn movements of the orchestra it becomes absurdly
ludicrous.

Ex. 56.
(*Intanto va facendo circolo colla verga, e pauroso.*)

[1] *Dorilla* fortunately supplies an Italian translation herself of her air,
" *Ic bin lipaber, ic libe, libe du*," which turns out to represent " Ich bin Liebhaber,
ich liebe, liebe Du,"—" *io sono amante, io amo, ama tu.*"

ORCONE.

Dai cu, cu, cu, dai cu - pi vor - ti - ci,

dai cu - pi vor - ti - ci dell' ombre or - ri - bi - li.

"Tigrane" is also interesting as being the first of Scarlatti's operas that shows a tendency towards modern orchestral writing. It contains a good many little dances and marches, but these are generally scored thinly, all the upper instruments playing in unison, or at most in two parts. But *Tigrane* has an air in Act I. accompanied by two horns, "*concerto di oubuoè*"[1] (*i.e.* oboes and bassoons in

---

[1] The spelling "*oubuoè*," which is regularly used by Scarlatti and his contemporaries, is as exact a representation as is possible in Italian of the French "*hautbois*," as it was pronounced at that time.

three-part harmony, with probably several instruments to each part) and strings, in which the horns are fairly prominent; and there are also airs with solo parts for the lute and the *violetta d'amore*. But on the whole the orchestration is old-fashioned, and it was not until later that Scarlatti adopted a style which we can recognize as consistently modern in spirit.

In 1718 Scarlatti produced his one comic opera, "Il Trionfo dell' Onore," at the Teatro de' Fiorentini. This theatre had for some years made a speciality of comic operas in Neapolitan dialect, the most prominent composer being Leonardo Vinci, who, if not actually a pupil of Scarlatti, was very much under his influence. It must be clearly understood that these comic operas were not *intermezzi*. It is true that by this time it had become fairly common to transplant the comic scenes from one opera to another. They were always a speciality of Naples, and if an opera by a stranger was to be performed there, some Neapolitan composer provided these, as Vignola did for Handel's "Agrippina." But the first occasion on which a series of comic *intermezzi* appears to have been recognized as an independent organism was the performance of Pergolesi's famous "Serva Padrona" in 1731, although we should perhaps give the honour to the *intermezzi* from Scarlatti's opera "Scipione nelle Spagne" (Naples, 1714), which was revived at Bologna in 1730 under the title of "La Dama Spagnuola ed il Cavalier Romano," and printed in a separate libretto, not incorporated with that of any other opera.

The Neapolitan "*cummedeja in museca*," however, is a full-sized opera in three acts. We should trace its descent from the pastoral operas and "*favole boscareccie*," such as "La Rosaura" and "Il Figlio delle Selve," and since the first recorded example of the new type, "Patrò Calienna de la Costa" (1709), seems to have been produced as a stop-gap, accompanied by the apologies of the management, it is possible that it was mainly written in dialect, because there was no time to turn the rough draft into

literary Italian.   Being a success, the experiment was
repeated, and a style was developed that depended for its
interest on the lively presentation of popular types of
character, with an occasional parody of the turgid style of
opera seria.   In the early comic operas all the characters
talk Neapolitan except those who are held up to ridicule
as Romans or Florentines; later the number of dialect
characters is reduced.   Scarlatti's opera presents a very
curious exception, since not one of the characters talks
Neapolitan or any other dialect.

The plot has a remarkable resemblance to that of
" Don Giovanni," except that the hero repents at the end,
without supernatural interference.   The scene is laid at
Pisa, and the time was probably the present day or any
period that happened to suit the *costumier's* convenience.
Riccardo, a young profligate from Leghorn, while visiting
his uncle *Flaminio*, arranges to elope with *Doralice*, niece
of *Cornelia*, an old lady whom *Flaminio* is anxious to
marry on account of her wealth.   The elopement is frus-
trated by *Leonora*, whom *Riccardo* has deserted, and her
brother *Erminio*, who is in love with *Doralice*.   *Leonora*
and *Erminio* are not unlike *Donna Elvira* and *Don Ottavio*,
but *Doralice* certainly has nothing in common with *Donna
Anna*, being quite ready to run away with *Riccardo*.
Rodimarte and *Rosina*, the servants of *Riccardo* and
Cornelia respectively, are ordinary *parti buffe*, but with
more part in the general action than usual; we see in
them the prototypes of *Leporello* and *Zerlina*.   Musically
they look as far forward as Rossini; even Mozart hardly
arrived at such exuberant humour as we find in their
duets—" *Or via dameggia*," with its absurd parodies of grand
opera, and " *Ferma, ferma, o cospettaccio*," a string of short
chattering, giggling phrases, evidently intended to be
spoken rather than sung, unified by a short violin-figure,
with now and then a real musical phrase to round off
a cadence.

I

Of the rest it is difficult to pick out single airs as illustrations. The music is always full of life and humour, sometimes in the orchestra, as when *Cornelia* scolds *Flaminio* for making love to her servant *Rosina*, sometimes in the voice-part itself, as in some of *Riccardo's* airs. This part, which is for a soprano, was sung by a woman, not by a *castrato*, and its florid phrases well suggest the hero's vanity and profligate cynicism.

Rosina's air " *Avete nel volto* " has a very arch effect of *aposiopesis* which is of interest from a technical point of view, besides exhibiting the characteristic charm of Scarlatti's light and playful style.

Ex. 58.

Rosina (Contralto).

A - ve - te nel vol-to, ch'è mol - to vi-va-ce, Si

Continuo.

dolce at-trat-ti-va ch'ar - ri - va, che piace, che ba-sta, ba-sta co - sì.

Indeed the whole opera is so fresh and so full of vitality that under favourable circumstances it might be quite possible to revive it, especially as it requires no elaborate scenery or stage effects, and contains no part for a *castrato* except *Erminio*, which is a very small one. Certainly its old-fashioned methods ought not to stand in its way when we see "La Serva Padrona" still remembered and performed in Italy.

Two serenatas belong to this period—"Pace, Amor, Providenza," and the "Seasons." The first of these appears to have been composed for the Emperor's nameday, with special allusion to the Peace of Rastatt (1714). The libretto is more than usually political. *Providence* quite early in the work informs *Peace* and *Love* that it is all very well for them to sing "*Viva amore*," but that it is really owing to him (*Providence* is a bass) that Charles is firmly established, not only on the throne of Naples, but on several others as well. *Love*, however, insists that it was he who "smoothed his path to the Iberian throne" and also presented Charles to "afflicted Germany." *Peace* appears to feel rather hurt at the other two taking to themselves all the credit of the recent diplomatic successes, and threatens to go away, but is restrained by *Providence*, and

"Now that the Ebro, Danube, and the Rhine
Haste with their tribute to the feet of Charles,"

we end with the usual chorus of jubilation. The music is of little interest.

The other serenata was composed in 1716 for the birth of the Archduke Leopold, who, however, died the same year. It is on a very large scale, having parts for five voices (the four seasons and Jupiter) and being scored for what was then a large orchestra. With regard to the score, however, there is some confusion, as the manuscripts exhibit divergencies. Each part is preceded by a *sinfonia*, the second having only the last two movements of the conventional form. The whole composition well illustrates the serenata style, which was intended to combine the brilliance of the stage with the elaboration of the chamber : but although it sometimes attains to a remarkable beauty, it is very often extremely tedious, especially at this period when Scarlatti's "brilliant" manner was occasionally inclined to superficiality. *Spring* has an attractive air, "*Canta dolce il Rosignuolo*," in the *Siciliana* style, the flute representing the nightingale with an unusual simplicity and restraint, and *Autumn* (contralto) has an air in the first part, "*Fuor dell' urna le belle onde*," with a very carefully written accompaniment for violins in unison, two violas, and two violoncellos. But the part of *Autumn* seems to have been sung by a singer who made a speciality of "rippling" effects, and by the end of the serenata they become most wearisome. The work is brought to a conclusion by a quintet in rondo-form ; some of its themes are graceful—it was hardly possible not to be graceful in $\frac{12}{8}$ time—but generally it exhibits Scarlatti's curious inability to grasp the possibilities of choral effect.

The birth of the Archduke was also celebrated with an opera, "La Virtù Trionfante dell' Odio e dell' Amore," preceded by a special prologue also by Scarlatti ; and it was probably in connexion with this that he received the honour of knighthood, as he is called *Cavaliere* for the first time in the libretto of "Carlo Re d' Allemagna," produced at the Carnival of 1716. It has been suggested that he was made a knight of the Golden Spur by the Pope, at the request of Cardinal Ottoboni. If this were the case, it is curious that he should not have been knighted earlier when he was living in Rome as Cardinal Ottoboni's Maestro di Cappella. In any case the order was no great honour, for Zedler [1] tells us that by 1677 it was sufficiently common for the Venetian ambassador to be "not a little surprised" at receiving it, while in later years it fell still lower in value, being scattered broadcast by all Papal nuncios and many other dignitaries of the Church. The Maltese cross on Scarlatti's tombstone suggests that he was a knight of Malta, but no documentary evidence in support of this has yet come to light.

Two oratorios, "San Filippo Neri" (1713) and the " Trinity Oratorio " (1715), present a curious contrast that seems to illustrate well Scarlatti's attitude towards sacred music. The libretto of the latter work is a discussion on the nature of the Trinity between *Faith*, *Divine Love* (soprano), *Theology* (alto), *Unbelief* (tenor), and *Time* (bass). Whether the arguments on either side are particularly convincing is not a question for the musical historian ; but however sound the doctrines may be, the operatic stanza is hardly a convenient literary form for their presentation, nor does the subject seem at all appropriate to musical treatment. Scarlatti has, if possible, surpassed his poet in dryness.

"San Filippo Neri," on the other hand, is one of his best oratorios. There is a real feeling of sincerity about it, though not all of it is in accordance with modern taste. The simile of a ship on a prosperous voyage leads St. Philip into vocal ripplings which are pretty, but rather out of place, and in the air " *Son come destriero* " the pawing and champing of both voice and violins throw Handel's frogs quite into the shade. But where genuine human feeling comes in Scarlatti rises to the occasion. There is something seraphic in the brilliance of *Charity's* high soprano airs ; *Faith* speaks with a large Handelian dignity, and the pathetic *recitativo stromentato*

---

[1] *Universal-Lexicon*, Halle and Leipzig, 1744.

in which the sufferings of the crucified Christ are
described

un a-mor con-trol-lò per tua sa-lu - - te

is worthily followed by the quiet and beautiful air in which St. Philip acknowledges the divine call.

Two masses "*alla Palestrina*" (1710 and 1716) show an advance upon previous work of the kind in the healthy feeling for modern tonality and the free treatment of discords.

Ex. 60. (1710.)

The *Missa Clementina II.* (1716) is the better of the two. Its style is dignified, with a firm sense of tonic relation, and the two *fugato* movements, "*In gloria Dei Patris*" and "*Et vitam venturi*," are full of vitality and breathe a thoroughly modern spirit. The same modern spirit is shown in the well-known *Laetatus sum*, for four voices,[1] which is as vigorous as any work of Leo.   It was probably composed as a study in counterpoint, as the only contemporary manuscript has no words, and is headed "*Modulatio sexti toni : tres cogitationes unaque Armonia*," referring to the three subjects, exhibited first separately and finally all together.   The Requiem is in a style similar to that of the other masses, and may perhaps be ascribed to this period.   It is not known for what occasion it was written ; possibly for the death of Clement XI. in 1721, though the mass for the accession of his successor, Innocent XIII., was merely dished up from old work ; and at so late a date we should expect a still more modern style. The Requiem is rather unequal, and seems to vary in quality with the character of the words.   Where they are merely liturgical, Scarlatti is dull ; where they touch some genuine human emotion, as in the *Requiem aeternam* the *Sanctus* and *Osanna*, Scarlatti is genuinely poetical.   The *Dies irae* is not set, being sung to the traditional plain-song.

The same poetical touch is seen in the two *Misereres* for five voices, strings, and organ in E minor (1715) and C minor (1716).[2]   These, like many other settings of psalms, are rather loose in tonality, but this is due as much to looseness of form as to modal survivals.   Indeed, form appears only in a free balancing of rhythmic sections and in the recurrence every now and then of fragmentary phrases which make for a vague unification of the whole, the idea being to express the words just as they come, as in Verdi's *Stabat Mater*, though there the strophic character of the poem necessarily gave a more symmetrical disposition to the music within the limits of single sections.

The other psalms are for the most part unsatisfactory. They have some beautiful moments, but are very unequal.   Generally they include some treatment of an ecclesiastical *canto fermo*, so that the trail of the modes

---

[1] Printed in Proske's *Musica Divina*.

[2] It is possible that these were written some ten years earlier, as suggested at the beginning of this chapter.

is still over their harmony, and though the style of
Palestrina is definitely abandoned, the new technique
of harmonic counterpoint is not yet quite perfected.
Leo has a complete mastery over it, but Scarlatti
does not always realize the necessity of individualizing
his parts in a polyphonic choral movement. It cannot
have been due to lack of skill, for his two-part writing
in the chamber-cantatas is not surpassed by J. S. Bach
himself, and the *Missa Clementina II.* shows that he
saw in what direction choral music had to go—indeed,
the final chorus of " S. Teodosia" pointed thither as
early as 1685. But in much of his choral writing the
parts cross and recross so often, and contrast so little
with each other, that the listener is quite unable to pursue
the development of a particular subject. The best of the
psalms is the *Laudate pueri Dominum* for five voices and
organ. It begins with a bass solo in E minor, practically
in unison with the *continuo*, varied by *coloratura*. It is
not in the style of an aria, but has the character of a fugue-
subject, and immediately gives a rough suggestion of a
fugal answer by repeating itself in the subdominant; it
then returns to a second repetition in the tonic, extended
by a coda. The other voices enter at " *Sit nomen Domini*,"
sung by the second soprano to the fourth tone as a *canto
fermo*, the other voices having free imitations. This
movement is also in E minor. " *A solis ortu*" and " *Laud-
abile nomen*" are set for soprano, alto, and tenor only, the
first theme being repeated at the end of nine bars, after
which the second is developed for twenty-five bars more.
The movement is gentle and melancholy in character, and
the " *A solis ortu*" has a despairing expression strangely
out of place in so cheerful a psalm of praise.

Ex. 61.

The "*Excelsus super omnes*" forms a welcome contrast, being in five-part harmony in C major, and the next section, "*et super coelos,*" though mostly in minor keys, is fairly vigorous and massive. It ends in C major, after which comes a duet, "*Quis sicut Dominus,*" for soprano and alto in the imitative manner of the chamber-duets. "*Suscitans a terra*" is set as a florid soprano solo, treated in a fugal spirit, like the opening bass solo, if one can conceive of a *fugato* for one voice. The *continuo* never imitates it at all.

Ex. 62.

It is followed by a well-developed *fugato* on "*ut collocet eum*" for all five voices,

Ex. 63.

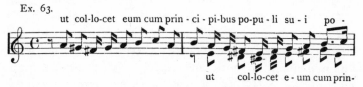

contrasted with which is "*Qui habitare fecit,*" a long movement in full harmony, falling into definite rhythmical periods. The *Gloria* is given out by the first soprano alone in a sort of *arioso;* "*sicut erat*" is sung to imitations on the *canto fermo*. The tonality of the motet is firm throughout, in spite of the use of an ecclesiastical *canto fermo*, so that it evidently belongs to a late period;

and in connection with this clear feeling for tonic relations
the oppressive melancholy of the work is the more strange.
It seems so sincere, so intimately tragic, that one cannot
regard it as a mere modal survival. Yet to interpret it
in a modern spirit as the expression of the composer's
personal feeling, strong though the temptation may be to
arrive in this way at a plausible explanation, would, I
think, be false psychology. However repugnant it may be
to leave a work of art as a wholly unexplained mystery, we
must always remember that we have no right to attempt
serious analysis of what we may imagine to be its emotional content until we have absolutely and entirely mastered
its structural organization down to the innermost details.

Three motets for double choir may safely be assigned
to this period, since we know that one of them, "*O
magnum mysterium*," was written in 1707. The "*Tu es
Petrus*" has always been a famous composition, and
thoroughly deserves its great reputation.[1] "*O magnum
mysterium*" is rather more archaic, though firm in tonality,
while "*Volo, Pater*" is a perfect specimen of the modern
style, masterly in its counterpoint, yet founded on a
subject that might have come from a chamber-cantata,
so melodious is its flow.

Ex. 64.

Operas and serenatas, motets and oratorios, are, however, left far behind by the chamber-cantatas that are
contemporary with them. Scarlatti had been appointed
master at the *Conservatorio dei Poveri di Gesù Cristo* in
1709, and it may have been his occupation as a teacher

[1] It has been reprinted several times.

that stimulated him to such extraordinary studies in advanced harmony as the chamber-cantatas exemplify. It was in 1712 that he made the celebrated exchange of cantatas with Francesco Gasparini. The details of the correspondence are not known. Apparently it began by Gasparini sending Scarlatti a setting of the cantata "*Andate o miei sospiri.*" Scarlatti replied to this composition, which is remarkable for nothing except its dryness, by sending two settings of the same words. The first is in G minor, headed "*in idea humana,*" and the last air has an alternative setting "*per intingolo.*" [1] The other setting is in F sharp minor, "*in idea inhumana,*[2] ma in regolato Cromatico, non è per ogni Professore.*"

The "human" cantata may fairly be taken to represent the best setting of the words that Scarlatti could conceive. The airs are melodious, and though their harmonies present nothing startling, they are quite modern in feeling. The most interesting movement from a historical point of view is the introductory *arioso* and recitative.

Ex. 65.

---

[1] *Intingolo* = a ragout.

[2] Scarlatti's habit of making an *h* that somewhat resembles an *E* (for a good facsimile of his handwriting see the catalogue of the library of the Brussels Conservatoire, vol. i.) led Burney and others to read this word as *in Eumana*, which, it was suggested, must have been an academic pseudonym!

This is comparatively simple, and shows at once that
the composer has just began to realize the possibilities of
the chord of the diminished seventh. It was by no means
a new chord; but Scarlatti is probably the first composer
who grasped what might be done with it considered as an
absolute chord, not as a suspended discord arrived at by a
contrapuntal process of preparation. And in the above
extract there are more diminished sevenths than those
marked $\flat^7_5$; the second chord of the fourth bar may be
safely regarded as implying an A flat and not a G. Scarlatti's figuring is always rather irregular; but by comparing
basses with voice-parts it is found to be a fairly general
rule, though not an absolute one, that $\sharp^6_4$ implies the third
inversion of the minor ninth, while the third inversion of
the dominant seventh is generally figured $^4_2$, and the dis-
cordant second prepared. The last bar of this example,
however, supplies an exception.

The next step is to go from one diminished seventh straight to another by a fall of a semitone.   This example

Ex. 66.

is from the second recitative of the same cantata.   A single diminished seventh will carry a modulation a fairly long way without obvious eccentricity of resolution, but two or more together can make the listener lose his bearings so completely that he does not know whether the next resolution be complicated or simple.

The second cantata was written with the deliberate intention of puzzling Gasparini.   Indeed to the modern reader it is not easily intelligible at first sight, even allowing for modern unfamiliarity with the style and the notation ; so we can imagine how Gasparini must have been bewildered by its amazing successions of chromatic harmonies, especially as Scarlatti, with a characteristic sense of humour, has started straight off with a third inversion of the supertonic seventh in the key of F sharp minor, and has left the bass unfigured. This at any rate was his intention, but either from force of habit, or possibly with deliberate irony, he has put in a harmless figure here and there in places where the most elementary pupil would have had no difficulty in supplying them instinctively.

The first recitative shows his methods.

Ex. 67.

Andante.

An - da - te, an - da - te o miei so - spi - ri al

cor, al cor d'I - re - ne, es - so del mio le

pe - ne sap - pia da voi; ben lo sa - prà se

di - te che per a - ver ri - sto - ro al suo do - lo - re

tut - to con voi sen vie - ne an - che il mio co - re. An -

-da-te, an-da-te   a quel bel se - no,

tan-to ch'un sol al-me-no es-sa n'ac-col-ga, pien del mio fo-co

o-gn'un di voi s'ag-gi-ri;   an-da-te, an-

-da-te al cor d'I-re-ne, an-da-te al cor d'I-re-ne, o miei so-spi-ri!

It is at once apparent that the accidentals make the music look more complicated than it really is. As it is, modern notation saves several of these, and three sharps to the signature would have saved several more. The sudden change to flats in the fourth bar might have been avoided by writing the second bass note as F double-sharp. Bar 8 shows a curious treatment of a $\frac{6}{4}$ chord, and we find an analogous case in the second recitative, which begins unmistakably on the second inversion of the chord of C sharp minor, and resolves it on to a chain of diminished sevenths whose basses descend by semitones.

Ex. 68.

Ma di che mi lu - sin - go? oh Dio ! che pen - so?

The diminished seventh is the key to the rest. But the close of the second recitative presents more striking progressions.

Ex. 69.

e pur sa quell' in - gra - ta, lo sa con suo pia - cer che

miei voi sie - te, e in - ten - de (ma s'in - fin - ge

qual suo bar-ba-ro cor) ciò.... che chie - de - te.

The modulation to A flat two bars before the end is extremely bold. The explanation must be sought in the words—though not merely as a piece of eccentricity on the word "*barbaro.*" The sentence includes a parenthesis— " and she understands (but that barbarous heart of hers feigns not to do so) that which ye ask." Scarlatti has ingeniously attempted to represent this rhetorical figure in

K

his music, for if we cut out what is in parenthesis, the music makes sense just as the words do, "*intende . . . ciò*" being on the same chord. Now probably Scarlatti's first instinct was to get "*barbaro*" on to a diminished seventh, so that we should read E natural for E flat, and the chord of F minor for that of A flat major. This would be a very characteristic progression. But the jump from F minor to the $\frac{4}{2}$ on G, which is attractive enough to our ears, was probably more than Scarlatti could manage. He would feel that the bass must descend to G from A flat. But the leap from E natural to A flat, whether the latter bears a $\frac{5}{3}$ or a 6, was awkward, and to flatten the E was an obvious way out of the difficulty. Whether the G on the fourth beat should bear a $\sharp\frac{6}{4}\!\!_2$ or a $\flat\sharp\frac{6}{4}\!\!_3$, I am not certain; the previous G must certainly bear a $\sharp\frac{6}{4}\!\!_2$, and Scarlatti probably contemplated the same chord following the parenthesis; but it is possible that he would have preferred eventually to soften the progression by using an inversion of his favourite diminished seventh.

Another progression common enough to us but unusual for Scarlatti is the resolution of the Neapolitan sixth on the first inversion of the supertonic minor ninth, on the word "*piacer*" in the preceding example. The Neapolitan sixth is, of course, plentiful in Scarlatti's work; indeed it is so conspicuous a mannerism of his that it may well have got its name from him. It appears frequently even in his earliest work, although in Stradella and Legrenzi it is employed very seldom, and even then with some timidity. The flat supertonic from which it is derived is characteristic of Neapolitan folk-song, as may be seen from the *canzonette* in the comic operas of Vinci and Leo;

Ex. 70. Vinci, " Le Ziten Galera " (1722).

Vor - ri - a re - ven-ta - re.... so - re - cil - lo........

Per met-te-re pa- u-ra a.... la Sia Anella,a la Sia A- nella,... ..

but this type of popular song had not yet been appropriated by serious composers. The rhythm is characteristically Neapolitan, and is never found in Scarlatti. It is much more probable that he found the flat supertonic in the songs of his native Sicily. Scarlatti was too good a musician to be much affected by the "assumption of simplicity by courtly persons who had become artificialized, and wanted a new sensation," which, as Mr. Fuller-Maitland[1] well points out, was a fashionable characteristic of the early eighteenth century, and which we can observe in our own day in the recrudescent craze for folk-song. But he did yield to it on rare occasions, and two examples have survived of airs specially described by Scarlatti as "*alla siciliana*," one in the opera "La Donna è ancora fedele," the other in the cantata "*Una beltà ch' eguale.*" Both of these are of the type which we associate with the name "*Siciliana*," flowing melodies in $\frac{12}{8}$ time; but that rhythm could hardly have been the essential of the Sicilian type, since the operas and cantatas are full of such airs, undistinguished by any special title. What distinguishes these two from the others is the frequent appearance of the flat supertonic. The characteristic cadence of the air "*Non mi tradir mai più*" in the opera shows it only tentatively; the raising of B flat to B on its last appearance was no doubt a concession to the audience, who would not have time in an opera to take in properly so unusual a melodic progression.

Ex. 71.

Mai più, mai più nè men per gio-co, per gio - co.

But in the cantata there was less need for such precautions, and Scarlatti has treated his theme much more freely. The characteristic interval appears, and is even allowed to distort the harmony of the conventional $\frac{6}{4}$ $\frac{5}{3}$ cadence; in-

[1] "Oxford History of Music," vol. iv. p. 63.

deed Scarlatti, having once impressed this distortion on the listener, shows how it can be ingeniously used to effect a striking modulation. Yet even here he has not introduced it at the end of the air, feeling that it would not give a sufficient impression of finality. The air is so interesting in its melody, harmony, and form that it is worth quoting entire.

Ex. 72.
Aria alla Siciliana.

I have purposely abstained from filling up the harmonies of the accompaniment. Scarlatti's figuring is always rather sketchy, and naturally so, since the system was
in theory and in practice one of convenience. Rousseau[1]

[1] *Dictionnaire de Musique*, art. *Accompagnement.*

and Marcello[1] tell us, each in his own characteristic way, how little attention was paid by Italians to the figures in accompanying ; and composers of that day were probably quite reasonable in trusting to the common sense and natural artistic instinct of players. But in this air there are several places where the bass might be harmonized in two or three different ways. Probably Scarlatti would have approved of any of them, and for that reason I have avoided suggesting that any particular way is the only right one.

I have not been able to identify this air with any recorded Sicilian folk-song, although it has a decidedly Sicilian character in its rhythms and its flat supertonic.[2] The Sicilian type of melody must not be judged by the "*Sicilianas*" of J. S. Bach and Handel, who had no connexion with Sicily, and merely imitated the airs in $\frac{12}{8}$ time that are common throughout Scarlatti's work, but which never bear the indication "*alla siciliana*" ; Scarlatti, as a Sicilian, realized, as his imitators did not, what characteristics were essential, and not accidental, to the native melodies of the island.

The "*Cantata inhumana*" represents the furthest point to which Scarlatti carried his harmonic audacities. In his later work he merely shows a completer mastery over the same material, with the result that it is less startling but more beautiful. There are no extravagant chords or progressions in the airs even of "*Andate o miei sospiri*" ; the first air is certainly difficult, but its difficulty arises from the closeness of its texture—the modulations are so tersely executed that the hearer has to make haste to get a firm footing in one key before Scarlatti twists him into another. Syncopations too and suspensions add to the complication. The second air is remarkably beautiful. In this, as in the air "*Cara tomba*" from "Mitridate Eupatore," the harmony gives poignance to the melody,

---

[1] *Il Teatro alla Moda.*

[2] I owe this information to Prof. E. P. Morello, librarian of the R. Conservatorio di Musica at Palermo.

but is never allowed to tyrannize over it, as it does in some of the still later cantatas.

A very beautiful use of chromatic harmony is to be found in the air "*Quante pene*" from the cantata "*Lontananza crudele*" (1713); such a phrase as this—

Ex. 73.

is quite in the spirit of Mozart, and there are many that remind us of J. S. Bach.

Even in the operas, where clearness was the first consideration, we find some new harmonic effect. Strange progressions and complicated modulations were not suitable to the theatre; but Scarlatti shows in "Scipione nelle Spagne" what an effect can be made with a *cadenza* on a diminished seventh,

Ex. 74.

- dol mio, oh Dio! nol deg - gio dir.

and the chord is made all the more striking by its appearance as the resolution of a deceptive cadence. There is a
somewhat similar case in " Il Trionfo dell' Onore," in
Riccardo's air, " *Sì, sì, che tutto goder mi farà,*" where a
single diminished seventh is dwelt upon for three bars,
and is additionally emphasized by a peculiarly insistent
rhythmic figure.

It will be observed that the main characteristic of
Scarlatti's new harmonic developments is that he considers
his music vertically as well as horizontally. He was, of
course, far from being the first composer to do so, and he
is equally far from being among those for whom the
vertical aspect of composition predominates. But he is
one of the first to apply the vertical principle to chromatic
chords, and especially to chromatic discords. There can
be no doubt that he was influenced in this direction by
the development of keyed instruments. The first impulse
was given by the organ, under the hands of such composers as Frescobaldi, and from the organ the style
extended itself to the *cembalo*. The invention of recitative, as well as the mechanical development of the instrument, must have greatly increased the importance of the
cembalo as an accompaniment to the voice, the lute
gradually retiring into the background. Alessandro
Scarlatti's compositions for the *cembalo* are of little importance and by no means represent him at his best; but
we can see from his toccatas how he grasped the possibilities of the instrument in this direction. The contrapuntal
style was the normal style of the day, and he therefore

writes mainly in contrapuntal forms; but his fugues for the *cembalo* are mere hollow shells. A subject stands out here and there, and there is a great deal of bustle and fuss, but he wastes no energy on inner parts which would never be heard clearly whether they were of contrapuntal value or not. If his fugues sound more or less like fugues, that is enough for him, as it was no doubt enough for most listeners. And scattered here and there among the quasi-contrapuntal passages we come upon slow successions of thick chords, often chromatic, played quite *ad libitum*, rattling up and down in varied arpeggios from one end of the keyboard to the other, or decorated by the right hand with passing-notes in his characteristic dactylic rhythms,[1] whilst the left hand sustained the harmony, giving the audience time to wonder what might come next, and into what new key the composer's carefully frenzied inspiration might take him—surely the precise musical equivalent of that florid luxuriance of adulation, expressed in the most extraordinary jumble of metaphor, which he pours forth without intermission in his correspondence with Ferdinand de' Medici.

The *Regole per Principianti* (*i.e.* in the art of accompanying from a *basso continuo*) show that Scarlatti was in favour of a free style of playing, perhaps more so than his contemporaries, as in introducing some of his rules he qualifies them with the words—"at any rate such is the style of the present writer." Most of the rules are such as are familiar to us all, and need not be quoted; and his rules for filling up a bass that is not figured amount to little more than would be carried out instinctively by any modern player who had a feeling for scholarship. But there are two rules which are specially interesting, and which he seems to have considered peculiarly character-istic of his own style. The second inversion of the dominant seventh, figured 6, and theoretically considered as a concordant second inversion of the "imperfect triad," is always to be given the fourth as well as the third in

---

[1] He gives an example in his *Regole per Principianti*.

practice, when the bass descends conjunctly. When the
bass ascends, the fourth is not to be sounded. He adds
as an excuse that the fourth prepares—or, as we should
rather say, anticipates—the fifth of the succeeding bass
note ; but his real reason seems to have been the best of
all reasons—"because it sounds well." [1]

He gives the same reason for his next rule :—

"It should be noted that for an agreeable style of
playing, every time that a perfect cadence is made, or
when the bass moves up a fourth or down a fifth, the
minor seventh is to be added to the major third of the
bass-note that proceeds in this way." [2]

Modern scholars have generally considered both these
licenses as foreign to the spirit of the music of Scarlatti's
time ; but Scarlatti's words leave no room for doubt, and
are further confirmed by actual examples in score in many
of his works, at least as regards the first of these two rules.
The dominant seventh as a cadence appears only in the
form of a passing-note, and it is conceivable that he also
wished it to be regarded as such in playing from a figured
bass. And we may see how conscious he was of his being
in advance of other composers in the words that follow
these two rules—"Other accidental circumstances required
by the harmony of the style of the present writer, and
considered by him to belong to the most dignified manner
of playing, cannot be described in writing." Indeed
dignity, notwithstanding harmonic licenses, is a very
essential quality of his style, as he never ceases to insist on
the "*nobile portamento delle mani.*"

---

[1] "*E da notare per bella maniera di sonare (e questo è secondo lo stile di chi
scrive nello presente libro) tutte le volte che accade la consonanza di 6ª maggiore
si aggiunge la 4ª sopra la 3ª di detta consonanza, perchè fà bel sentire, oltre di
essere preparativa della 5ª nota del basso susseguente, quando questo discende per
un tuono; ma quando ascende per un tuono non si aggiunge detta 4ta come si è
detto.*"

[2] "*È da notarsi similmte che per modo grato di sonare, tutte le volte che si
fanno cadenze ò pure movimento del basso di 4ª in sù ò 5ª in giù, alla 3ª
maggiore della nota del basso ch' è per moversi di dª maniera, vi si aggiunge la
7ª minore perchè fà buon sentire.*"

CHAPTER V

ALTHOUGH "Il Trionfo dell' Onore" was produced at the Teatro de' Fiorentini in 1718, and "Cambise" at the Teatro S. Bartolomeo the following year, Scarlatti seems during these years to have had more interests in Rome than in Naples. He obtained leave on October 18, 1717, to go to Rome for the following Carnival;[1] and he apparently stayed on there for the next few years, since he received no stipend as Maestro di Cappella at Naples, although he retained the title—Francesco Mancini acting as Vice-Maestro until Scarlatti's death, on which he succeeded by right to the post of *Primo Maestro.*

At Rome Scarlatti produced a very interesting series of operas at the "*Sala degli illustrissimi Signori Capranica,*" and it is probable that Prince Ruspoli was also concerned in the management, since the autograph score of "Griselda," the last of the series—and indeed the last of all Scarlatti's operas—states that it was written for him. The first of the series was "Telemaco," produced in 1718, which was followed in 1719 by "Marco Attilio Regolo." "Tito Sempronio Gracco" and "Turno Aricino" were revived in 1720 with so much new music that they may be counted as new operas.

"Telemaco" is very unequal. Much of it is very tedious, though the comic scenes are among the best that Scarlatti ever wrote. But we see the beginning of a new style in *Calipso's* fine opening air, "*Dio del mar,*" which

---

[1] Naples, R. Archivio di Stato, *Mandati dei Vicerè*, vol. 336, fol. 44.

has a Mozartian breadth of melody, and still more in the
noble duet for *Minerva* and *Nettuno* in the prologue. This
movement is on a much larger scale than anything that
preceded it, and was evidently written with a large theatre
in view. Both melody and harmony are remarkably
dignified and simple, and produce a striking effect of
grandeur and serenity—one might almost say, an effect
of distance. The arrangement of the orchestra is novel
for the time: *Nettuno* is accompanied generally by the
main body of the strings, and *Minerva* by a smaller body
of strings placed on the chariot in which she descends
from heaven. There is also a "*concerto di oubuoè,*"
and a pair of horns. This is the first time that
Scarlatti uses horns, except for a single air and a sort
of fanfare in "Tigrane," and he turns them to very good
effect here; indeed they are the life and soul of the
movement.

Note.—The horn parts are given in Scarlatti's notation an octave above the notes actually sounded.

This use of the horns seems to have been a happy inspiration, for they appear in every subsequent opera, generally associated with a harbour-scene, in which some characters arrive in a ship and disembark followed by their suite. On such occasions there is always a "*sinfonia per lo sbarco*" in the manner of a march, in which the horns take a prominent part, the players being placed on board the ship, like the trumpeters in "Mitridate." No doubt the *impresario* considered that the ship also was a happy inspiration, as it could be used again every year.

"Marco Attilio Regolo" is an advance upon "Telemaco" as a whole, though it contains nothing as great as the duet mentioned above. Its airs are generally broad and dignified; and it is interesting to find four airs broken off abruptly in the middle by the interruption of another character. This must have been rather a risky proceeding with an audience that came mainly to hear the singers, though it required an audience trained to the *Da Capo* form to realize its full dramatic value. The opera also contains many pieces of *recitativo stromentato*, one of which is remarkably fine. *Attilio* has escaped from the

Carthaginians by a feigned death, which even his wife *Fausta* believes to be genuine. She comes by night to weep over his tombstone, *Attilio* himself watching her in concealment, undecided whether to endure her grief in silence or to risk recapture by making himself known to her. The recitative, which is unfortunately much too long for quotation entire, and to which extracts would hardly do justice, well illustrates the importance that was given to declamation in Scarlatti's day. Over fifty bars in length, and followed by an aria of which the middle section is also *recitativo stromentato*, it illustrates every variety of passion. The accompaniment is very vigorous and full for its period, but the simplicity of the means employed would demand a first-rate actress to make the most of it.

Another interesting feature of the opera is the introductory ballet of Carthaginians accompanied " with the noise of bagpipes and castanets and rattles in the manner of barbarous nations," in which it is evident that Scarlatti has done his best to get something like local colour. He made a similar attempt in " Tigrane " with a ballet of Scythians, but it is not so characteristic as this example.

Ex. 76. *Strada di Cartagine ornata di varij trionfi. Ballo di Giovani Cartaginesi. Comincia prima il ballo con strepito di Zampogne e Gnaccare e Sistri all'uso di barbare Nazioni.*

Of "Tito Sempronio Gracco" and "Turno Aricino"
only fragments remain, so that it is impossible to judge of
either opera as a whole. But the airs that have survived
are often singularly beautiful. They have all the masterly

L

technique of Scarlatti's fourth period, all its brilliance of dramatic effect, together with an increased sense of dignity and spaciousness, as well as a sincerity of expression that is often extremely touching.   A very characteristic mannerism at this time is the use of an introductory vocal phrase sung *ad libitum;* not, as in the earlier operas, a fragment of the initial phrase of the air, but designed rather as a contrast to what follows, like the beautiful opening of Beethoven's pianoforte sonata in F sharp major.   Employed in every air, it would have been wearisome in the extreme ; but Scarlatti has exercised a wise restraint, and reserves it as a rule for airs of a pathetic character.

That he was able to count upon singers of high dramatic ability is shown by the frequent opportunities that he gives for free declamation or for extemporary *cadenzas.* The beautiful air " *Queste son pene* " in " Turno Aricino " supplies several examples of this.

Here it is evident that the word " *lasci* " (Scarlatti also writes " *lasciata* ") means that the music was to be left as it was written ; where the voice is marked " *solo* " the singer was no doubt free to do what she pleased. The final cadence in this air, as in many others, imperatively demands an extemporized *cadenza* of some distinction. The short extract given will also serve to show the change in Scarlatti's general style; his chamber-music seems to have reacted upon his music for the stage, and his later operas contain many airs of great pathos, besides some in which more energetic passions find an intensity of expression never attained in the Neapolitan operas of the preceding ten years.

Ex. 79. *Moderato.*

Dil - lo al mio be - ne, dil - lo, dil - lo,

Viol. 1 & 2.

Viola. Basso. (*Violoncello & Viola.*)

lasci

par - - - la, par - la per me.

p *f*

(*tutti bassi.*)

solo

Son pe - - ne ques - te, dil - lo,

p

6 6♭6 4 ♮3

(*Violoncello & Viola.*)

dil - lo, quest' è do - lo - re, par - la, par - la, ques-

- te son pe - ne

*   Scarlatti's last opera "Griselda" (1721) shows him at his fullest maturity. The libretto was by Apostolo Zeno, and is fairly good, though there is not sufficient material for three acts. The story of "Patient Grizzel" is in some ways effective for operatic treatment, as it affords well-defined and strongly coloured characters; but this very reason is also a drawback. *Gualtiero* is so incredibly tyrannical and *Griselda* so incredibly patient that we can get up little sympathy for such obviously stagey figures. *Ottone* is the blackest possible of villains; *Roberto* and *Costanza* are merely picturesque puppets, and *Corrado* hardly even that. Scarlatti has made the most of the characters, such as they are, *Griselda* and *Costanza* being the most successful. The finest example of dramatic expression is *Griselda's* air in the second act, "*Figlio ! tiranno ! oh Dio !*" when *Ottone* has threatened to kill her child before her eyes unless she yields to his desires. Here the composer has shown a truly wonderful ingenuity in making the conventional aria form serve as a vehicle for

the most passionate appeals of *Griselda* to her son, to *Ottone* and to heaven, the short declamatory phrases being so arranged as to make up together a perfectly logical and formal movement.

Ex. 80.
Andante moderato.

al figlio

GRISELDA.

Fi-glio!

Viol.
I & 2.

Viola.
Basso.

(Viola e Violoncello.)

ad Ottone

Ti-ran-no! oh Dio!

al figlio

Dite che far poss'io, che?

ad Ottone

dite che far poss'io, che?

(tutti senza cembalo.)

no!

Especially good is the contrast in the last few bars between her despairing aside, her silent glance at her child, and
the rush of splendid indignation that concludes the section.
The second part of the air is more conventionally melodious,
yet even here there is a great variety of expression.

A characteristic feature of these last operas is the
concerted movement which finds a place in each of them.
The septet in " Eraclea," quoted in an earlier chapter, finds
its development at last, after being forgotten for nearly
twenty years. Yet even now Scarlatti does not seize the
opportunities that were offered for a developed finale. The
second act of " Il Trionfo dell' Onore " ends with a quartet,
but it is ineffective, and does not even serve to conceal the
want of a strong dramatic situation at the fall of the curtain. The duets in the same opera are far superior to it
in dramatic vitality. The second act of " Griselda " ends
with a trio which is more interesting musically ; but the
characters are not well defined. There is much more characterization in the quartets in "Telemaco" ("*Sdegno—amor—
destino*") and in the third act of "Griselda" ("*Non fu mai colpa
amor*"). But even these are hardly conceived dramatically,
any more than the septet in " Eraclea." " Turno Aricino "
and " Marco Attilio Regolo " both contain quartets that are
merely double duets, with no particular conflict of interests ;
and the type is most beautifully exemplified in the melodious
" *Idolo mio ti chiamo* " in " Tito Sempronio Gracco." It is
significant that the contemporary manuscript calls it an
" *Aria a quattro* " ; the voices enter at first singly, one
carrying on the phrase as another drops it,[1]

---

[1] The unimportant parts for strings and oboes in this and the following
example are omitted to save space.

all four uniting voluptuously on a diminished seventh just
before the close.

With these operas may be classed the oratorio "La Vergine Addolorata" (1717) and two serenatas, one for the peace of Passarowitz[1] (1718) and the other (apparently unfinished) for the marriage of the Prince of Stigliano (1723). The oratorio deals with the Passion, as witnessed by the four *interlocutori*, the Virgin, St. John, Nicodemus, and a

[1] The lines

> "*Il Trace agricoltor*
> *Ben presto piangerà*
> *Che i campi suoi vedrà*
> *Preda del fuoco,*"

and

> "*Si, si, sperar ci giovi*
> *Veder l'Aquile altere*
> *Di Bizanzio rubella sulle rovine*
> *Un di fermarsi il nido,*"

evidently refer to the expedition to Thessalonica, projected by Prince Eugene and his allies the Venetians to satisfy the "zealous Christians" who wished to see Turkey more permanently crippled now that there was so good an opportunity (Muratori, *Annali d'Italia*).

Jewish priest.   The treatment is interesting for comparison
with other oratorios on the same subject.   Scarlatti's
youthful Latin " Passion according to St. John" told the
story simply through the mouth of the Evangelist ; here
we deduce the story from the meditative utterances of
some of the principal characters concerned in it.   The two
schemes are seen in combination in the " Passions" of
J. S. Bach, with the addition of the chorales, which are of
course peculiar to the Lutheran Church.   Indeed in this
later oratorio of Scarlatti there are many places where one
is conscious of a similarity of feeling with the " Matthäus-
Passion," especially in the final trio representing the *Pietà*,
which corresponds closely in spirit with the chorus " *Wir
setzen uns mit Thränen nieder.*"

The serenatas are generally good, but their principal
interest lies in their treatment of the orchestra, which at
this period of Scarlatti's career begins to show something
of that importance which has been assigned to it in more
modern times.   As early as " L'Amor Generoso" we can
see here and there a vague tendency towards modern
orchestral writing.   It has already been pointed out
(Chapter II.) that the Venetian composers before Scarlatti
had made some advance towards treating the orchestra on
harmonic rather than contrapuntal principles.   Scarlatti's
early opera overtures show that he realized the effect of
broken chords played by the strings, as in the extract from
" La Rosaura" quoted in the "Oxford History of Music,"
vol. iii. ; but after his return from Rome, where he had
had the opportunity of studying Corelli's methods, he
begins to carry this effect still further, by employing
genuine violin-figures, instead of arpeggios of a type almost
equally well suited to any instrument.   As the violin style
gets more and more differentiated, so it becomes more and
more impossible for the trumpets and oboes to play in
unison with the strings, and in this way Scarlatti begins to
realise that the contrast of the style between phrases
suitable for wind instruments and phrases suitable for
strings enhances the contrast of colour.

The overture to " Griselda" will illustrate some of
Scarlatti's methods.

The balance of instruments is of course still old-fashioned, and we must not forget that there would be some five or six oboes playing. The frequent crossing of the parts is a relic of still older times ; it was a habit that Scarlatti scarcely ever shook off, greatly to the disadvantage of his instrumental style. Such gaps as there are in the harmony would be well filled up by the two *cembali*, and though the movement is not undeserving of Marcello's satire—"the overture shall consist of a *Tempo francese*, or *prestissimo* of semiquavers in the major key, which of course must be followed by a *piano* in the same key, with the minor third, ending with a minuet, gavotte, or gigue in the major key again, avoiding in these forms fugues, suspensions, subjects [*i.e.* for imitation], &c., as being old-fashioned things quite out of modern use,"[1] —it shows a keen sense of orchestral effect, and certainly would get as much noise out of the instruments as they could make. If we cannot admire it much as serious music, it is at any rate of great importance in the development of the symphonic style.

[1] *Il Teatro alla Moda*, p. 23. " La Sinfonia consisterà in un *Tempo Francese*, o *prestissimo di semicrome in Tuono con terza maggiore,* al quale dovrà succedere al solito un *Piano* del medesimo *Tuono* in *Terza minore,* chiudendo finalmente con *Minuetto, Gavotta* o *Gigha,* nuovamente in *Terza maggiore,* e sfuggendo in tal forme *Fughe, Legature, Soggetti, &c.,* come cose *antiche* fuori affatto del *moderno* costume."

Scarlatti himself must certainly have felt that this sort of writing was only suitable for theatre-music that had to make itself heard somehow above the noise of general conversation, for in his instrumental chamber-music he holds rigidly to the contrapuntal style. His *Sonate a quattro*, *i.e.* string quartets, composed some time during the last ten years of his life, are if anything less modern than Corelli's, at least in form. The fugues which form their principal movement are more developed than Corelli's —sometimes indeed to a very tedious extent—and there is a certain modernity in the brisk little minuets that have something of the spirit of Beethoven's *scherzos*,[1] but in general structure they look backward to the old *Sonata da chiesa*, not forward to the chamber-music of the classical period.

The same attitude is to be observed in Scarlatti's twelve symphonies [2] or concertos for orchestra. These interesting works were begun on June 1, 1715; over how long a period their composition extends cannot be definitely decided, but it is not likely that they cover a period of more than twelve months at the outside. The instruments employed are strings, with a few wind instruments; the first has two flutes, the second a trumpet and a flute, the third one flute, the fourth a flute and an oboe, the rest one flute only. In form they come between the quartets and the opera-overtures; the first movement is an *allegro* like those of the later overtures, spirited and energetic, but short and rather formless; it generally ends suddenly on

---

[1] A more detailed account of these quartets will be found in the *Monthly Musical Record* for November 1903. They are not of sufficient importance to the general history of music to require a full analysis here.

[2] The autograph manuscript of these interesting compositions was recently discovered by Mr. W. Barclay Squire in the Music Library at Buckingham Palace. They are headed thus :-

Cominciate al P⁰ Giugno 1715   *D' Alessandro Scarlatti*
Sinfonia Prima, di concerto Grosso con due Flauti.

No other date is given throughout the volume. Each symphony is numbered in the handwriting of the composer, who signs his name with the title *Cavaliere* at the head of No. 5 and of Nos. 7–12. I describe them here by kind permission of Sir Walter Parratt.

the dominant. It is followed by the usual transitional *adagio*, generally in ¾ time, sometimes starting with the character of a slow movement, but sooner or later relapsing into the conventional series of modulations serving as a framework for thematic treatment of some unimportant figure. The third movement is a fugue, sometimes on two subjects, always developed at great length, and showing traces of a feeling that is symphonic rather than contrapuntal in its episodes, though it never falls into what might be truly classed as sonata form. It is followed by a second *adagio*, transitional like the first and serving merely as an introduction to the march or dance movement which concludes the composition. Compared with the quartets, the symphonies show less solidity and severity of workmanship ; the style is often hollow, though effective. The slow movements, instead of being definitely contrapuntal, are more melodious and modern in spirit ; the final movements are more elaborate in form, but sometimes almost rowdy. Indeed, the material is hardly ever either beautiful or original, and the interest of the work lies entirely in the skilful development of themes which are themselves of slight intrinsic merit.

Scarlatti's feeling for orchestral colouring in a modern sense is best seen in some of the arias, more particularly in the *ritornelli*. In his middle period he did not get much beyond dividing his strings into *concertino* and *concerto grosso*, with sometimes nightingales and other birds *ad libitum* in the manner of a toy-symphony, and these extravagances are confined to the serenatas and oratorios. It may also be pointed out that even where he divides his strings in this way, he shows little or no feeling for the true spirit of the concerto. His object seems merely to get a contrast of *piano* and *forte* in a rough way from players who were not much accustomed to such refinements ; there is hardly ever any attempt to counterbalance the superior weight of the orchestra by the superior agility of the individual soloist.[1] In the operas, at

[1] Compare Mr. D. F. Tovey's interesting essay, *The Classical Concerto*.

any rate until his last ten years, he pays less attention to instrumental detail. Later in life he was very
likely influenced by such singers as Vittoria Tesi-Tra-
montini, who was not at her best in *coloratura*, but had a
great dramatic personality and a great voice, since his arias
are not only less florid and more expressive, but also more
elaborately scored. Thus in the serenata ("Filli, Clori,
Tirsi") for the Peace of Passarowitz we find an air
charmingly accompanied by two flutes, violins all in unison,
violas, two violoncellos, and *continuo*, the score being most
carefully managed so as never to let the mass of violins
overpower the other instruments except where they have to
play a broad *cantabile* melody, in which they are supported
by the *cembalo*, thus contrasting well with the lighter tones
of the answering pairs of flutes and violoncellos.

The trumpet is the first wind instrument to appear in
Scarlatti's scores, and naturally so, as its technique was the
most advanced of all. Scarlatti's treatment of it differs
very little from that adopted by J. S. Bach and Handel,
except that he is less lavish in the use of scale-passages.
Airs with trumpet *obbligato* were an almost invariable feature
of all operas and oratorios, and Scarlatti's are often remarkable for their keen dramatic sense ; they seldom give
the impression of being a show piece for the player, the
instrument generally playing either a broad sustained
melody or a series of reiterated notes which suggest its
military character much more forcibly than the florid runs
of Handel's trumpet-arias. The oratorio "La Vergine
Addolorata" makes a very striking use of the trumpet
in one of the airs, and also in a recitative given by the
Virgin, which is suddenly interrupted by a single D on the
trumpet—the signal for the procession to Calvary—blown
loud and growing gradually softer, while St. John takes up
the recitative on a different chord.

The horns were a new ingredient of the orchestra
when Scarlatti first introduced them into "Tigrane" in
1715, and after this first experiment had been successful
it was natural that they should be given considerable

prominence.   In the later operas they nearly always have passages of some length to play by themselves un-accompanied, so that their characteristic tone might be heard to the fullest advantage.   Probably they were played by the trumpeters, just as now the *cor anglais* is often played by one of the oboe-players, since the horns and trumpets are never used together.

The oboes and bassoons seldom have parts of much individuality.   We occasionally find an oboe solo some-times effectively contrasted with a solo flute, as in the charming duet, "*Vaga ninfa semplicetta*," which ends the first part of the serenata for the Peace of Passarowitz ; and in the serenata for the Prince of Stigliano there is a very amusing air in which the bassoons imitate the bellowing of an angry bull.   But for the most part the "*concerto di oubuoè*" seems to have been regarded as a single mass of sound valued more for its sonority than for its peculiar quality of tone.   Indeed, setting aside the advantages resulting from later improvements in the mechanism of the instrument, the characteristic personality of the oboe could scarcely be realized until the advent of its rival, the clarinet.   It is in the serenata for the Prince of Stigliano that Scarlatti approaches nearest to a modern treatment of wind instruments.

The overture, scored for trumpets, oboes, and strings, is of little interest, but there is an effective pastoral symphony played in the distance by wind instruments only—two flutes, two oboes, two horns, and two bassoons, the last being supported by the double-basses as in many of Mozart's compositions for wind-bands.   This is followed by two pretty little choruses of shepherds, two sopranos, alto, and tenor, accompanied by the same instruments. One of the most interesting pieces of scoring is the old shepherd's first air, "*Mentre quel solco ara il bifolco*," attractive also from the cheerful rusticity of its melody, which quite suggests the "impatient husbandman" of Haydn's "Seasons."   Only flutes and oboes are used in addition to the strings, though perhaps the bassoons would

play with the *continuo;* but even with these small means a
very picturesque variety of colour is achieved.

Ex. 85.

M

Ex. 86.

Per le cam - pa - gne pas - cen - do

l'a - - - - gne, dan - -

-zɔn,   dan - zan tal - o - ra le nin-fe an - co -

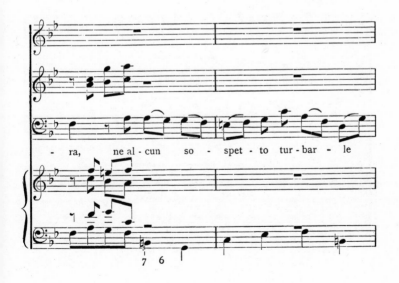

- ra,   ne al - cun   so - spet - to tur - bar - le

One of the most interesting works of Scarlatti's latest period, though contributing little that is remarkable from an orchestral point of view, is the second Mass in A for soli, chorus, and orchestra. The most authoritative extant manuscript, a score in the Biblioteca Casanatense at Rome, written out by a copyist but with a heading in Scarlatti's handwriting, has parts for five voices only, with vague directions as to when the music is to be sung by the chorus and when by solo voices. Santini, however, appears to have been in possession of an incomplete set of parts from which he prepared a score, filling up the missing portions from the score in the Biblioteca Casanatense, and in this he indicates what was probably the correct distribution of the voices. The mass was composed at Rome in 1720 for Cardinal Acquaviva for performance on St. Cecilia's Day, being coupled with a setting of the Gradual "*Audi filia et inclina aurem*" for five voices, oboes and strings. The complete autograph of this motet is bound up with the score at Rome. Santini's score of the mass inserts it between the *Gloria* and the *Credo*.

The mass cannot be considered a great work; taken as a whole it wants breadth and dignity, and for success of effect is far surpassed by Leo's compositions in the same style. But it is of importance as a forerunner not only of Leo's masses, but of J. S. Bach's Mass in B minor. It shows a much greater mastery over the new style than Scarlatti's first mass with orchestra, and certain movements show clearly that the composer must have had a fairly definite idea of the kind of effects that would be most suitable to this material. Moreover it exhibits in certain movements a poetical seriousness of a type which is not characteristic of Leo, in spite of all his severity and grandeur; indeed it is this quality almost as much as any other that gives the work its marked affinity to that of Bach.

The first movement does not look very dignified on paper, but with the support of the organ it would be very much more solid; and the *soli* and *ripieni* are at any rate laid out so as to make an effective contrast.

Ex. 87.

The *Cum Sancto Spiritu* is set to a well-developed fugue of some length in quite a modern style ; the subject and its counter-subject are well contrasted, and the strings have a definite figure of accompaniment which is kept up the whole time.

Ex. 88.

Towards the end, when we should expect a coda, a new subject is brought in on the word *Amen;* but the two subjects are never worked together. Whether Bach ever knew this mass it is impossible to say ; but there is a decided resemblance to Bach's style in the tranquilly melodious *Crucifixus*, though not to his setting of those particular words :—

Ex. 89.

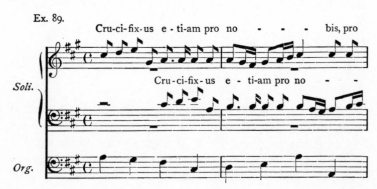

and still more so in the *Qui tollis*, as regards both the melodic outline of the bass solo and the carefully worked suspensions of the accompaniment.

Ex. 90.

Qui tol - - - - - lis pec-

-ca - - ta, pec-ca - - ta, pec-

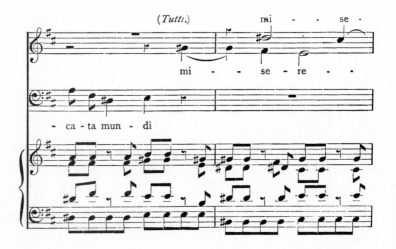

(*Tutti.*)

mi - - se -

mi - - se - re - -

-ca - ta mun - di

Besides the Gradual "*Audi filia*," which contains some brilliant and effective writing, several other works for Saint Cecilia's Day seem to have been composed at this date: there is a rather florid setting of the Psalm "*Laetatus sum*," for five voices and orchestra, with a fine dignified *Gloria* followed by a most Bacchanalian *Amen*, and also a simple and attractive setting of the hymn "*Jesu corona virginum*" for five voices and strings, as well as a *Magnificat* and minor pieces unfortunately incomplete. A more interesting composition is the *Stabat Mater* for soprano and alto, two violins and *continuo*. Pergolesi's more celebrated setting of the same words is said to have been composed as a substitute for it, and it is not surprising that Scarlatti's was forgotten, since it has little of the grace and charm of the younger composer's. But it probably served as a model to Pergolesi, and though it can seldom be called attractive, it is sincere in expression, as well as interesting from a technical point of view. It is evidently one of Scarlatti's very latest works, as it employs turns of phrase more characteristic of the next generation than of his own, and the *appoggiatura*, rare even in his latest operas, frequently appears here. But the general spirit of the work is essentially severe, and seems to aim almost painfully at the expression of the words, never descending to the superficial prettiness of Pergolesi. The first stanza is a duet full of strange modulations in long-drawn phrases; the *Cujus animam* is a soprano solo, the style of which is characteristic of the whole hymn.

Ex. 91. *Moderato e dolce.*

The movements for two voices are generally more or less contrapuntal; the airs, which are always in binary form, often have curious experiments in expression in the accompaniment. We see this in the "*Sancta Mater*":—

Ex. 92.

and the beautiful "*Fac me vere*" is very remarkable for the persistence with which the syncopations are carried on.

Ex. 93.

Contralto.

Fac me ve - re te - cum fle - re, Cru - ci -

Violini unis.

Continuo.

\- fix - - o con do - le - - re

"*Fac ut portem*" and "*Fac me cruce*" are set as recitatives which make a very effective contrast, and the work concludes with a well-developed fugue on *Amen*.

On the whole the style of the *Stabat Mater* has more affinity with the chamber-cantatas than with either the oratorios or the motets. Few chamber-cantatas can be ascribed with certainty to Scarlatti's closing years; internal evidence is not always a safe guide where the chamber-music is concerned, particularly in the last fifteen

years of Scarlatti's life, after he had pushed harmonic
audacity as far as "*Andate o miei sospiri.*" But we can
see that in the work of his old age he had more fully
mastered the science of modulation. His harmony moves
more easily and sounds more genuinely modern, especially
when helped by the use of more modern instrumental
figures in his basses. On the other hand, his melody
sometimes suffers; it even comes perilously near being
unvocal in the Bach-like tortuousness of its *coloratura*, as
may be seen in the cantata "*La dove a Mergellina*" (1725).

Ex. 94.

pre - gio   del - la   bel - tà.

Here we can see that for the moment Scarlatti's interest has been entirely absorbed in the sequential development of a figure, complicated by a cross-rhythm quite worthy of Brahms. In another late cantata, "*Nel centro oscuro*," there is an air which is obviously nothing but a labyrinthine study in modulations, the composer quite frankly trying to see how many he can get into the short space of a single aria. The result strikes the hearer at first as more curious than beautiful; yet it is not without a certain poetic feeling, like the two well-known preludes of Beethoven, modulating through all keys.

Short extracts cannot do justice to these later cantatas. Many of them are written round some interesting problem of form or harmony, and all require an alert and sympathetic listener to fully appreciate their severely intellectual beauty. Scarlatti seems, indeed, to have desired less to make a thing perfectly beautiful of its kind than to use the most intellectual form at his disposal to sketch the shadowy outlines of ideas more profound than his contemporaries were capable of penetrating. Even a German theorist like Heinichen considerered his harmony as extravagant, and from the account given by Quantz[1] it seems that he was regarded at Naples rather as a celebrity to be admired at a respectful distance than as an actual creative force in the artistic life of his time.

He probably remained in Rome until after November 1721, since in that month he composed a Pastorale at the request of the Portuguese Ambassador to celebrate the entrance of the new Pope Innocent XIII. into the Vatican. In 1722 he appears to have paid a visit to Loreto, where he is supposed to have written an *Ave Maria* and the psalm "*Memento Domine David.*" But he must have been at Naples in 1723 for the wedding of the Prince of Stigliano, and probably he remained there until his death. Hasse became his pupil in 1724, although he does not appear to have been teaching regularly at any of the

[1] In Marpurg's *Historisch-Kritische Beiträge zur Aufnahme der Musik*, Berlin, 1744-1762.

Conservatorii at this time.   Hasse's amiable disposition
seems to have won the old man's friendship, as it did that
of many other musicians in later years, Porpora always
excepted.   It was only after some persuasion on his part
that Scarlatti could be induced to receive Quantz, then on
a visit to Naples.   "My son," he said to Hasse, "you
know that I cannot endure players of wind-instruments;
for they all blow out of tune."   But he yielded eventually,
and Quantz gives an account of the interview, telling us,
however, less about Scarlatti than about himself.   "Scarlatti let me hear him on the harpsichord,[1] which he played
in a learned manner, although he did not possess as much
agility of execution as his son.   After this he accompanied
a solo for me.   I had the good fortune to gain his favour,
and he composed a couple of flute solos for me."

It is significant that although Quantz makes some
rather extraordinary assertions about Scarlatti (it must be
admitted that he offers them with a touch of incredulity),
he never mentions any single one of his compositions by
name.   When we read not only that Scarlatti has written
a vast quantity of operas ("*eine grosse Menge Opern*"),
but that "they say he has set the Mass two hundred
times in addition to Vesper Psalms and other church
music ; and indeed a certain Neapolitan gentleman boasted
of possessing four thousand [2] pieces of his composition,
mostly solo cantatas, to many of which he had written the
words himself," it seems fairly clear that the musical
gossips of Naples were not averse to trying how much the
"*gemüthlicher Sachse*" could be made to swallow.

It must have been in the early part of 1725 that
Scarlatti received Quantz.   On October 24 of the same
year he died, from what immediate cause is not known.   The
Gazzetta di Napoli [3] recorded his death a few days later.

"In the course of last week there died [4] the celebrated

---

[1] This has been curiously perverted by later historians into a statement
that Scarlatti was a performer on the harp.   Quantz's word "*Clavicymbel*"
leaves no room for misunderstanding.

[2] Not four hundred, as quoted in Grove's Dictionary.

[3] No. 45, October 30, 1725.

[4] "*Rese l'anima al Signore.*"

Cavaliere Alessandro Scarlatti, to whom music owes much for the numerous works with which he enriched it."

It is the laconic and conventional eulogy that is paid at his death to a great man who has been forgotten by his own generation.

He was buried in the church of Montesanto, in the musicians' chapel dedicated to St. Cecilia; his epitaph, said to have been written by Cardinal Ottoboni, is on the marble slab just under the gate, and runs as follows :—

HEIC · SITUS · EST

EQVES · ALEXANDER · SCARLACTVS

VIR · MODERATIONE · BENEFICENTIA

PIETATE · INSIGNIS

MVSICES · INSTAVRATOR · MAXIMVS

QVI · SOLIDIS · VETERVM · NVMERIS

NOVA · AC · MIRA · SVAVITATE

MOLLITIS

ANTIQVITATI · GLORIAM · POSTERITATI

IMITANDI · SPEM · ADEMIT

OPTIMATIBVS · REGIBVSQ

APPRIME · CARVS

TANDEM · ANNOS · NATVM · LXVI · EXTINXIT

SVMMO · CUM · ITALIAE · DOLORE

IX · KAL^AS · NOVEMB^EIS CIƆIƆCCXXV

MORS · MODIS · FLECTI · NESCIA

Of Scarlatti's personal character it is practically impossible to form an estimate. Contemporary records are singularly deficient in anything that can give us an idea of him as a man. His correspondence with Ferdinand de' Medici is voluminous, but its elaborately complimentary style effectually disguises the individuality of the writer. Such personal recollections of him as were handed down by Quantz and Geminiani have been seized upon by historians with avidity, but they really amount to hardly anything, and their scantiness has given them a fictitious value. Even his attitude towards his art is difficult to determine. Not until a century later did music begin to be regarded as the intimate expression of the composer's personal feelings ; it was only the romantic period of the

N

nineteenth century that required an autobiographical explanation of every bar. Roughly speaking, the intellectual side of music was all that a composer was expected to provide in Scarlatti's day; the appeal to the emotions was the legitimate province of the singer.

To us Scarlatti's music often seems conspicuously devoid of emotional qualities, compared with that of his contemporaries, such as Purcell, Handel, and J. S. Bach. But he certainly was very susceptible to emotion through the medium of poetry, for he writes to Ferdinand de' Medici full of enthusiasm for Stampiglia's libretto of " Il Gran Tamerlano" :—

" It is almost impossible, even merely reading the drama, not to feel stirred by the various passions which it exhibits. I confess my weakness ; at some passages, while I was composing the music for them, I wept." [1]

And in judging of his emotional qualities, it must not be forgotten that Scarlatti speaks a musical language to which we are little accustomed. To most lovers of music at the present day Schumann, Wagner, and Brahms represent the normal style of musical expression. Italian music is out of fashion, and since Beethoven's day the only non-German composers who have taken a permanent hold upon the musical public in England are those who have been largely influenced by Teutonic methods. In the eighteenth century the converse was the case. The Italian influence is the strongest bond of unity even between non-Italian composers such as Purcell, J. S. Bach, Haydn, and Mozart, and we cannot enter into their music at all deeply without some sympathy with Italian methods of expression. Scarlatti is of course wholly and entirely Italian, and those to whom Italian music is an unfamiliar language will naturally fail to understand the poetic beauty of his work.

Yet it must be frankly admitted that it is difficult to form a right judgment of his intrinsic merits as a composer. Though more than half his operas are lost, the amount that remains is still enormous, and bewildering in its

[1] Archivio Mediceo, *Filza* 5903, No. 204.

variety.   Are we to judge him by the pedantic eccentrici-
ties of his later chamber-music, or by the be-wigged and
powdered tunes of his Neapolitan operas?   Here again
we must forget modern conditions and take into consideration the circumstances of his life.   Bach, a church organist
in Central Germany, scarcely known outside his own
immediate circle, might write what he pleased as long as
he was content to perform his works as best he could with
limited means, and leave the rest to posterity ; Handel,
tyrannizing in musical matters over a land that was ready
meekly to accept his word as law, had even greater
advantages, provided that he did not push his learning
too far.   Scarlatti's case was in some ways less fortunate.
He had to write to make a living, and to write in competition against other musicians for audiences that had been
trained to musical drama for nearly a hundred years.   More
genuinely and more lavishly enthusiastic over opera than
any other nation, then as now, provided that it conforms
to their particular standard, the Italians are the least
patient of audiences towards opera that does not.   Court
patronage, though encouraging in some respects, had its
drawbacks.   It is clear that Scarlatti was glad enough
to escape from the Spanish Court at Naples ; but whether
Pratolino was really more of "a safe harbour" to him may
be doubted.   Ferdinand was an amateur musician of some
ability, but though this may have been an advantage to
Scarlatti, it must also have been irksome to him to have to
write and rewrite his operas in accordance with the prince's
taste.   Ferdinand[1] complained of the melancholy nature
of Scarlatti's music, as well as of its difficulty, and Scarlatti
protests vigorously in his letters that " Lucio Manlio " and
"Tamerlano" contain nothing melancholy, "even in the
places where it seems that such a character is indispens-
able."   On the whole Scarlatti seems to have done his
best for his art under difficult conditions.   His work
certainly shows a steady improvement from beginning to
end in technique at least, if the development of its poetical

[1] Archivio Mediceo, *Filza* 5903, No. 497.

side is irregular; and we can surely find a good proof of the loftiness of his aspiration and attainment in the great gulf that separates him from his immediate followers.

Alessandro Scarlatti is always regarded as the founder of the school of Naples; but it seems that Neapolitan chauvinism has somewhat exaggerated his connection with it. Roughly speaking, he certainly is the founder of the style which was developed by Leo, Vinci, and the rest; and certainly Naples would have had little chance of becoming a great musical centre if Scarlatti had not been induced to settle there, practically to monopolize the stage of S. Bartolomeo from 1684 to 1702 and from 1709 to 1719. But however considerable his indirect influence must have been, he was never very much in demand as an actual teacher. It is noticeable that the men who have had the greatest reputation as teachers were seldom thought much of as composers. Gaetano Greco and Nicola Fago il Tarentino, especially the latter, did far more than Scarlatti for the actual training of the next generation.

It is conceivable that Scarlatti may have been too exacting a teacher for clever boys who would soon realize that mechanical accuracy in counterpoint was sufficient for the church and natural facility of melody for the theatre. He is said to have insisted on not cramping his pupils with rules, wishing that they should develop their own ideas freely. As we have already seen in his "*Regole per principianti*," his ultimate reason for every exceptional progression is always "*perche fa buon sentire*"—"because it sounds well;" and such a passage as that on page 180 of this book shows that he was supremely indifferent to conventional prohibitions. A man of this temperament is not suited to be a teacher of beginners, and it is only a few enthusiasts who will be content to listen to his advice after they think that they have reached maturity. The early part of the eighteenth century was not conducive to the production of such types, least of all in the kingdom of Naples.

The difference between the later operas of Scarlatti and those of Leo, Vinci, and Pergolesi is very striking.

Scarlatti always seems to struggle more or less against the formalization of the opera, although to the modern reader this is not very apparent at first sight ; the next generation not only accepted its formalities but exaggerated them, until that intolerable state of affairs was reached when every air had its first part in a developed binary form, often full of a *coloratura* interesting at most for its difficulty, and still further extended by the lengthiest of *ritornelli* both at the beginning and in the middle. We see a faint tendency towards the type in *Roberto's* airs in "Griselda"; but the style had already been pushed further by the younger composers, especially by Vinci, when Scarlatti's opera came out, and it is probable that he wrote the airs only as a concession to popular taste. Everything seems to point to the fact that Scarlatti's influence in Naples was practically exhausted by about 1718. "Cambise" (1719) was the last opera which he produced there, and his works do not appear to have been revived there later, as they were at Rome and Bologna. The Neapolitan school of composers which professed to regard Alessandro Scarlatti as their head imitated him only during his second Neapolitan period, of which "Tigrane" may be taken as the representative opera. Even then his direct influence was slighter than might have been expected. His music evidently did not altogether suit popular taste, and it was through inferior composers like Mancini and Sarro, much less melodious, but more obviously commonplace in their rhythms, that the new style was developed to the stage at which we find it in Leo and Vinci. Leo's serious operas are his least interesting work ; like Vinci and Logroscino, he is at his best in *opera buffa*, in which all three inherited a good portion of Scarlatti's sense of humour. Vinci is on the whole the best of Scarlatti's immediate followers in the field of serious opera. His distinguishing quality is a swift, incisive vigour, enhanced by *coloratura* of real brilliancy ; but he very often becomes dry and stagey. Durante stands rather apart from the rest, as he confined himself to music for the church and chamber. He exhibits a larger share than any of the others of Scarlatti's poetry and tenderness of style; and we may trace Scarlatti's influence through him at second-hand in Pergolesi and Jommelli. Pergolesi's nature was not masculine enough for him ever to reach anything approaching the grandeur of Scarlatti, or even his humour; the best features of his comic operas are the sentimental airs. But the famous air in " L'Olimpiade "—" *Se cerca, se dice* "—has a touch of Scarlatti in the pathetic expression of its broken phrases skilfully woven into the texture of a formal design.

It is a significant fact that Scarlatti was the last great writer of chamber-cantatas. Those of the next generation are comparatively few, and seldom interesting. Pergolesi's are on the whole the best, and these are hardly to be classed as chamber-music, all having accompaniments for strings, on a much larger scale than Scarlatti's. Durante arranged a series of twelve duets from Scarlatti's later cantatas, taking recitatives and *ariosi* and expanding them in a more or less contrapuntal style. But these were intended, as Burney tells us, only as advanced "*studij* for singers, in which the passages being echoed in fugue excited emulation in performance, and furnished an opportunity of comparing the rapidity and neatness of the execution, as the comparative speed of two coursers is best known by their *running a trial*."

As the ideal form of chamber-music the cantata died with Alessandro Scarlatti. Probably the rise of instrumental music threw it out of fashion, as well as the increase in the number of amateur players and singers, which was a prominent factor in the development of music for the *cembalo*. Villarosa's judgment on Scarlatti's cantatas, though dating from a hundred years later, nevertheless probably represents with fair accuracy the opinion of the previous century :—

" But what music has he left that could be listened to to-day? His style was great, it is well understood; but his taste was always dry, nerveless and scholastic. If it

had not occurred to Francesco Durante to arrange some of
his pieces for two voices, soprano and alto, combining them
in a masterly manner, the name of Scarlatti would be no
more heard among us." To the modern reader it is
Durante's arrangements that appear "dry, nerveless and
scholastic," while the original movements, restored to their
proper places, are full of life and poetry.

On Handel Scarlatti's influence was strong at the
beginning, but not very lasting or profound. Certainly
the change of style that took place in his music after his
visit to Italy is very noticeable ; " Rinaldo " is as definitely
Italian as " Almira " was definitely German in its manner.
But although he began by modelling his phrases on Scarlatti after his visit to Italy, he very seldom enters thoroughly
into Scarlatti's style. There are several reasons for this.
His acquaintance with Scarlatti lasted a very short time,
and his age made him more suited to the companionship
of Domenico, whose influence can also be traced in much of
his work. Moreover, Handel, though only twenty-three
when he came to Italy, was a fully fledged composer. He
was not very familiar with the Italian style, but his Italian
Dixit Dominus is in some ways stronger than anything
of Scarlatti's in that line : Handel had had a Protestant
organist's training, which taught him to build up his music
on a strong harmonic framework. But in spite of the
advantages of that wonderful German faculty for translating
and assimilating the work of other countries which accounts
for much of the greatness of Handel, Bach, Gluck, and
Mozart, Handel had also the drawbacks of his nationality.
He set Italian as he set English, like a foreigner, never
approaching that delicate intimacy of declamation which is
as characteristic a quality of Scarlatti as it is of Purcell.
And it must be remembered that a literary appreciation of
this kind may take effect not only in impassioned recitative, but also in the most melodious and florid of arias.
Handel's *coloratura* is fairly effective in many cases, but
it is commonplace in detail ; a florid passage by Handel
is as different from one by Scarlatti as a *cadenza* of Liszt

is from a *cadenza* of Chopin. Handel seems to nail his *coloratura* to his framework; Scarlatti's often gains a priceless charm by its wayward independence. Handel often reminds us of some prudish nymph of Rubens, clutching her drapery tightly about her, anxious and ungraceful; Scarlatti recalls Tintoretto's Venus, her loose transparent girdle fluttering crisply to the breeze, serving its whole purpose in the delicate contrast that it makes with the pure firm line of her perfectly poised and rounded form. Besides Scarlatti, two other Italian composers exercised an equally strong influence on Handel: the eclectic Steffani, from whom Handel learned to write overtures and dances in what we may call an Italian version of the style of Lulli, and Bononcini, who in spite of his bad reputation among Handel's admirers seems to have been the real originator of what is commonly described as the "Handelian style." Bononcini even influenced Scarlatti himself, as we have seen, and it is therefore not surprising that a man of Handel's temperament should have seized more readily on the salient mannerisms of Bononcini and Steffani than on the more intricate subtleties of Scarlatti's music.

Domenico Scarlatti was to some extent a pupil of his father, though he also studied with Bernardo Pasquini and Francesco Gasparini. At a first glance there seems the strongest possible contrast between father and son. Domenico's operas and cantatas are as devoid of character and interest as Alessandro's tiresome toccatas for the *cembalo*. But if we compare Alessandro's arias with Domenico's sonatas, we shall find that they have much in common, after eliminating such qualities as are purely accidental to the two personalities, depending merely on the form in which their music is cast. We must not expect *cantabile* melodies in the *Esercizi per Gravicembalo* any more than wild leaps and rattling arpeggios in the *Cantate a voce sola*. But it certainly could not have been from Gasparini or Pasquini that Domenico got his genius for neatly organized forms, his extraordinary modulations, his

skill in thematic development, his quaint mannerism of
reiterating a characteristic figure, and above all his
astonishing Beethovenish sense of humour.

Among Scarlatti's pupils Hasse has a peculiar interest
and importance. His later work bears little resemblance
to his master's, for like all his contemporaries he too was
obliged to conform to the taste of his generation. But he
doubtless derived from Scarlatti his careful workmanship,
especially with regard to accompaniments, and the beautiful declamation and dramatic feeling of his *recitativo
stromentato*. He is moreover the principal connecting
link between the school of Naples and the school of
Vienna, and if he did no more than his fellow-pupils to
carry on the letter of the Scarlatti tradition, probably none
did so much for the propagation of its spirit as the devoted
disciple who told Burney "that the first time Scarlatti saw
him, he hastily conceived such an affection for him, that he
ever after treated him with the kindness of a father." [1]

Indeed the real importance of Scarlatti lies not in his
direct influence on his immediate followers, but in his relation to the whole development of classical music. "Eraclea"
may be said to divide his work at the meeting of the centuries. Before 1700, he had gathered up all that was best of
the tangled materials produced by that age of transition and
experiment, the seventeenth century, to form out of them a
musical language, vigorous and flexible as Italian itself,
which has been the foundation of all music of the classical
period. Lesser composers contributed their part to this
great work, but Scarlatti is so much the most fertile, and
maintains even at his lowest so high a standard, that the
main glory of the achievement is certainly due to him.
His best pupil, we may safely say, is Mozart. Almost
all those characteristics of style that we are accustomed
loosely to consider as essentially Mozartian, were learned
by Mozart from the Italians of the preceding half-century.
Indeed, Mozart to some extent repeated the work of
Scarlatti, uniting in himself the massive strength of Leo,

[1] *The Present State of Music in Germany, &c.*, vol. i. p. 348.

the sweetness of Durante and Pergolesi, the swift energy of Vinci and the racy humour of Logroscino, together with that divine beauty of melody which belonged to Scarlatti alone. Nor was this Italian influence confined to his early years ; " Die Zauberflöte," in some ways the most German of his operas, is also the opera in which he shows the most marked affinity to Scarlatti. , The *Queen of Night, Tamino,* and *Pamina* are all characteristic figures of the Italian stage, treated quite in Scarlatti's manner ; and *Papageno* and *Papagena*, however typically Viennese they may be from a psychological point of view, are certainly nothing but Italian *parti buffe* as far as their place in the opera is concerned.

The history of the classical period is the history of musical form from the aggressive symmetry of Haydn to the masterly freedom of Beethoven. For this development Scarlatti prepared the ground. Large symphonic forms he never used ; the airs and duets of his later operas and cantatas represent the widest schemes of design that he could conceive for single movements. It is natural to think that this was mainly due to his innate sympathy with the voice and his comparative indifference to instrumental music. This, however, is probably not the sole reason. Scarlatti, as we have seen, always cherished the contrapuntal tradition in serious music, both vocal and instrumental, although his counterpoint is seldom in more than two parts ; hence in his instrumental music the tendency towards modern symphonic forms is apparent only in his dances, marches, and similar movements. Even in these he becomes contrapuntal whenever the occasion demands a serious style : the last movement of the overture to " La Vergine Addolorata," composed as late as 1717, is thoroughly polyphonic, and not in the least orchestral in a modern sense, although its dance form is as clearly defined as that of the march in " Il Prigioniero Fortunato." In the chamber-cantatas, however, it was easier to extend his forms on modern lines ; and we see clearly from such examples as are quoted in Chapter III. how much he was influenced in this direction by the words which he set. Long before Scarlatti, composers had found it necessary to repeat the words of a song in order to bring the music to a sufficient length. Once repeat the words in their entirety, and common sense demands a more or less well-defined binary form. The further the words are extended by the repetition of single words or phrases within a section, the more complicated must the musical organization become ; and such complication is peculiarly characteristic of Italian music, because the genius of the Italian language has always delighted in the symmetrical grouping of words and the antithetical inversion of phrase. The breaking up of the words into small groups would naturally tend to the breaking up of the music into contrasting subjects, and this would be still further assisted by the necessity of bringing out to the full the opposition and interaction of the voice and the violoncello. For it is noticeable that in all Scarlatti's cantatas the violoncello has a strongly individualized part, the menial duty of accompaniment being left to the *cembalo*. Practical considerations of course restrained music for solo voices within shorter limits than were possible for purely instrumental movements ; but within these limits there is not only a perfect proportion of main divisions, but every bar displays the most subtly ingenious organization of figure, and this too carried out with a richness of detail that is noticeably deficient in the instrumental music of his time. We must admit that consciously or unconsciously Scarlatti did as much as any composer to bring about that degradation of the musical drama that preceded the reforms of Gluck ; but when we view the history of European music as a whole, it must appear that his sins with regard to musical drama were far outweighed by his priceless contribution to the development of pure music. For we may call him not only a great architect, but a great poet as well ; formal and rhetorical as his music may seem to us, he nevertheless speaks the language of passion as sincerely as any later composer. He may almost be said to have invented it, for none of his predecessors or contemporaries can show the same absolute mastery over it. Monteverdi, Cavalli, Heinrich Schütz and Purcell may give us single phrases, even single movements which are often astonishingly modern in their effect ; Scarlatti never. His music is either frankly the music of his own time, or else, like Mozart's, it is music for all time. Whenever he does anything new he does it with the perfect ease of an accomplished master ; even in the chamber-music, where he is openly attacking a problem, he is fully conscious of his power to solve it. He is entirely devoid of the hysterical romanticism which makes wild experiments in the vague hope of expressing the inexpressible ; musical composition is for him a science, "the daughter of Mathematics." [1] Well did Cardinal Ottoboni describe him for his own age when he wrote upon his tombstone " *musices instaurator maximus.*" We, some two centuries later, tracing the development of his art through Haydn, Mozart, Beethoven, and Brahms along those lines which he was the first clearly to lay down, may legitimately interpret the words—Father of Classical Music.

[1] Letter to Ferdinand de' Medici, May 1, 1706. (Archivio Mediceo, *Filza* 5903, No. 196.)

CATALOGUE OF THE EXTANT WORKS OF ALESSANDRO SCARLATTI

CATALOGUE OF THE EXTANT WORKS
OF ALESSANDRO SCARLATTI

With the Libraries where the MSS. are to be found.[1]

B. Berlin, Royal Library.
BA. Bologna, Accademia Filarmonica.
BC. Brussels, Conservatoire Royal de Musique.
BF. Brussels, Royal Library (Fétis' collection).
BL. Bologna, Liceo Musicale.
BM. London, British Museum.
Bod. Oxford, Bodleian Library.
C. Cambridge, Fitzwilliam Museum.
Cas. Rome, Biblioteca Casanatense.
Cec. Rome, Biblioteca S. Cecilia.
Chr. Oxford, Christchurch.
Cor. Rome, Biblioteca Corsiniana.
D. Dresden, Royal Library.
Dar. Darmstadt, Grand-Ducal Library.
F. Florence, R. Istituto Musicale.
FN. Florence, National Library.
LA. London, Royal Academy of Music.
LB. London, Buckingham Palace.

LC. London, Royal College of Music.
M. Munich, National Library.
MC. Montecassino.
Mil. Milan, R. Conservatorio di Musica.
Mod. Modena, Biblioteca Estense.
N. Naples, R. Conservatorio di Musica.
Pad. Padua, Biblioteca del Santo.
Pal. Palermo, R. Conservatorio di Musica.
PC. Paris, Conservatoire de Musique.
PN. Paris, Bibliothèque Nationale.
RB. Rome, Biblioteca Barberini.
S. Münster in Westphalia, Santini's collection.
Sch. Schwerin, Grand-Ducal Library.
V. Venice, Biblioteca Marciana.
Vat. Rome, Vatican Library.
W. Vienna, Imperial Library.
WM. Vienna, Gesellschaft der Musikfreunde.

I. OPERAS.

II. ORATORIOS.

III. SERENATAS AND CANTATAS FOR FESTIVALS.

IV. MADRIGALS.

V. CHAMBER-CANTATAS FOR TWO VOICES.

VI. CHAMBER-CANTATAS FOR ONE VOICE.

VII. MASSES.

VIII. MOTETS.

IX. INSTRUMENTAL MUSIC.

X. THEORETICAL WORKS, &c.

[1] This catalogue does not include modern printed editions, or MS. arias from unidentified operas.

I. OPERAS

L'Aldimiro ovvero Favore per Favore.
Libretto: *BL.* (Gubbio, 1687), *BC.* (Rome, 1688). Fragments: *BM.* Produced previously at Naples.

L'Amazone Corsara (in the scores, Guerriera).
Score: *MC. M. Cec.* Libretto: *N.* (Naples, Royal Palace, 1689).

L'Amor Generoso.
Score: *BM.* Libretto: *N.* (Naples, Royal Palace and Teatro S. Bartolomeo, 1 October 1714).

Amor non vuol Inganni. *See* Gli Equivoci nel Sembiante.

L'Amor Volubile e Tiranno.
Score: *BC. D.* Libretto: *BL. N.* (Naples, S. Bartolomeo, 1709.)

L'Anacreonte Tiranno.
Score: *S.* Libretto: *N.* (Naples, 1689), *BC.* (Pratolino 1698).

L'Analinda. *See* Le Nozze con l' Inimico.

L'Ariovisto.
Fragments: *S.* (about 1700?)

Arminio.
Libretto: *N. BL.* (Naples, S. Bartolomeo, 19 November 1714). *BC. BL.* (Rome, Sala Capranica, 1722).

La Caduta dei Decemviri.
Score: *BF. BM. N.* Libretto: *BC. N.* (Naples, S. Bartolomeo, 1697). Fragments: *D.*

Cambise.
Score: *N.* ("Opera 111"). Libretto: *N.* (Naples, S. Bartolomeo, 4 February 1719).

Carlo Re d'Allemagna.
Libretto: *BL. N.* (Naples, S. Bartolomeo, Carnival 1718). Fragments: *BC. D.*

Il Ciro.
Score: *BC.* (autograph, October 1711). Libretto: *BL.* (Rome, 1712). Fragments: *S. N.*

Clearco in Negroponte.
Score: *Mod.* Libretto: *BC. Mod. N.* (Naples, Royal Palace, 21 December 1686).

Il Consiglio dell' Ombra. *See* L' Emireno.

Dafni e Galatea.
Fragments: *D. PC.* (Naples, 1700).

Dal Male il Bene.
Score: *B. MC.* (partly autograph). Libretto: *BC.* (Naples, Royal Palace, 1687). Fragments: *BM.*

La Dama Spagnuola ed il Cavalier Romano. *See* Scipione nelle Spagne.

La Didone Delirante.
Fragments: *N.* (Naples, 1695 or 1696?).

La Donna ancora è fedele.
Libretto: *BC.* (Naples, S. Bartolomeo, 1698). Fragments: *D. Sch.*

L' Emireno ovvero Il Consiglio dell' Ombra.
Libretto: *BC.* (Naples, S. Bartolomeo, 1697). Fragments: *D.*

L' Equal Impegno d'Amore. *See* Il Tigrane.

Gli Equivoci in Amore ovvero La Rosaura.
Score: *BM.* (two copies, representing two different performances). Libretto: *BC.* (Rome, at the French Embassy, 1690), *N.* (Naples, Royal Palace, 1690). Fragments: *F. N. PC. RB. S.*

Gli Equivoci nel Sembiante ovvero L' Errore Innocente.
Score : BC. BL. Mod. V.
Libretto : BL. (Rome, 1679; Bologna, 1679; Ravenna, 1635), BC. (Monte Filottramo, 1680), Mod. (Rome, 1679). Fragments : W.

L' Eraclea.
Libretto : N. (Naples, 1700), BC. BL. (Parma 1700). Fragments : BF. D. LB. N. PC.

L' Errore Innocente. See Gli Equivoci nel Sembiante.

Il Figlio delle Selve.
Score : PC. Libretto : BC. (Rome, 1687).

Flavio.
Libretto : BL. N. (Naples, S. Bartolomeo, 6 November 1688).

Il Flavio Cuniberto.
Score : Chr. Libretto : BC. (Rome, Teatro Capranica, 1698), N. (Rome, n.d.), FN. (Pratolino 1702). Fragments : S. (Pratolino, 1702. These 16 airs are not in the Chr. MS.) Ademollo mentions a performance at Rome (Teatro Tordinona) in 1695.

Gerone Tiranno di Siracusa.
Score : Chr. (composed 1692). Fragments : N. It was performed at Rome in 1694, and probably produced at Naples earlier.

Il Gran Tamerlano.
Libretto : FN. (Pratolino, 1706).

La Griselda.
Score : B. BC. M. S. ("Opera 114"). Libretto : BL. (Rome, T. Capranica, Carnival 1721). Fragments : BM. (Acts I. and III. autograph), PC.

L' Honestà negli Amori.
Score : Mod. Libretto : BL.

BC. (Rome, 6 February 1680). Fragments : Cas. PC:

L' Humanità nelle Fere ovvero Il Lucullo.
Libretto : BL. (Naples, S. Bartolomeo, 1708). Probably produced before elsewhere, since the libretto mentions additions by Vignola.

L' Infedeltà Fedele. See La Rosmene.

Gli Inganni Felici.
Libretto : BC. N. (Naples, Royal Palace and S. Bartolomeo, 1699). Fragments : D.

Laodicea e Berenice.
Score : PN. Libretto : Mod. N. (Naples, S. Bartolomeo, 1701). Fragments : BM. BF. N. PC.

Lucio Manlio l' Imperioso.
Libretto : FN. (Pratolino, 1705).

Marco Attilio Regolo.
Score : BM. (autograph). Libretto : BL. BC. N. (Rome, T. Capranica, Carnival 1719). Fragments : BC. BM. (with title " Annibale ") PC.

Massimo Puppieno.
Score : MC. Libretto : N. (Naples, S. Bartolomeo, 26 December 1695).

Il Mitridate Eupatore.
Score : B. PC. Libretto : BL. V. (Venice, Teatro S. Giovanni Crisostomo, 1707).

Le Nozze con l' Inimico ovvero l'Analinda.
Score : PN. Libretto : BC. (Naples, S. Bartolomeo, 1695). Fragments : BM. D.

Odoardo.
Libretto : BC. (Naples, S. Bartolomeo, 1700). Fragments : D. N. PC.

L' Olimpia Vendicata.
Score : London, in possession of F. G. Edwards, Esq. Libretto : *BC. N.* (Naples, S. Bartolomeo, 1686). Fragments : *BM. N. PC.*

Il Pastor di Corinto.
Score : *BF.* Libretto : *BC.* (Naples, S. Bartolomeo, 1701). Fragments : *D. PC.*

Il Pirro e Demetrio.
Score : *BF. N.* Libretto : *N.* (Naples, S. Bartolomeo, 1694), *BC.* (Rome, 1696). Fragments : *BM.* Performed in London 14 December 1700 in an English adaptation by Swiny and Haym.

Il Pompeo.
Score : *BF.* Libretto : *BC.* (Rome, Teatro Colonna, 1683; Naples, Royal Palace and S. Bartolomeo, 1684), *N. BL.* (Leghorn, 1688). Fragments : *Bod. PC. S. V.*

Il Prigioniero Fortunato.
Score : *BM. N.* Libretto : *BL. BC.* (Naples, S. Bartolomeo, 14 December 1698). Fragments : *D. PC. S. PN.*

La Principessa Fedele.
Score : *BF.* Libretto : *BL. N.* (Naples, S. Bartolomeo, Carnival 1710). Fragments : *S.* (partly autograph).

La Rosaura. See Gli Equivoci in Amore.

La Rosmene ovvero L' Infedeltà Fedele.
Score : *S.* Libretto : *BC.* (Naples, S. Bartolomeo, 1688). Fragments : *BM. F.*

Scipione nelle Spagne.
Score : *BM. BF.* Libretto : *N.* (Naples, S. Bartolomeo, 21 January 1714). Fragments : *MC.* The comic scenes were

revived at Bologna in 1730 with the title " La Dama Spagnuola ed il Cavalier Romano."

La Statira.
Score : *BM. BC. D. M.* Libretto : *BC.* (Rome, Teatro Tordinona, 1690). Fragments : *N. S.*

Telemaco.
Score : *PC. S. W.* (autograph). Libretto : *BL. BC.* (Rome, T. Capranica, 1718; " Opera 109"). Fragments : *F.*

La Teodora Augusta.
Score : *Chr. F.* Libretto : *BC.* (Rome, T. Capranica, 1693).

Teodosio.
Libretto : *N.* (Naples, S. Bartolomeo, 1709). The libretto does not mention Scarlatti, but the *Gazzetta di Napoli* names him as the composer.

Il Tigrane ovvero L' Equal Impegno d'Amore.
Score : *F. N. LB.* Libretto : *BL. N.* (Naples, S. Bartolomeo, Carnival 1715; " Opera 106 "). Fragments : *S.*

Tiberio Imperatore d' Oriente.
Fragments : *N. PC.* (Naples, Royal Palace, 8 May 1702).

Tito Sempronio Gracco.
Libretto : *N.* (Naples, S. Bartolomeo, 1702, and Rome, T. Capranica, 1720), *BL. BC.* (Rome, 1720). Fragments : *D. N.* (Naples, 1702), *PC. S.* (Rome, 1720).

Il Trionfo dell' Onore.
Score : *BM.* (" Opera 110 "). Libretto : *N.* (Naples, T. dei Fiorentini, 1718).

Il Trionfo della Libertà.
Libretto : *BL. N. V.* (Venice, S. Giovanni Crisostomo, 1707). Fragments : *BF.*

o

Turno Aricino.
  Libretto: *FN*. (Pratolino, 1704),
  BC. *BL*. (Rome, T. Capranica,
  1720). Fragments: *PC*. *S*. *B*.
  (Rome, 1720). It is possible
  that the setting produced at
  Pratolino in 1704 was not Scar-
  latti's.

La Virtù negli Amori.
  Libretto: *BL*. (Rome, 18 No-
  vember 1721).
La Virtù Trionfante dell' Odio e
  dell' Amore.
  Libretto: *BC*. *N*. (Naples, Royal
  Palace, 3 May, 1716).

OPERAS WRITTEN IN COLLABORATION

La Santa Genuinda.
  Score: *BM*. *M*. *PC*. Libretto:
  BC. *M*. (Rome, 1694). Act I.
  by Giovanni del Violone, Act
  II. by A. Scarlatti, Act III. by
  C. F. Pollarolo.

Giunio Bruto ovvero la Caduta dei
  Tarquinij.
  Score: *W*. Act I. by Carlo
  Cesarini, Act II. by Antonio
  Caldara, Act III. by A. Scar-
  latti.

ADDITIONS TO OPERAS BY OTHER COMPOSERS

Odoacre (Legrenzi).
  Libretto: *N*. (Naples, S. Barto-
  lomeo, 1694).
La Pastorella (Act I. by Cesarini,
  Act II. by Giannino, Act III.
  by Bononcini).
  Fragments: *BM*. Represented
  by marionettes in the palace of
  the Venetian ambassador at
  Rome in 1705.
Il Porsenna (Lotti).
  Fragments: *MC*. Performed at
  Naples in 1713.
  Aiace, Comodo Antonino, Etio,

*Muzio Scevola,*and *Penelope la Casta*
were ascribed by Florimo and others
to A. Scarlatti without any apparent
documentary evidence. The libretti
are without any composer's name,
and no scores or fragments by Scarlatti are known.

  Il Medo and *Rodrigo* (scores in
PC.) have been ascribed to A. Scarlatti by modern hands. *Il Medo*
is certainly by a much later composer, and *Rodrigo* is identical with
an opera by Stradella (*Mod*.),
called by Catelani *Il Floridoro*.

II. ORATORIOS

Agar et Ismaele Esiliati. Rome,
  1683. *W*.
La SS^{ma} Annuntiata (about 1710?).
  BF.
L'Assunzione della Beatissima Ver-
  gine (about 1705?). *S*. *W*. *See*
  La Sposa dei Sacri Cantici.
S. Casimiro Re di Polonia (Vienna,
  1713, probably not first per-
  formance). *W*.

La Concettione della B.V. (Rome,
  1703, according to Florimo).
  PN.
La Conversione di Maddalena. *See*
  Il Trionfo della Gratia.
Davidis Pugna et Victoria (Rome,
  1700). Libretto: *BL*.
San Filippo Neri (Foligno, 14 May,
  1713, probably not first perfor-
  mance). *BF*. *S*. Libretto: *BL*.

La Giuditta (about 1690?). *N.*

Il Martirio di S. Teodosia (Modena, 1685). *PN. BF. Mod. W.* Libretto: *BL. Mod.* Fragments: *Cor.*

Cantata per la Notte di Natale (Rome, Palazzo Apostolico, 1705). *S.*

Pastorale per la Natività del Bambino Gesù (Rome, 1705?). *S.*

Passio secundum Johannem (about 1680?). *N.*

La Passione di N. S. G. C. (Rome, 1708). *Cas.*[1] Libretto: *BL.*

Il Sedecia Re di Gerusalemme (1706). *BC. Cas. D. M. W.* Fragments: *S.*

La Sposa dei Sacri Cantici (Naples, 1710, according to Florimo).

PC. A slightly different version of L'Assunzione.

La SS^ma Trinità (1715). *N.* (autograph).

Il Trionfo della Gratia ovvero la Conversione di Maddalena. (Rome, 1685; Modena, 1686; Mantua, 1695; Bologna, 1696, 1699, 1704; Vienna, 1701, 1707). *D. Mod.* (partly autograph). Libretto: *BC. Mod.* Fragments: *Cor.*

[La Vergine Addolorata] (1717). *BC.* Fragments: Westminster, Chapter Library. So called by M. Gevaert: neither score has a title.

La SS^ma Vergine del Rosario (about 1705?) *S.*

Of *I Dolori di Maria Sempre Vergine* (Rome, 1693), *Il Martirio di S. Cecilia* (Rome, 1709), and *Il Sagrificio d'Abramo* (Rome, 1703), ascribed to A. Scarlatti by Fétis, Florimo, and others, I have found no trace.

Ademollo mentions an *Oratorio per la Notte di Natale* (Rome, 1695), and Croce an Oratorio for St. Joseph's Day, *Il Trionfo del Valore* (Naples, 1709), but I have found neither libretto nor music.

III. SERENATAS AND CANTATAS FOR FESTIVALS, &c.[2]

Achille e Deidamia (very early, and probably not Scarlatti). *N.*

Diana ed Endimione (about 1680–1685?). *MC.*

Il Genio di Partenope, la Gloria del Sebeto, il Piacere di Mergellina (Naples, 1696). *MC.*

Venere, Adone ed Amore—"*Per l'apertura di Posilipo*" (Naples, 1696). *MC. Chr.*

Venere ed Amore (Naples, about 1695–1700?). *BF.*

Clori, Lidia, Filli (about 1700?). *BC.*

Clori, Dorino, Amore ("*Cantata a Napoli alla presenza di Filippo V. Re delle Spagne,*" probably 1702). *B. S.*

Il Giardino di Amore (about 1700–1705?). *B. S.*

---

[1] According to the catalogue; but the MS. is not to be found. The Royal Library at Dresden possesses the score of an oratorio attributed to Scarlatti, which corresponds partly with the libretto, but it is probably a rearrangement of Scarlatti's original by a later composer, probably Hasse.

[2] These compositions scarcely ever have definite titles; I have therefore given them the names of their characters, and arranged them (as far as was possible) in chronological order.

Endimione e Cintia (Rome, 1705).
B. S.

Amore e Virtù ossia il Trionfo della Virtù ("*scritta per il Principe Ruspoli,*" Rome, 1706). *B. S.*

Clori e Zeffiro (1706). *B. S.*

Fileno, Niso, Doralbo (Rome, 1706). *S.*

Le Muse Urania e Clio lodano le bellezze di Filli (1706). *S.*

Venere, Adone e Amore (Rome, 1706). *S.*

Venere avendo perduto Amore lo ritrova fra le Ninfe e Pastori

dei Sette Colli (Rome, 1706). *B. S.*

Pace, Amor, Providenza (Naples, probably 1714). *B.*

Primavera, Estate, Autunno, Inverno e Giove (Naples, 1716, for the birth of the Archduke Leopold). *BM. M. N.*

Filli, Clori, e Tirsi (Naples, 1718?). *B. S.*

Erminia, Tancredi, Polidoro, e Pastore ("*Per l' ecc^{mo} Sig^r Principe di Stigliano in occasione de' suoi Sponsali,*" Naples, 1723). *MC. N. LC.*

IV. MADRIGALS

Arsi un tempo e l'ardore (SS.A.T.B.). *WM.*

Cor mio deh non languire (SSSS.A.). *B. BL. BM.* (Add. 14166) *C. M. N. S.* Also printed in Martini's *Saggio di Contrappunto.*

Intenerite voi lacrime mie (S.A.TT.B). *BM.* (Add. 31412).

Mori mi dici (SS.A.T.B.). *N.*

O morte agli altri fosca, a me serena (SS.A.T.B.). *WM.*

O selce o tigre o ninfa (SS.A.T.B.). *BM.* (Add. 31412).

Or che da te mio bene (S.A.T.B.). *N.*

Sdegno la fiamma estinse (SS.A.T.B.). *BM.* (Add. 31412).

V. CHAMBER-CANTATAS FOR TWO VOICES

(Accompanied by Continuo alone unless additional instruments are mentioned.)

The asterisk (*) denotes a work of which the authorship is doubtful.

A battaglia, pensieri, a battaglia (S.A., trumpet, 2 violins, 1699). *WM.*

Ahi che sarà di me (Floro e Tirsi) (SS., 2 Sept., 1707). *C. N. S.*

Amica, hor che Aprile (Filli e Clori) (SS., 2 violins). *Bod. BM.* (Add. 31488, 31506) *S. WM.*

Bel Dorino—amata Clori (Clori e Dorino) (S.B., 2 violins). *Sch.*

Che più farai arciero amor (Clori e Dorino (S.B.). *Sch.*

Cleopatra mia Reina (Marc'antonio e Cleopatra (S.A.). *S.*

Clori mia—Dorino caro (Clori e Dorino) (S.B.). *Sch.*

Crudel perche privarmi (SS.). *F.*

{ Di quel seno al bel candore
{ Di quegli occhi al dolce foco
(S.A.). *WM.*

*Dimmi crudel e quando (S.A.). *BL.*

Disperate pupille hor si piangete (S.B.). *Sch.*

Dove fuggi o bella Clori (Clori e Lidio) (S.A.). *N.*

Another setting (S.A., 2 violins). *S.*

*Due cori a me fan guerra (SS.; perhaps by Lotti). *N. Pal.*

E pur vuole il cielo (S.A., 1706?). *BL. BM.* (Add. 31491). *C. S.*

Il ciel seren, le fresche aurette (La Primavera, Clori e Lisa) (SS.). *S.*

Lasciami sospirar, io voglio piangere (Dorindo e Fileno) (S.B.). *PC.*

Lisa, del foco mio (Clori e Lisa (SS., 28 Feb. 1706). *C.N.PC.S.*

Mentre sul carro aurato (Clori e Mirtillo). *PC. S.*

*No che lungi da quel volto (SA.; perhaps by Lotti). *N. Pal.*

No, non ti voglio no (S.A.). *S.*

O come bello con onde chiare (Tirsi e Clori) (SS.). *S.*

O penosa lontananza—o felice lontananza (S.B.). *S. Sch. W.*

Ombre romite e solitarie piante (S.A.). *M.*

Or per pietà del mio crudel destino (S.A.). *B.* (incomplete?).

Perche sospiri o Niso (Doralba e Niso) (S.A.). *D.*

*Quando un Eroe che s'ama (S.A.). *BL.*

Questo silenzio ombroso (S.A., 17 Sept. 1707). *BM.* (Add. 14166, 31412). *C. N. PC. S.*

*Son pur care le catene (S.A.). *BL.*

*Tirsi che fa il tuo core (SS.; perhaps by Lotti). *N. Pal.*

Viva, viva mia libertà (SS.). *PC.*

VI. CHAMBER CANTATAS FOR ONE VOICE

(1) ACCOMPANIED BY CONTINUO WITH OTHER INSTRUMENTS

All' hor che stanco il sole (S., 2 violins). *PC.*

Alma tu che dal Cielo (S., 2 violins, 12 Sept. 1709, sacred). *BM.* (Add. 34056).

Amanti anch' io son preso (S., violin solo). *S.*

Appena chiudo gli occhi (S., violin). *N. PC.*

Appena giunse al forte campo. (Oloferne) (B., 2 violins). *BM.* (Add. 14166, incomplete).

Ardo, è ver, per te d'amore (S., flute). *N.* (incomplete).

[1] Augellin sospendi i vanni (S., 2 violins). *B.* (autograph).

Augellin vago e canoro (S., 2 flutes, 26 June 1699). *S.*

Ben mio, quel verme alato (S., 2 violins). *BM.* (Add. 31506).

Clori mia, Clori bella (S., flute, 18 June 1699). *S.*

Correa nel seno amato (S., 2 violins). *BM.* (Add. 31506) *N. Pal.*

Da dupplicati oggetti (S., 2 violins, viola). *N.*

Dall' oscura magion dell' arsa Dite (L' Orfeo) (S., 2 violins). *PC. S.*

Dove fuggo, a che penso? (S., violin solo.) *N. PC. S.*

E con qual core, oh Dio (S., 2 violins). *S.*

Ebra d'amor fuggia (L'Arianna) (S., 2 violins). *N. PC.*

Era l' oscura notte (S., 2 violins). *S.*

Ferma omai fugace e bella (A., 2 violins and viola, Dec. 1724). *Rome, Comm. Carlo Lozzi* (autograph).

Fida compagna del tuo alato amante (S., 2 violins). *B. N. PC.*

---

[1] See under Cantatas with *continuo* alone.

Fileno, oh Dio ! Fileno, di quest' anima amante (S., 2 violins). *BF.*

Fileno, quel Fileno, tutto fè (S., 2 violins). *S.*

Fillì che fra gl' orrori (S., 2 violins, 1706). *S.*

Filli, tu sai s' io t' amo (S., 2 flutes, April 1701). *S.*

Hor che di Febo ascosi (S., 2 violins, 1704). *N. Dar. S.*

Imagini d' orrore (B., 2 violins, 16 July 1710). *PC.* (autograph).

* Lagrime dolorose dagli occhi miei. (T., 2 violins). *PC.*

*Mentre Clori la bella presso un ruscel sedea (S., 2 violins). *S.*

Mentre Clori la bella sotto l' ombra d' un mirto (S., 2 flutes). *S. WM.*

Mentre un Zeffiro arguto (S., 2 violins). *S.* The same for B. with a different Sinfonia. *Sch.*

· Mi contento così (T., 2 violins). *PC.*

Mia Dorinda, mia vita (S., violin, 1706). *S.*

Mirtillo anima mia, già che parti. (S., 2 violins). *S.*

Nel silentio commune (S., 2 violìns, viola). *BM.* (Add. 14163).

Nella stagione appunto (S., 2 violins). *S.*

Nella tomba di Gnido (S., 2 violins). *S.*

Notte ch' in carro d' ombre (S., 2 violins). *S. W.*

Oh di Betlemme altera (S., 2 violins, viola, sacred). *BM.* (Add. 14165).

Per l' ondoso sentiero (S., 2 violins). *PC.*

Perche, perche tacete regolati concenti (A., 2 violins). *S.*

Perde al vostro confronto (S., 2 violins). *S.*

Piangete o mie pupille (S., 2 violins). *PC.*

Piango, sospiro e peno (A., 2 violins). *BM.* (Add. 31506).

Prima d' esservi infedele (S., 2 violins). *MC.*

Qual' ora io veggo la vezzosa Irene (S., 2 violins). *N. PC.*

Quella pace gradita (S., flute, violin, violoncello). *S.* (autograph).

Siete uniti a tormentarmi (A., 2 violins). *D.*

Silentio, aure volanti (S., 2 violins). *Bod. S.*

Solitudini amene, apriche collinette (S., flute). *D.*

Sotto l' ombra d' un faggio (B., 2 violins). *N. PC.*

Sotto l' ombra d'un faggio (S., 2 violins. *MC. PC. LA.* (incomplete).

Sovra carro stellato (S., 2 violins). *N.* (incomplete).

Sul margine d' un rivo (S., 2 violins). *PC. S.*

Sulla sponda del mare (L' Olimpia) (S., 2 violins, viola). *W.*

Sull' ora appunto che col carro d' oro (La Fenice) (S., 2 violins). *Dar. S.*

Sulle sponde del Tebro (S., trumpet, 2 violins). *BM.* (Add. 31487) *S. WM.*

Tiranna ingrata, che far dovrò (B., 2 violins). *N.*

Tirsi pastore amante (S., 2 violins). *PC. S.*

Tra speranza e timore (B., violin) *BM.* (Add. 14166).

Tu che una dea rassembri (S., 2 violins). *S.*

Tu resti, o mio bel nume (B., 2 violins). *N.*

Tu sei quella che al nome (A., flute, 2 violins). *MC.* (incomplete).

(2) ACCOMPANIED BY CONTINUO ALONE

(All for Soprano unless another voice is mentioned.)

*A chi t'inganna, bella tiranna. *Mil. N. PC.*

A piè d'un verde colle. *BF. LC. N. S.*

*A placar la mia bella. *BF.*

A privarmi del bel. *LC. Mil. S.*

A soffrire impara o core. *S.*

A te Lisa gentile (alto). *BC.*

A voi che l'accendeste. *D. N.* (incomplete) *S.*

Abbandonar Fileno dovea. *RB.* (alto) *S.*

Abbandonato e solo (Il Nerone). *BC. M. S.*

Ad altro uso serbate. *N.*

Agitato mio core (1704). *Pal. S.*

Agitato sen cade (La Sofonisba). *Mod. S.*

Agli strali d'amore. *BF.*

Ah ben l） vedi o core. *N. S.*

Ah che pur troppo è vero. *Mil.*

Ah fuggi, si, mio core. *BF. S.*

Ah, Mitilde vezzosa (29 July 1712). *LC. S.*

Al fin m'ucciderete (1718). *B. BM.* (Add. 14165, 31508) *D. LA. M. Mil. N. PC. S. W.*

Al fine o Clori amata. *Pal. S.*

*Al mormorio d'un vago ruscelletto. *N.*

Al mormorio dell' onda. *C. S.*

Al pensiero miei sguardi (July 1706). *S.*

Al voler del bene amato. *BM.* (Add. 14164) *Pal. PC.*

Alba che neghittosa. *BM.* (Add. 14165) *S.*

All' hor che il Dio di Delo (La Gelosia). *BM.* (Add. 14165) *S.*

All' hor che il fier leone. *PC.*

Alle Trojane antenne (La Didone). *S.*

Alme voi che provaste. *BM.* (Add. 14215, 31509) *N. PC. S.*

*Amai dolce mia vita. *S. W.*

Amanti sospirate, Amore è morto. *N.*

Amici, s'è vinto. *BM.* (Add. 34056).

Ammore brutto figlio de Pottana (in Neapolitan dialect). *S.*

Amo e negar nol posso (Dec. 1704). *S.*

Amo, ma l'idol mio (9 June, 1702). *BM.* (Add. 14227) *PC.* (alto) *S.* (alto, autograph).

Amo, peno e languisco. *RB.*

Amo, peno, gioisco. *N. Pal. S. Sch. W.*

Amor, che fia di noi. *PC.*

Amor con l'idol mio (3 April 1702). *PC. S.*

Amor, Mitilde è morta. *BM.* (Add. 14212) *N. PC. S.*

Amor, t'intendo, si (1701). *N.*

Amor, tu che si bella fiamma accendesti. *PC.*

Amore, o mi togli le fiamme. *BM.* (Add. 14228).

Andate o miei sospiri (G minor, 10 March, 1712). *BM.* (Add. 14220) *LA. LC. N. S.*

MSS. without the additional air in $\frac{12}{8}$ time. *BM.* (Add. 31509) *Mil. PC.* Rome, *Comm. Carlo Lozzi* (autograph fragment).

Andate o miei sospiri (F sharp minor). *BF. BM.* (Add. 14220) *LA. LC. Mil. N. PC.* Rome, *Comm. Carlo Lozzi* (autograph).

The same cantata set by Gasparini. *BM.* (Add. 14220) *LA. LC. N. S.*

Api industri che volate. *Mil. PC. Sch.*

[1] Appena chiudo gli occhi. *N. PC.*

Ardea per Coridone Clori. *LC.*

Arder per due pupille. *M. Mil. PC. S.*

Ardo, ardo d'amore. *BC. BM.* (Add. 14163) *LA. Mil. Sch.*

Ardo tacito amante. *PC. S.*

Arse felice un tempo. *BM.* (Add. 31512).

Assiso in verde prato. *S.*

Augelletti semplicetti. *M.* (incomplete) *PC.* (incomplete) *S. W.*

[2] Augellin sospendi i vanni. *BC. PC. S.*

Augellino prigioniero, ferma oh Dio. *S. W.*

Aure io son di voi geloso. *Pal.*

Barbara e ingrata Fille. *Pal. Rome, Comm. Carlo Lozzi* (autograph), *S.*

Bei prati freschi rivi. *BM.* (Add. 31512) *LC. M. PC. S.*

Bei prati verdi colli. *S.*

Bella, dunque n'andrai. *BM.* (Add. 31508).

Bella, per te d'amore. *N. N.* (alto) *Pal.* (alto).

Bella quanto crudel, spietata Irene (June 1717). *LC. S.*

Bella Rosa adorata (Sept. 1704). *S.*

Bella se quella face. *PC.*

*Belle pupille care. *S.*

Ben che o sirena bella. *BM.* (Add. 14220) *N. PC. S.*

Ben che porti nel volto. *BF.*

Ben che vezzosa Irene. *N.*

Ben folle è chi non parte. *BF. Mod.*

Biondi crini che in fronte. *S.*

Boschi amati che cingete. *PC.*

Cara sempre agli occhi miei. *BF. BM.* (Add. 14163).

*Care selve a voi ritorno. *LC.*

Care selve gradite. *B. BM.* (Add. 31509).

Caro Fileno mio, quanto mi spiace. *S.*

*Caro laccio, dolce nodo. *B.*

Cerca nel cor di mille (10 August 1706). *BA.* (autograph) *BC.* (alto).

Cerco, nè so trovar beltà fedel. *Pal.*

Ch'io da te mi divida. *Pal.*

Che fai mio cor. *BM.* (Add. 31512, incomplete).

Che le dolcezze estreme. *LC.*

Che mai sarà di me. *M.*

Che più tardi o Ninfa bella. *PC.*

*Che pretendi o tiranna. *S.*

Che Sisifo infelice (25 July 1706). *S.* (autograph).

Chi batte al mio core? *PC.*

Chi m'insegna ov'è quel bene. *S. W.*

Chi vedesse la ferita. *PN. S.*

Chi vidde mai o chi provò. *S.*

Chiudetevi per sempre. *B. N.*

Chiusa tra fosche bende. *BM.* (Add. 14164).

Cinta dei più bei fiori. *N.*

*Cinta di rai splendea. *S.*

Cleopatra la bella, la Venere d'Egitto (Lamento di Cleopatra). *PC.*

Clori allor ch'io ti vidi (17 April 1702). *S.* (autograph).

Clori, bell' idol mio, Clori mia vita. *PC. S. W.*

Clori, Clori spietata, mio crudel tesoro. *Mil.*

Clori, Clori superba, e come mai. *N. S.* (See *Cruda Irene su-*

---

[1] See under cantatas with *continuo* and other instruments.
[2] Ibid.

perba, of which this is a different version.)

Clori, mi sento al seno. *S.*

Clori, mia cara Clori, moro. *BM.*
(Add. 31508).

Clori vezzosa e bella (alto). *BM.*
(Add. 14212) *F. LC. N.*

Clorinda è bella. *N.*

Colui che fisso mira (April 1696).
BM. (Add. 14163) *S.* (alto).

Come il fuoco alla sua sfera. *Sch.*

Come potesti mai. *Chr.*

Come può non esser bella (15 Feb.
1702). *S.* (autograph).

Come vago augelletto (1701). *N.*

Come volubil gira la ruota. *BM.*
(Add. 31512) *PC.*

Con non inteso affanno. *S.*

Con trasparente velo (13 Dec.
1702). *B.* (autograph) *BM.*
(Add. 14225) *S. W.*

Cor di Bruto e che risolvi. *PC.*

Coronate il bel crine. *PC.*

Cruda Irene superba. *Mil. N.
PC. S.* (See *Clori, Clori superba*, of which this appears to
be a corrupt version.)

Crudelissimo amore. *N.* (incomplete).

Crudo amor, che vuoi da me.
BL.

D'un platano frondoso. *M.*

Da che Tirsi mirai. *BM.* (Add.
14220) *Pal.*

*Da l'arco d'un bel ciglio (alto).
Pal.*

Da qual parte celeste (20 Oct.
1702). *S.* (autograph).

Da quel dì che Matilda. *LA.*

Da quell'hora fatale (1716). *LC.
N.*

Da sventura a sventura (1690?).
BL. C. (incomplete) *N. PC.*
(incomplete) *W.* (*C.* has a
MS. of the first air with accompaniment for four strings.)

Da turbini di pene. *LC.*

*Da voi parto amati rai (bass). *B.*

Dagli strali d'amore vivea lieto
(13 Sept. 1701). *S.*

Dal bel volto d'Irene. *BM.* (Add.
14165) *Mil. N.*

Dal colle al pian discesa. *BF. M.*

Dal crudele Daliso. *PN.*

Dal dì che amor m'accese. *N.*

Dal dì che l'empio fato. *LC. N.*

Dal grato mormorio. *BM.* (Add.
31509).

Dalla fida compagna abbandonata.
PC.

Dalla speme deluso. *Mod. S.*

Dalle pene amorose. *Rome,
Comm. C. Lozzi.*

Dalle Tirrene sponde partì Fille.
Mil.

Dammi amore. *Bod.*

Deh per merce. *BM.* (Add. 14164)
LC. S.

Deh torna amico sonno (22 Sept.
1716). *N. PC.* (autograph?).

Del faretrato nume Amor tiranno.
BF. Mil. N. PC. (autograph?).

Del lacrimoso lido (17 June 1699).
BM. (Add. 31487) *S. Sch.*

Del mio seno la costanza. *BM.*
(Add. 14163).

Del Tebro in su le sponde. *Mil.
N. PC.*

Del Tirreno alle sponde. *BM.*
(Add. 14211) *PC. S. W.*

Del Tirreno sul lido (alto). *S.*

Della spietata Irene fur l'accese
pupille. *S.*

Delle patrie contrade. *LC.*

Dentro un orrido speco. *W.*

*Di che avete paura? *N.*

Di cipresso funesto. *N. Pal. PN.*

Di colore de' cieli. *Pal.*

Di due vaghe pupille nere. *PC.*

Di me che sarà? *V.*

Di pensiero in pensier. *BM.*
(Add. 14165).

Diedi a Fileno il core (1705).
BM. (Add. 14165) S. S. (alto).
Dimmi Clori superba. M. Mil.
PC. S.
Dimmi, mio ben, perche. PN.
Doppo lungo penar (bass). BM.
(Add. 14166).
Dorisbe i miei lamenti. PC.
Dormono l'aure estive. BM. (Add.
14165, 31508) LC. N. PC. S.
WM.
Dove alfin mi traeste? (L'Arianna).
B. LC. N. Mil. PC. (auto-
graph ?).
Dov' è Filli, dov' è? Chr. Pal.
Dov' io mi volga o vada. LC.
Mil.
Dove in grembo. See Ove in
grembo.
Dove l' eneta Dori alla reggia. N.
Dove xestu cor mio? (in Venetian
dialect). D.
Due nemici tiranni (1722). BF.
N. PC.
Dunque ingrato spergiuro. B.
BM. (Add. 14212) Mil. N.
PC. WM.
Dunque perche lontano. M.
Dunque sperar non lice. PC.
E come, oh Dio, lontana. Pal. S.
E come e come, oh Dio, tacito. M.
E come ohimè poss' io. N. PC.
È 'l gran pena l' amare. LC.
È la speme un desio tormentoso.
S.
E lungi dal mio bene. BM. (Add.
31512)
E penar deggio ancora. BL.
(alto) M. S.
*E pur e pur è vero. BF. S.
E pur odo e non moro. LC. N.
E pur tenti il ritorno. LC. MC.
S. (versions vary).
È pure il gran tormento. B. (alto)
BM. (Add. 31508) LC. PC.
(alto) S. (alto).

E quando ingrata Nice. Mil. N.
PC. W.
E quando io veggio. LC. (incom-
plete).
E quando mai cessate. Pal.
E satio ancor non sei. LC.
E sia pur vero. BM. (Add. 14229)
N.
E sino a quando, Amor. LC.
E sino a quando, o stelle. Pal.
È viva al diletto la mia rimem-
branza. PC.
Ecco che a voi ritorno. B. BM.
(Add. 14212, 14225, 14229)
C. N. Mil. PC.
Entro a più foschi horrori. PC.
Entro romito speco. BM. (Add.
31509) LC. Mil. N. PC.
(partly autograph).
Era già l' alba (Europa rapita).
PC.
Era giunta quell' ora (29 Nov.
1704). S.
Era la notte e già sorgea dal mare.
N.
Era l' oscura notte. Florence,
Comm. A. Kraus. S.
Eurilla, amata Eurilla. BC. BL.
BM. (Add. 31518) D. LC. PC.
Eurilla, io parto, addio. Pal.
Eurilla, oh Dio, nel seno palpita.
Pal.
Facile sembra a un core l'amar. S.
Farfalla che s' aggira (La Pazzia).
B. BC. BM. (Add. 31510) N.
Mil. PC. S.
Farfalletta innocente se correndo.
BM. (Add. 31510) S.
Fatto d'amor seguace. BM. (Add.
31510) PC.
Fiamma che avvampa. BM. (Add.
31509) Mil. N.
Fiero acerbo destin dell' alma mia.
N. PC.
Fileno, ove ten vai? (1705) BM.
(Add. 14165, 31510) LC. S.

[1] Filli adorata, ah ben comprendo.
BM. (Add. 31510).
Filli adorata e cara, che fosti e sei.
B. BM. (Add. 14220, 31510)
LC. N. PC. S.
Filli adorata e cara, io parto. *BM*.
(Add. 31510).
Filli altera e spietata. *BM*. (Add.
31510).
Fille che del mio core (May 1700).
N.
Filli crudel, dunque tu parti. *BM*.
(Add. 31510) *S.*
Filli, di questo cor parte più cara.
WM.
Fille, dolente Fille. *BM*. (Add.
31510) *N. PC.*
Fille, mia cara Fille (18 Nov. 1704).
BM. (Add. 31510) *LC. S.*
Filli mia, Filli cara (15 Jan. 1702).
BM. (Add. 31510) *S.*
Fille mia, perche piangi. *S.*
*Filli mia, tu mi consoli. *D.*
Filli, mio ben, mia vita (May 1704).
BM. (Add. 31510) *PC.*
Fille, tu parti, oh Dio. *LC. Mil.*
N. PC. S. W.
Fiumicel che del mio pianto. *BM*.
(Add. 31510).
Flagellava nel Cielo (Il Narciso).
PC.
Fonte d' ogni dolcezza (12 March
1709). *BM*. (Add. 31510) *N.*
Fonti amiche, erbe care. *BM*.
(Add. 31510).
Forse di Sirio ardente. *BM*. (Add.
31510).
Fra mille semplicetti augei canori
(14 August 1701). *S.* (auto-
graph).
Fra tante pene e tante (23 June
1705). *BM*. (Add. 31510)
S.

Frangi l' arco e lo stral (27 August
1706). *BM*. (Add. 31510).
Fu d' oro il primo dardo. *BM*.
(Add. 31510, 31512).
Già di trionfi onusto (Il Ger-
manico). *BL. N. Pal. PN. S.*
Già per lunga stagion bersaglio.
BM. (Add. 31487) *S.*
Già sorge l' alba (Dorisbe caccia-
trice). *S. W.*
Già sul carro dorato. *M. PC. S.*
Già vicina è quell' hora (15 June
1699). *BL. Bod. Pal. S.*
Giacea d' un mirto all' ombra. *LC.*
Giacea presso alla sponda. *BM*.
(Add. 14163).
Giù di Vulcan nella fucina eterna
(1698). *S.*
Giunto è il fatal momento (1705).
BM. (Add. 14165) *S.*
Goderai sempre crudele. *BM*.
(Add. 14164) (incomplete).
Ha l' humore stravagante. *PC.*
Ho una pena intorno al core.
BM. (Add. 31512) *M. N. S.*
Il cor che vive oppresso. *Mil. N.*
PC.
Il genio di Mitilde. *BC. BM*.
(Add. 14229) *Mil. N. PC.*
WM.
Il mio sol non è più meco. *S.*
Il più misero amante. *N.*
Il rosignuolo se scioglie il volo
(alto in F major) (19 Dec.
1698). *BL.* (printed by Étienne
Roger, Amsterdam). *Pal.* (so-
prano). *S.*
Il rosignuolo se scioglie il volo
(alto in F minor) (26 August
1700). *BM*. (Add. 14165)
S. W.
Il timido mio core. *B. Mil. N.*
PC.

---

[1] The name Phyllis appears in both forms—*Filli* and *Fille*. I have thought it
better to disregard the variation in arranging this list.

In amorosi ardori. *BM.* (Add. 31508).

In bel sonno profondo. *LC. N.*

In che giammai t' offesi. *S.* (autograph).

In due vaghe pupille. *BM.* (Add. 14211).

In placida sembianza. *BF.*

In solitaria soglia. *N.*

In traccia del suo bene. *PC.*

In vano, amor tiranno. *N. S.*

Ingiustissimo amor. *BF. BM.* (Add. 14215) *LC. MC.*

Io ben so che siete arciere (1704). *Mil. PC. S.*

Io che ad un tronco. *BF. LC. PC.*

*Io che con aurea luce. *BF.*

Io che dal cor di Fille. *BM.* (Add. 14220, 31509; 14213, alto). *Mil. N. PC.* (also alto) *S.*

Io credei che felice. *Mil.*

Io m' accendo a poco a poco. *Pal.*

Io morirei contento. *LC. Mod. S. W.*

Io non v' intendo o stelle. *S.*

Io per Dori mi struggo. *N. W.* (both incomplete).

Io son Neron l' imperator del mondo (1698). *S.*

Io son pur solo. *LC. Mil. N.*

*Io t' amerò e nel mio petto. *BF.*

Irene, idolo mio. *LC.*

L' armi crudeli e fiere. *BM.* (Add. 29249).

L' huom che segue una speranza. *PC.*

La beltà ch' io sospiro (16 August 1701). *BM.* (Add. 29249). *PC. S.* (autograph).

La cagion delle mie pene. *BM.* (Add. 29249).

*Là dei sassi Latini. *N.*

Là dell' Arno sull' onda. *BM.* (Add. 29249).

Là dove a Mergellina (1725). *BF. LC. Mil. MC. N. S.*

Là dove al vivo argento. *LC.*

La face d' amore ch' il core m' ardè. *BM.* (Add. 34056).

La fortuna di Roma (Il Coriolano). *BC. BM.* (Add. 29249, 31488) *PC. S.*

La gran madre d' amore. *PC.* (autograph?)

La grazia, la sembianza (22 Feb. 1702). *BM.* (Add. 29249) *PC. S.*

La libertà perduta (incomplete). *BF. MC.* See *Talor per suo diletto*, of which this is a fragment.

Là nel bel sen della regal Sirena. *BF. BL.*

La speranza che lusinga. *PC.*

La vezzosa Celinda. *Mil. N.*

Langue Clori vezzosa. *N. S.*

Lascia di tormentar (1709). *BM.* (Add. 29249, 31507) *LC. N.*

Lascia più di tormentarmi (1688). *PC.*

*Lasciami alquanto piangere (May 1716). *D.*

Lasciate ch' io v' adori (October 1705). *BM.* (Add. 14165, 29249) *N. S.*

Lasciate homai lasciate. *BL. N.*

Lasciato havea l' adultero superbo. *S.*

Le vaghe tue pupille. *BM.* (Add. 29249, 31512) *M. PC. S.*

Leandro, anima mia, Ero t' attende. *BM.* (Add. 29249) *Pal. S.* (alto).

Libertà del mio cor. *LC.*

Lidia, in van mi condanni. *BM.* (Add. 29249).

Liete placide e belle (1709). *BM.* (Add. 29249) *LC. N. S.*

Lieti boschi, ombre amiche (18 August 1704). *BM.* (Add. 29249) *S.* (alto).

Lontan dalla sua Clori. *BM.* (Add. 31509) *Mil. N.*

Lontan dall' idol mio. *BM.* (Add. 29249, Harl. 1273) *Bod. Chr. Pal.*

Lontan dal suo tesor. *Mil.*

Lontan dal tuo bel viso. *MC.*

Lontananza che fai (27 Nov. 1701). *BM.* (Add. 29249, incomplete) *S.* (autograph) *W.*

Lontananza crudele deh perche (4 Oct. 1713). *LA.*

Lontananza crudele tu mi trafiggi. *N. Pal.*

Lontananza non risana. *Pad.*

Lontananza tiranna che da te mi divide. *PC.*

Luci care al mondo sole. *PN. S.*

Luci siete pur quelle. *BM.* (Add. 29249).

Lumi che in fronte al mio bel sole (4 Dec. 1703). *BM.* (Add. 29249) *M. MC.* (incomplete) *Mil. PC. S.*

Lumi dolenti lumi. *B.* (alto) *BM.* (Add. 29249) *C. LC. Pal.*

Lunga stagion dolente (25 August 1706). *BM.* (Add. 29249) *N. S.* (autograph).

Lungi dal ben ch' adoro. *F.*

Lungi dall' idol mio. *B.*

Lungi dalla cagion per cui sospiro. *BM.* (Add. 14165, 29249) *F. S.*

M' ha diviso il cor dal core. *B. BM.* (Add. 34056).

Mal fondati sospetti. *PC.*

Mal sicuro è il fior nel prato. *BM.* (Add. 34056).

Mentre affidan al mar di Cupido. *Mod. S.*

Mentre al sonno chiudea. *S. W.*

Mentre da questo monte. *S.*

Mentre Eurillo fedele (infelice). *N. S.*

*Mentre in un dolce oblio. *BF.*

Mentre un zeffiro altero. *LC. N. PC.*

Mesto, lasso e ramingo (June 1704). *S.*

Mi nasce un sospetto. *LC. PC.*

Mi parto, Eurilla, addio (alto). *B. PC. S.*

Mi tormenta il pensiero (alto). *Pal. S. Sch.* (also for bass) *W.*

*Another setting. *S.*

Mia Chimene adorata (1710). *BM.* (Add. 14225) *LC. N. PC.*

Mie speranze fallaci. *S.*

Mira o Filli quella rosa. *M. PC. S.*

Mitilde, alma mia, se udiste mai (3 July 1720). *BF. LC. M. N. PC.*

Mitilde, anima mia, dove sei? *M.*

Mitilde, dove sei? *BC.* (incomplete) *F.*

Mitilde, mio tesoro, e dove sei? *S.*

Mitilde, oh quanto dolce e lusinghiero. *S.*

Morirei disperato. *BM.* (Add. 14164) *LC. N. S.*

*Mostri deh non temete. *S. W.*

Nei languidi respiri. *BM.* (Add. 14227) *C.*

Nei tuoi lumi, o bella Clori. *BM.* (Add. 31512) *M. Mil. PC. S.*

Nel centro oscuro. *F. N. PC.*

Nel dolce tempo (27 May 1712 or 27 Sept. 1716). *LC. Mil. N. PC.*

Nel mar che bagna al bel Sebeto (bass). *N.*

*Nel profondo del mio core. *S.*

Nel sen degli antri. *N.*

Nel suo fido caro nido. *S. W.*

Nelle arene del Tago (24 July 1698). *S.*

Nice mia, un solo istante. *BM.*
(Add. 31509) *S.*

Ninfa crudel, deh vieni. *BC.*
BM. (Add. 14215).

Ninfe e pastori che nel cor nutrite
(1712). *N.*

No, non deggio, è troppo cara.
LC. N. S.

No, non lasciar canora e bella
(20 Nov. 1704). *S.*

No, non posso fingere di non amar
BM. (Add. 34056).

No, non vorrei vivere fra le catene.
PC.

Non è come si dice (20 August
1701). *S.* (autograph) *W.*

Non è facile ad un core. *B. BM.*
(Add. 14165) *N. S.*

Non han core is not a cantata, but
from La Rosaura, Act III.,
Scene 7. *BM.* (Add. 31488)
F. LC. N.

*Non mi credi, deh perche? *S.*

Non per pioggia del cielo. *BF.*
(incomplete).

Non più contrasti (contese) nò (6
Oct. 1721). *B. BF. LC. M.*
N. PC. S.

Non posso già nè voglio. *LA.*

Non temo disastri. *PC.*

Notte cara a un cor che langue
(1705). *BM.* (Add. 14165)
S.

Notte cara, ombre beate. *BM.*
(Add. 14164, incomplete) *N.*
Pal. W.

Notte placida e lieta. *LC.*

O che mostro, o che furia (20 July
1709). *BM.* (Add. 34056). *N.*
(incomplete).

Oh che pena è la mia (1704). *BM.*
(Add. 31512) *M. PC. S.*

O Clori, ahi bella Clori. *S.*

O de' pastori diletto stuolo. *BM.*
(Add. 29963).

O de' regni di Dite Eumenidi. *BC.*

O di fere e d' augelli cheti ricetti.
BF. S.

O di lucida notte inclita imago.
PC.

Oh Dio, che viene amore. *N.*

O dolce servitù. *Florence, Comm.*
A. Kraus.

O Flora, anima mia. *BM.* (Add.
14190).

Oh Mitilde, fosti meco tiranna
(1711). *BC. LC.*

Oh Mitilde, oh del core (9 Dec.
1708). *S.*

O pace del mio cor. *BF. LC. Mil.*
MC. N. PC. S. WM.

O pace del mio cor (another setting). *B. C.*

O sol degli occhi miei. *BM.*
(Add. 34056). *LC. N.*

O sventurata Olimpia. *N.*

O voi di queste selve habitatrici
(1717?) *BM.* (Add. 14220,
14229, 31509) *LA.* (alto)
Mil. N. PC. WM.

Occhi miei ch' al pianto avvezzi
(alto). *B.*

Omai dal cielo al più sublime
punto. *PC.*

Or che a me ritornasti. *N.*

Or che barbara sorte. *PC.*

Or che di te son privo. *BM.*
(Add. 14215) *PC.*

Or che di Teti in seno. *LC. PC.*

*Or che graditi orrori. *S.*

Or che graditi orrori (a different
cantata). *LC. S.*

Or che in petto d'Eurilla. *M.*
PC. S.

Or che lungi son io. *BM.* (Add.
14220). *M. Mil. N. PC.*
(versions vary).

Or che su legno aurato. *N.*

Ove al Sebeto in riva. *LC. N.*

Ove fuor del mio seno. *BM.*
(Add. 31512) *M. PC. S.*
WM.

Ove il fiorito impero mostra. *M.*
Mil.
Ove in grembo alla pace. *BL.*
LA. Pal. S.
Ove placido e cheto. *PC.*
Parla mia pena omai. *BM.* (Add.
14165, 31511) *B.* (alto).
Parte da me Cupido. *PC.*
*Pastor d' Arcadia, è morta Clori.
LC.*
Pastorella   innamorata. *BM.*
(Add. 31508).
Pastori amici, amiche pastorelle.
LC.
Peno e del mio penar (4 Sept.
1705). *BM.* (Add. 14165,
31511) *S.*
Pensier che in ogni parte. *M. PC.*
Pensier che sei inflessibile (12
Feb. 1702). *BM.* (Add.
31511) *S.*
Pensieri, pensieri, oh Dio qual
pena. *S. V.*
Penso che non ho core (1705).
BM. (Add. 31511) *M. Mil.
Pal. PC. S. W.*
* Per destin d'ingrato amore
(tenor). *PC.*
Per farmi amar da tutte. *BM.*
(Add. 34056).
*Per formare la bella che adoro. *D.*
Per prova di mia fede (alto). *B.*
Per queste dell' antica Alba famosa.
BM. (Add. 31511).
*Per saettar un seno. *S.*
Per saettar un seno (another
setting). *BM.* (Add. 31508).
Per te, florida bella (July 1708).
BM. (Add. 31511).
Per un momento solo. *B.* (alto)
BM. (Add. 31511, 31512)
M. Mil. N. PC. S.
Per un vago desire. *B. LC. Mil.
N. PC.*
Perche mai, luci amorose (April
1700). *N.*

Perdono, amor, perdono (6 June
1702, alto). *PC. S.* (auto-
graph).
Perdono, amor, perdono (another
setting). *BM.* (Add. 31509,
(incomplete), 31511). *N. PC.*
Perfida Filli ingrata (27 July
1705). *BM.* (Add. 14165,
31511) *LC.* (versions vary).
Piagge fiorite, ameni prati. *N.*
Piagge fiorite e amene, io parto
(28 August 1716). *N.*
Piangi la tua sventura (1 July
1706). *B. BM.* (Add. 31511).
LC. M. N. S. (versions vary).
Piango ogni ora del mio core. *BM.*
(Add. 31511).
Piango sospiro e peno. *LC.*
Più che penso all' idol mio. *BM.*
(Add. 31511) *Pal. S.*
Più non si puote amar. *BM.*
(Add 31511). *PC.*
Più veggio Lidia mia. *BM.* (Add.
31511) *PC.*
Poi che a Tirsi infelice. *N.
Mil.*
Poi che cessano al fin. *BM.*
(Add. 31511) *LC.*
Poi che l' Ercole Argivo (Lisimaco
Re di Traccia). *PC.*
Poi che la bella Clori (1699). *N.*
Poi che riseppe Orfeo. *BM.*
(Add. 31511).
Porto il cor incatenato. *PC.*
Preparati o mio core (alto). *BM.*
(Add. 31511).
Presso a un limpido fonte. *BM.*
(Add. 31511) *LC.*
Presso il balcon dell' incostante
Nisa (15 June 1699). *S.*
*Pria che desto ai nitriti. *BF.*
Primavera sei gentile. *BM.* (Add.
31511).
Pur al fine la vincesti. *BL.*
Qual bellezza divina. *BC. Mod.
PN.*

Quale al gelo s'adugge. *BM.*
(Add. 14165) *S.*
Qual' or l'egre pupille. *M.*
Qual' or miro la bella. *N. S.*
Quando amor vuol ferirmi. *BA.*
(incomplete) *N. S.*
Quando che ti vedrò. *Pal.*
Quando credeva il core (16 Oct.
1701) *Pal. S.* (autograph)
*Quando Lidia amorosa. *N.*
Quando l'umide ninfe. *LC.*
Quando satia sarai. *S.*
Quando stanche dal pianto. *BM.*
(Add. 31512).
Quando veggio un gelsomino.
BM. (Add. 14227).
Quante le grazie son (4 June 1703).
W.
Quanti affanni ad un core. *B.*
BM. (Add. 31487, 31518) *N.*
Pal. RB. PC. Sch.
Quanto io v'ami. *N.*
Quanto, o Filli, t'inganni (10 May
1702). *S.*
Quanto piace agli occhi miei. *LC.*
N. PC. (versions vary).
Quanto vezzosa e quanto. *BM.*
(Add. 14163).
Quel cor che a te già diede.
Sch.
Quel piacer che nell' amarti. *LC.*
Quel ruscelletto o Clori. *B. LC.*
Quell' augello che vola d'intorno.
S.
Questa, questa è la 'selva. *N. PC.*
Queste torbide e meste onde
(1717). *BM.* (Add. 14215)
LC. N. PC.
Questo di bei giacinti serto. *BM.*
(Add. 31512) *LC.*
Qui dove a piè d'un colle. *N.*
PC. S.
Qui dove alfin m'assido (Il rossig-
nuolo). *BC. BM.* (Add. 14220)
LC. N. PC. (versions vary).
Qui dove aure ed augelli. *LC.*

Qui vieni ingrata Fille. *BM.*
(Add. 14229) *LC. Mil. N.*
*Reggie paludi, addio. *N.*
Reggie soglie, alte moli (18 Oct.
1720). *LC. M. N. PC.*
Ritardati momenti, egre dimore.
PN.
Rondinella torna al lido (1701).
N.
Rondinella torna al nido. *Sch.*
S'io t'amo, s'io t'adoro (June
1704). *S.*
Sanno, o Filli adorata (24 August
1716). *N.*
Sarà pur vero, o stelle? *LC.*
Sarei troppo felice (30 April 1702).
S. (autograph).
Saresti ben tiranna (fragment).
BF. MC.
Sazio di più soffrire. *S.*
Sciolgo in lacrime amare. *LC.*
N. PC.
Sciolta da freddi amplessi (Marito
vecchio, sposa giovane). *M.*
PC. S.
Scompagnata tortorella. *LC. M.*
PC. S.
Scorgo il fiume (La Primavera).
BM. (Add. 14165, 31512) *N.*
PC. S. (alto).
*Sdegno fiero ed amore. *BM.*
(Add. 31518).
Se a goder torna il mio core. *S.*
Se a quel fiero dolor. *BM.*
(Add. 31512) *LA. Mil. M.*
PC. S.
Se amassi da dovere. *LC.*
Se amor con un contento. *BM.*
(Add. 31512) *S.*
*Se credete all' amor mio. *N.*
*Se dalla cruda Irene. *LC.*
Se d'Elisa spietata il bel sembiante.
N.
Se mai Clori gentile. *LC. Mil. N.*
PC. S.
Se per amor quest' alma. *MC.*

Se tu parti io morirò (L'Armida). *PC.* (autograph?).

Se vagheggio nel mattino (1709). *LC. S.*

Sedea Eurillo un giorno. *LC. Pal.*

Senti, bella crudele. *LC. PC.*

Senti, bell' idol mio (1705). *BM.* (Add. 14165) *S.*

Sentite, o tronchi, o sassi. *Bod. Pad.*

Sento nel core certo dolore. *BM.* (Add. 31512) *M. Mil.* (alto) *PC. S.*

Senz' alma, senza cor. *S.*

Serba il mio cor costante. *PC.*

S' accinge Eurillo al canto. *BM.* (Add. 31518).

Si, conosco, o Mitilde. *B. N.*

Si, t' amo, o mio Daliso. *BF.* (incomplete).

Si, t' intendo, t' intendo, tu vuoi. *B.* (alto) *M. Mil. PC. S.*

Siamo in contesa la bellezza ed io (4 May 1702). *S.* (autograph).

Solitudini amene. *LC. PC.*

Solitudini care in voi spera. *BM.* (Add. 14213, 31509) *Mil. N. PC. Rome, Comm. C. Lozzi. S.*

Son contenta di soffrire. *S.*

Son io, barbara donna. *BM.* (Add. 14213) *S.*

Son le nere pupillette (12 March 1702) *Pad. PC. S.*

Son pur care quelle pene. *LC.*

Son quest' ultimi momenti. *BM.* (Add. 14211) *Bod. PC. S.*

Sono amante e m' arde il core. *S.*

Sono un alma tormentata. *N.*

Sopra le verdi sponde. *N. Pal.*

Sopra le verdi sponde (11 Feb. 1712—a different setting). *LC.*

Sorge l' alba. *MC.*

Sorta fin dallè piume (8 Jan. 1702) *S.*

Sovra il margine erboso. *S.*

Spero che avrò la pace. *BM.* (Add. 34056).

Spesso suol l' alma mia. *Pal.*

Spiega l' ali il mio pensiero (1702 or 1704). *M. Mil. PC. S.*

Splendeano in bel sembiante (bass). *PC.*

Sta presente il mio tesoro. *BM.* (Add. 14220).

Stanco di più soffrire. *LC.*

Stravagante è l' amor. *LC. PC.*

Stravagante non è l' amor. *N. PC.*

Strali, facelle, Amore. *BM.* (Add. 14165).

Su bel seggio di fiori. *S.*

Sul margine d' un rio. *Mod.*

Sul margine fiorito d' un tumido ruscello (13 Dec. 1704). *BM.* (Add. 14225) *S.*

Sulla sponda fiorita d' un rio pargoleggiante (L'Adone). *BM.* (Add. 14164) *BL. PC.* (autograph?).

*Sulla sponda fiorita di limpido ruscello (20 August,1710). *BM.* (Add. 14215) *N.*

Sulle fiorite sponde. *F. LC.*

Sulle sponde d'Abbido (Il Leandro) (1693). *N. PC.*

Sulle sponde del Reno. *BM.* (Add. 31518).

Taccio e tacendo io moro. *S. W.*

Taci, taci, infedele (infelice) amore (1720). *LC. N. PC.*

Talor per suo diletto. *BF. LC. S.*

Tanti affanni e tante pene. *S.*

Tanto strano è l' amor mio (April 1697). *S.*

Temo d' amarti poco. *S.*

Tenebrose foreste. *N. PC.*

The beauteous Melissa. *BM.* (printed in London about 1709).

Ti vorrei credere speranza. *BM.* (Add. 31508).

Tiranna di mia fè. *V.*

*Tirsi mentr' io dormiva. *M.*
Tormentatemi pur, furie d' amore.
BM. (Add. 31488).
Torna al sen dolce mia pace. *V.*
*Tra l' ombre più secrete. *BF.*
Tra le pompe fiorite. *S.*
Tra queste ombrose piaggie (1709).
LC.
Tra solitarie balze. *F.*
Tra verdi piante ombrose. *Mil.*
PC.
Troppo care, troppo belle. *M. PC.*
S. W.
Troppo ingrata Amaranta. *LC.*
Mil. N.
Troppo oppresso dal sonno. *LC.*
Tu mi chiedi s' io t' amo. *LC.*
Tu mi lasciasti, o bella (April
1698). *Pal. PC. S.*
Tu parti, idolo amato. *N.*
Tu parti, idolo amato (another set-
ting—1702). *Mil.* (alto) *N.*
S. (alto).
Tu resti, o mio bel nume (22 April
1706). *S.*
Tutto acceso d' amore. *BM.*
(Add. 14163) *Pal.*
Udite, o selve, o fiumi. *N.*
Un cervello frenetico ch' amò.
PC.
Un giorno Amor la benda si
disciolse (1709). *LC.*
Un' incredula speranza. *LC.*
Un sospiro d' un amante (La Luc-
cioletta). *BM.* (Add. 31507).
Un sol guardo di Clori. *BM.*
(Add. 31507).
Un spietato destino. *Pal.*
Un Tantalo assetato. *LC. N.*

Una beltà ch' eguale. *BM.* (Add.
31507) *PC. Sch.*
Va pur lungi da me. *BM.* (Add.
31507).
Vaga Elisa, la tua rimembranza
(June 1708). *BM.* (Add.
31507).
Vaghe selve beate. *BL.*
Vaghe tende adorate. *PN. S.*
Vaghi fonti di luce. *BM.* (Add.
31507) *M. PC. S.*
Vago il ciel non saria. *S.*
Vedi, Fille, quel sasso. *B. BF.*
Mil. N. PC. S.
Veggio l' idolo mio. *BM.* (Add.
31507, 31512).
Venite, amici, e con ghirlande.
BM. (Add. 31507).
Venne ad Amor desio. *BM.* (Add.
14165, 31507).
Vi comanda un cenno solo. *BM.*
(Add. 34056).
Viddi un giorno un fiumicello. *PC.*
Vieni, vieni, o caro Mirtillo (June
1708). *BM.* (Add. 31507).
Voi ben sapete. *BM.* (Add.
31507).
Voi giungeste o vaghi fiori (I Fiori).
BM. (Add. 31507) *M. PC. S.*
Vorrei, Filli adorata, farti palese
(21 Nov. 1705). *B.* (alto) *BM.*
(Add. 31507) *PC.*
Vorrei ma non posso amarti. *N.*
Vuoi ch' io spiri, tra i sospiri (20
Sept. 1699). *PC. S. Sch. W.*
Vuoi più Filli crudele. *N.* (alto).
Zeffiretto che indrizzi il tuo volo
(14 Dec. 1702). *B.* (autograph)
BM. (Add. 31507) *LC. S. W.*

VII. MASSES

(1) UNACCOMPANIED, OR WITH ORGAN ALONE

1. Missa Clementina. I. (1703), SS.A.T.B., and SS.AA.TT.B. in Agnus Dei.

Ex. 95.

B. BF. BM. (Add. MS. 32071), Dar. F. M. (4 copies, one supposed to be autograph), S. Sch. Vat. W.

2. Mass (in Canon), S.A.T.B.

Ex. 96.

B. N. (4 copies), S. (printed by Otto Braune, Berlin and Potsdam, transposed a third higher).

3. Mass for Cardinal Ottoboni (1706), S.A.T.B.

Ex. 97.

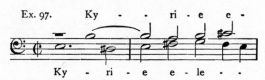

B. (wants Agnus), BM. (Eg. 2464) (parts Add. MS. 31519), M. (wants Agnus), PC. S. Vat. (autograph).

The Berlin MS. and British Museum Add. MS. 31519 exhibit considerable differences from the other MSS. and have probably no authority. Printed by Proske from the autograph.

4. Mass in Canon, SS.A.T.B. (Agnus SS.AA.T.B.).

Ex. 98.

B. BL. C. F. PC. (autograph?).

5. Missa Clementina II. (1716), SS.A.T.B.

Ex 99.

B. M. (copy from N.), Mil. N. (Kyrie, Gloria, Credo and fragment of Sanctus), Vat.

6. Mass, S.A.T.B., composed for Innocent XIII. (1721).

Ex. 100.

PC. copied from a MS. in Cec. not to be found there now.   Fragments: BL. BM. (Add. 14166—dated 1710) Mil. N. Probably Scarlatti used up old material for this.

7. Requiem Mass, S.A.T.B.

Ex. 101.

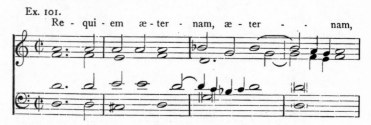

BC. M. PC. S.
Printed in Lück's "Sammlung Ausgewählter Kompositionen für die Kirche," and Choron's "Choix de Musique Réligieuse."
8. Mass, SS.A.T.B. and organ in E minor "in IV. tono."

Ex. 102.

S.

(2) With other Instruments

9. Mass, SS.A.T.B., S.A.T.B., two violins and continuo in A (1707—for Christmas). *S.*

Ex. 103.

10. Mass, SS.A.T.B. (soli), SS.A.T.B. (ripieni), two violins, viola and continuo in A. *Cas.* (partly autograph—1720). *S.*

Ex. 104.   Ky - ri - e   *Vl.*

* Credo, S.A.T.B. (soli and chorus), 2 oboes, 2 horns, strings and organ in B flat. *N.*

VIII. MOTETS

Adorna Thalamum tuum Sion. S.A.T.B. (January 1708). *BM.* (Add. MS. 34054—autograph parts), *S.* (also a copy to the words "Collaudabunt multi sapientiam eius").

Audi filia et inclina aurem (Gradual for S. Cecilia's day), SS.A.T.B.,

2 violins, viola, oboes, and
organ (October 1720). *Cas.*
(autograph) *S.*
Ave Maris Stella, S.A.T.B. and
continuo. *N. B.*
Ave Regina Coelorum, SS. and
continuo (1722). *N.*
Beatus vir qui timet Dominum,
SS.A.T.B. and organ. *S.*
Benedicta et venerabilis es,
SS.A.T.B., 2 violins, viola,
and continuo (4 July 1720).
S.
Cantantibus organis Cecilia (antiphon for St. Cecilia's Day), *S.*,
oboe, 2 violins, viola and continuo. *S.* (incomplete).
Concerti Sacri, printed in separate
parts by E. Roger at Amsterdam :—
I. Rorate coeli, *Canto solo con
v. v. per ogni Santo.*
II. Jam sole clarior, *Canto solo
con v. v. per Santo Sacer-
dote.*
III. Infirmata vulnerata. *Alto
solo con v. v. per il San-
tissimo e per ogni tempo.*
IV. Totus amore languens. *Alto
solo con v. v. per ogni
Santo e per il Santiss.*
V. Mortales non auditis. *A 2
Canto ed Alto con v. v. per
la Beata Vergine.*
VI. Quae est ista. *A 3 C. A. T.
con v. v. e Organo per ogni
Festività della Natività.*
VII. Diligam te. *A 3 C. A. T.
con v. v. per il SS. e per
ogni tempo.*
VIII. Properate fideles. *A 4 C. A.
T. B. con v. v. per il San-
tissimo.*
IX. Est dies. *A 4 C. A. T. B.
con v. v. per ogni Santo e
Santa.*

X. Salve Regina. *A 4 C. A. T. B.
con v. v.*
BF. Cas. (wants 2nd violin part).
MS. parts of I., II., and frag-
ments of others are in *LC.*, and
MS. scores of X. in *BF.* and
M.
Confitebor tibi Domine, SS.A.T.B.
and organ. *S.*
Constitues eos principes, S.A.B.
and organ (1716). *S.*
De tenebroso lacu, A., 2 violins,
viola, and continuo. *BM.*
(Add. MS. 31508).
Dextera Domini fecit virtutem,
S.S.B. and organ (1715). *S.*
Diffusa est gratia, SS. and organ.
S.
Dixit Dominus, SS.A.T.B. and
organ. *D. S.*
(Another setting). *S.*
Dixit Dominus,SS.A.T.B.,2 violins,
viola, oboes, and continuo.
Cas. (incomplete) *S.* (incom-
plete).
Domine refugium factus es nobis,
SS.A.T.B. *M. S. W.*
Exultate Deo adjutori nostro,
S.A.T.B. *M. S. W.*
Iste est panis, S.A.T.B. *S.* (in-
complete).
Jesu corona Virginum (*Inno per
S. Cecilia*), S.A.T.B., 2 violins,
viola, and continuo (October
1720). *Pal.* (autograph), *Cec.
S.* (incomplete).
Laetatus sum, S.A.T.B. *BM.*
(Add. MS. 14166) *M. W.*
(Another setting). *Cas.* (incom-
plete).
Laetatus sum, SS.A.T.B., 2 violins,
viola, and continuo (August
1721). *B.* (autograph) *S.* in-
complete, partly autograph).
Lauda Jerusalem Dominum,
S.A.T.B. and organ. *S.*

Laudate Dominum omnes gentes, S.A.TT.B., 2 violins, 2 violas, violoncello and continuo. *B. S.*

Laudate Dominum quia benignus, S.S.B. and organ. *S.*

Laudate pueri Dominum, SS.A.T.B. and continuo. *D. S.*

Another setting for S.solo, S.A.T.B., 2 violins and continuo. *S.* (incomplete).

Magnificat, SS.A.T.B. and organ (1st tone). *S.*

Magnificat, SS.A.T.B. and orchestra in D major. *S.* (incomplete).

Memento Domine David, S.A.T.B. *B. BL. BM.* (Add. MS. 14166) *D. M. Mil. N.* (autograph) *PC. S.*

Miserere, S.A.T.B., SS.A.T.B. (1680). *Vat.*

Miserere, SS.A.T.B., 2 violins, viola and continuo in E minor (1714?). *B. S.*

Miserere, SS.A.T.B., 2 violins, viola and continuo in C minor (1715?). *BS.*

Nisi Dominus ædificaverit, S.A. soli, S.A.T.B. rip., 2 violins and continuo. *B. BM.* (Add. MS. 34118) *W.*

Nisi dominus ædificaverit, S.A.T.B. and organ. *S.*

O magnum mysterium, S.A.T.B., S.A.T.B. (1707). *D. S.*

Sacerdotes Domini incensum et panes, S.A.T. and organ (offertorio per il Corpus Domini). *S. W.*

*Salve Regina, S.A., 2 violins and continuo. *Mil. N.*

Salve Regina, S.A.T.B. (1703). *London, W. Barclay Squire, Esq.*

Sancti et justi in Domino gaudete, S.A.T.B., S.A.T.B. *S.* (incomplete).

Stabat Mater, S.A., 2 violins and continuo. *F.*

Te Deum, SS.A.T.B., 2 violins, viola, 2 oboes and continuo. *Cas.*

Tu es Petrus, S.A.T.B., S.A.T.B., and organ. *B. BC.* (autograph?) *BL. BM.* (Add. 14166, 31481; Eg. 2454, 2459) *C. M. Mil. N. PC. S.*

Tui sunt caeli et terra, SS.B. and organ. *S. W.*

Valerianus in cubiculo Cæciliam, A., 2 violins, viola, oboe and continuo (antiphon for St. Cecilia's Day). *S.* (incomplete).

*Veritas mea et misericordia, S.A.T.B. *S.*

Vexilla regis prodeunt, SS., 2 violins and continuo. *Mod.* (autograph).

Volo Pater ut ubi ego sum, S.A.T.B., S.A.T.B., and organ. *S.*

IX. INSTRUMENTAL MUSIC

Toccatas[1] and other pieces for cembalo. *B. BM.* (Add. 14244, 32161) *Mil. MC. N. S. W.* (some doubtful).

Sonate a quattro, 2 violins, viola and violoncello. *S. D.* (incomplete). Parts of these are also included in a set of six con-

[1] The MSS. exhibit such confusion that it is impossible to give a detailed list here. The volume (in private hands) described by Mr. J. S. Shedlock in the *Sammelband der Internationalen Musikgesellschaft*, Jahrgang vi. No. 1, will probably throw some light on the correct arrangement of movements; the article appeared too late for me to do more than mention it here.

certos for strings.   *C. BM.*
(printed parts, and fragments
in Add. MS. 32587).
Suite for flute and cembalo in F
(16 June 1699).   *S.*
Suite for flute and cembalo in G
(June 1699).   *S.*
Sonata for 2 flutes, 2 violins and
continuo in A.   *S.*
Sonata for flute, 2 violins and
continuo in F.   *S*

Sonata for 3 flutes and continuo
in F.   *S.*
Twelve Symphonies for Orchestra
(begun 1 June 1715).   *LB.*
(autograph).
*Sonata for flute, 2 violins and
continuo in D.   *BL.*
*Six Preludes and Fugues for cem-
balo.   *MC.*
*Six Concertos for cembalo.   *BM.*
(Add. 32431).

X. THEORETICAL WORKS, &c.

Fifteen fugues in two parts.   *N.*
Canon for two voices.   *BM.* (Add.
14166).
Studio a quattro sulla nota ferma.
BM. (Add. 14166).
Varie partite obligate al basso.
MC.

Regole per principianti.   *BM.*
(Add. 14244, 31517) *MC.*
Discorso sopra un caso particolare.
Printed in Kirnberger's *Kunst
des reinen Satzes.*

ADDITIONAL NOTES

Pages 6–7. *Parentage, and date and place of birth*

Ulisse Prota-Giurleo, in his privately-printed *Alessandro Scarlatti " il Palermitano "* (Naples, 1926), established that Palermo was the composer's birthplace, but did not himself go to Sicily to discover the actual date of birth. This was first ascertained, from the parish registers, by Paolo Dotto and published by him in the *Giornale di Sicilia* (Palermo) for September 3–4, 1926. The entry refers to " Pietro Alessandro Gaspare Scarlata ", born on May 2, 1660, and baptised next day. More recently Ottavio Tiby has made a much more thorough search through the parish registers of Palermo and published the results in an article, " La famiglia Scarlatti ", in the *Journal of Renaissance and Baroque Music* (Rome) for June, 1947. The composer's father, Pietro Scarlata, was born at Trapani and married Eleonora D'Amato, of Palermo, on May 5, 1658. They had eight children in all, the others being Anna Maria Antonia Diana (*b.* February 8, 1659), Anna Maria (*b.* December 8, 1661), Melchiorra Brigida (*b.* October 5, 1663), Vincenzo Placido (*b.* October 15, 1665), Francesco Antonio Nicola (*b.* December 5, 1666), Antonio Giuseppe (*b.* January 15, 1669) and Tommaso (precise date of birth uncertain). Anna Maria Antonia Diana died on October 28, 1659, at the age of eight months, and her first two Christian names were given also to her younger sister.

Page 8. *Early family history*

Prota-Giurleo's researches in Neapolitan archives produced some documentary evidence about the early lives of several members of the family.

In statements made before her marriage in May, 1688, Alessandro's sister Melchiorra declared that she left Palermo in 1672, aged about nine, for Rome, where she stayed for ten years, until 1682, when she came to Naples. She had lived at Naples for six years and was about twenty-five years old. Melchiorra supplied official confirmation of her statement about her stay in Rome. The *Curia Romana*, in an accompanying document, vouched for the fact that she had lived in Rome from June, 1672 to September, 1682.

In a declaration before his marriage, early in 1690, Francesco Scarlatti said he was about twenty-two years of age, a native of

Palermo, and had been brought as a boy of six or seven to Naples, where he had lived for sixteen years, never having left the city. In a statement relative to Anna Maria Scarlatti's second marriage in February, 1699, her youngest brother, Tommaso, declared that he was aged twenty-two, born at Palermo, and came to Naples so young that he did not recall anything about it. Before his own marriage on May 30, 1701, he said he was about twenty-four, and had lived at Naples since infancy, never having left the city. Thus, according to his own accounts, Tommaso was born at Palermo about 1677 and was brought to Naples, say, between 1678 and 1682.

Alessandro himself, on the occasion of the second marriage of Anna Maria, in February, 1699, stated that he and Anna Maria left Palermo together for Rome, where they lived for seven or eight years, before he left her in Rome " with other relatives of ours " and came to Naples. We know from other sources that Alessandro came to Naples towards the end of 1683 and settled there in 1684, so if he only lived in Rome seven or eight years he and Anna Maria came together from Sicily in 1676 or 1677. This is improbable, though not quite impossible ; as Dent himself suggested, in discussing Prota-Giurleo's booklet in the *Monthly Musical Record* for November, 1926, it seems likely that Alessandro gave false information on this occasion owing to his sister's desire, at her second marriage, to pass herself off as younger than she really was. One of the documents says : " The bride . . . says she is only twenty-nine years old." She was thirty-seven.

The accuracy of the statements of Melchiorra and Francesco can be checked, since Tiby discovered their precise dates of birth. Melchiorra, born at Palermo on October 5, 1663, told the truth, and Francesco, born there on December 5, 1666, was not far out in his estimate of his own age. Tiby blames him, saying that in his marriage documents in 1690 he declared he was about twenty-two, when in fact he was twenty-four, " whence we see that it is not only women who make mistakes about their age ! " But this is rather superficial and takes no account of Francesco having been born at the end of 1666 and having married at the beginning of 1690 (the precise date is unknown, but his first child was born on December 23 of the same year). He was, in fact, just twenty-three, which is not far removed from " about twenty-two ". It seems to have been not uncommon at this period for people to be unaware of their precise birthdays. Perhaps the " name-day " was celebrated instead, but as Francesco probably grew up as an inmate of one of the Neapolitan Conservatorii it is unlikely that much fuss was made of him on either occasion.

What of Tommaso ? Tiby, having failed to find the registra-
tion of his birth or baptism, falls back on the formula " born at
Palermo between 1669 and 1672 " for this youngest of the
Scarlattis, the latter date depending on the generally accepted
account of the family's migration from Sicily. According to this
the father, Pietro, " left Palermo in 1672 with his . . . children,
and established himself at Rome ; the two youngest sons,
Francesco and Tommaso, were not taken to Rome, but left at
Naples, where both remained until they were grown up. This
suggests that Pietro or his wife may have had relatives at Naples,
who would take charge of them."[1] Now Melchiorra's statement
is consistent in itself and supported by an official declaration, so
we may be certain that she, at any rate, came to Rome in June,
1672. Alessandro must have been there at about the same time
if he was, as tradition has it, a pupil of Carissimi, who died on
January 12, 1674. He himself says Anna Maria came with him.
Therefore it does seem likely that Alessandro, Anna Maria, and
Melchiorra came to Rome together in June, 1672, probably to stay
with those " other relatives of ours ". The parents, however,
would seem not to have come, for Tommaso's statements imply
that he was born at Palermo in 1677. There seems no reason why
he should have lied about his age. If he was actually born before
the supposed general migration of 1672 he must have been under
the impression that he was twenty-two when he was actually, at
least, twenty-seven, and according to Tiby's formula, anything
between twenty-seven and thirty. This is hard to believe.
Tommaso's two statements are so difficult to reconcile with the
accepted story that they have been quietly ignored and a suitable
date of birth fabricated for him. The process began with Prota-
Giurleo. He produced the entry concerning his death : " A primo
agosto 1760. Tomaso Scarlato morì d'anni 95 . . . " This gives
the impossibly early date of 1665 for his birth. Such statements
of age in parish registers of deaths seem to have been the results
of the merest guess-work ; when they can be checked from the
registers of births they are nearly always found to be wrong. But
Prota-Giurleo just assumed that the parish priest wrote 95 in error
for 85, giving 1675 for the birth. In the booklet edited by S. A.
Luciani on the occasion of the Scarlatti Festival at Siena in 1940
Tommaso's birth is given as 1665 in one place and 1675 in another ;
Della Corte and Gatti give 1675 ; Dent and Loewenberg in *Grove*,
third and fourth editions, gave *c.* 1670, which was a convenient
formula to bring him into line with the rest and with the theory

[1] Dent in Grove's *Dictionary of Music and Musicians*, fourth edition.

of a general migration in 1672.   But this was only done by ignoring Tommaso's own statements.

The Neapolitan relatives, unlike the Roman ones, are purely hypothetical. It seems almost certain that Francesco and Tommaso came to Naples not to stay with relatives but to enter one of the Conservatorii to which, having been born in the Kingdom of Naples, they had the right of entry (the Conservatorio dei Figliuoli Dispersi at Palermo had not yet begun to provide a musical education for its inmates). Now that we know precisely when Francesco was born, we can see that his statement implies that he was sent to Naples between the end of 1672 and 1674, though of course he may easily have been a little out in his reckoning; Tommaso would seem to have followed considerably later, say between 1678 and 1682, possibly as an orphan after the death of his parents in Sicily.   (Nothing is known about the parents' deaths, except that the father was dead when Alessandro got married.) Salvatore Di Giacomo noted an entry in the registers of the Conservatorio di Sant' Onofrio at Naples, concerning shoe repairs for one "Scarlati" in 1689. The reference is probably to Tommaso.

One may surmise that the parents were poor and that those of the children with evident musical gifts were sent to places where they could be best developed.   For the Scarlattis there were two such places : Rome, where they had relatives ; and Naples, where free education for poor male children was available in the Conservatorii. It may seem unnatural for the parents to have dispersed their children in this way, but it is unwise to assume that the seventeenth-century attitude in such things was the same as our own.   The letters of Salvator Rosa, for example, show a positively Chinese harshness : if the child was male he kept it ; if it was female it went straight into the foundling hospital. And, in any case, even those who hold (without evidence) that Pietro Scarlatti accompanied his elder children to Rome must admit that he sent the younger ones to Naples.

Page 8.   *Scarlatti's teacher in Rome*

Documents from the archives of the Arciconfraternità del SS. Crocifisso, published by Domenico Alaleona in the appendix to his *Studi sulla storia dell'oratorio musicale in Italia* (Turin, 1908), include one of January 27, 1679, concerning the commission of a Latin oratorio from "il Scarlattino alias il Siciliano ". This supports the tradition that he was a pupil of Carissimi, whose oratorios were written for this same confraternity.

Page 8. *Marriage in Rome*

The results of researches in Roman archives by Pasquale Fienga were published in two articles in the *Revue Musicale*.[1] Fienga discovered that Alessandro was married to Antonia Anzalone, a native of Rome, in the church of Sant' Andrea delle Fratte on April 12, 1678—before his eighteenth birthday. Their first child, Pietro Filippo, was born on January 5, 1679, before any of his operas, or the above-mentioned oratorio, had been performed.

Pages 9 & 23-4. *Scarlatti's first opera*

Gli Equivoci nel Sembiante was produced in February, 1679, at the Teatro Capranica, before being given privately at the Collegio Clementino.

Page 8. *Neapolitan operatic history*

The company of the *Febi Armonici* was Roman, rather than Venetian, and included Francesco Cirillo, born at Grumo Nevano, near Naples, and brought up in Rome, afterwards composer of some of the earliest native Neapolitan operas. The company enjoyed in Rome the protection of the Spanish Ambassador to the Vatican, Count d'Ognatte, who called them to Naples after he had been appointed Viceroy in that city.

Pages 8, 31, & 34. *Scarlatti's earliest connexions with Naples*

On the basis of later researches, rather unsatisfactorily summarised in his " Breve Storia del Teatro di Corte e della Musica a Napoli nei Secoli XVII–XVIII " (in the volume *Il Teatro di Corte del Palazzo Reale di Napoli*, Naples, 1952), Prota-Giurleo states that the Neapolitan Duke of Maddaloni made Scarlatti's acquaintance in the course of a visit to Rome in May and June, 1679, and attended a performance of *Gli Equivoci nel Sembiante*. This opera was performed in the Duke of Maddaloni's own Palazzo at Naples in March, 1680, quite possibly under Scarlatti's own direction. The opera was also produced at the Royal Palace on December 21, 1681.

Scarlatti's first original work for Naples was the opera *Psiche, ovvero Amore innamorato*, unknown to Dent, performed at the Royal Palace on December 23, 1683, and subsequently at the Teatro San Bartolomeo. A document published by Prota-Giurleo (" Breve Storia . . . " pp. 37–8) shows conclusively that the composer was in charge of the whole season of opera at Naples. Even if he did not direct the performances of *Gli Equivoci nel Sembiante* in 1680 and 1681, or come to visit his sister Melchiorra

---

[1] " La véritable patrie et la famille d'Alessandre Scarlatti " (January, 1929), and " Giuseppe Scarlatti et son incertaine ascendance directe " (February, 1932).

or his younger brothers, the date of his first connexions with Naples can certainly be advanced to 1683.

Page 34. *Appointment at Naples*

Prota-Giurleo (*op. cit.*, p. 39) states that he found no documentary evidence for Scarlatti's appointment as Maestro di Cappella to the Royal Chapel at Naples. Dent gives the date of appointment, February 17, 1684, together with his source : Archivio di Stato, *Scrivania di Razione e Ruota de' Conti*, vol. iii, fol. 82 *verso*. Among Dent's manuscript Scarlatti files, which he allowed me to examine when I was revising his *Grove* articles, was a long list of extracts from these archives in the hand of Cav. Giacomo Leo. It included this one concerning the appointment, with this reference.

It was after Ziani's *death*, on February 12, that Scarlatti got this post.

Pages 34–35. *Francesco Scarlatti*

We now have more information about Francesco, and the suggestion that his twenty-six years' service at Palermo was an invention on his part is no longer acceptable. He secured permission to return to Sicily in February, 1691, and remained there as Maestro di Cappella of some unidentified institution (not the Royal Chapel) for a quarter of a century. Doubts about this long residence at Palermo have been dissipated by Tiby's discovery of documents concerning his family and the death (in 1706) of his wife. His application for the post in Vienna was published by La Mara (" Briefe alter Wiener Hofmusiker ", in *Musikbuch aus Österreich*, VII Jahrgang, 1910) (June 29, 1715, after the death a few months earlier of Marc' Antonio Ziani in Vienna) :—

Holy, Imperial and Royal Catholic Majesty!

The Maestro di Cappella of your Imperial and Catholic Majesty having passed on to another life, if your Maestro di Cappella Fux should succeed to that post, I should venture (in that case) humbly to petition for a most clement glance towards my person, who for twenty-six years have held the position of Maestro di Cappella at Palermo, with the universal approbation of all virtuosi and composers of music.

If you should consider me worthy of so much honour, as would be (in the above-mentioned case) that of being deemed capable of succeeding to the post of the same Maestro di Cappella, I should hold it the utmost glory were my poor notes put to the test, in Church as in the Theatre and in your Majesty's Chamber, the which I would willingly submit to the judgment of anyone skilled

in the Art, and I would undertake to make known the insufficiency
of my talent ; meanwhile, hoping for such most clement favour,
prostrate before your Royal and Imperial Throne I consecrate
myself for ever,
> your Holy, Imperial and Royal Catholic Majesty's most humble
> and most
>> reverent servant and subject,
>> Francesco Scarlatti.

Apparently he succeeded only too well in making known the
insufficiency of his talent, for he did not get the job. He seems to
have returned to Naples and the service of the Royal Chapel. He
certainly drew his salary there in February, 1719. And then, a
little later, we find him in London. He gave a concert at
Hickford's Room on May 1, 1719 (more than a year before that
mentioned by Dent) and is mentioned in a letter from James
Brydges, Duke of Chandos, to Dr. Arbuthnot, of January 21, 1720 :[1]

" In my lre of yesterday I forgot to desire you wou'd send
Scarlatti's Brother down whom you recommended to me and let me
know wt Terms he will come to me upon."

As he does not appear on the list of musicians employed in the
Canons Concert it seems that Francesco did not take up this
engagement.

It is now considered improbable that Domenico Scarlatti was
in London for the production of *Narciso* in 1719.

Francesco gave another concert at Hickford's Room on
March 16, 1724, and it is probable that he was the " Signior
Scarlotti " for whose benefit a concert was given at " Mr. Johnson's
Great Room ", Dublin, on February 13, 1741.

Pages 24, 35-7, & 108. *A Libel on Anna Maria*

Alessandro's sister Anna Maria has acquired a certain notoriety
owing to two dubious episodes in the family history. There is,
however, something to be said in her defence.

Dent mentions that Scarlatti was in bad odour with the Court
of the Vicar in Rome in 1679, on account of the secret marriage of
his sister with an ecclesiastic. It was assumed that this was Anna
Maria, because at the time she was the only known sister of
Alessandro, but since then Prota-Giurleo has introduced us to
Melchiorra, and it may equally well have been this sister who
incurred the displeasure of the Papal authorities (" marriage " is
here probably a relative term). It is true that Anna Maria was

---

[1] In the Huntington Library, San Marino, California.

the elder sister and Melchiorra was aged only fifteen years and four months, but that is quite old enough for a Sicilian girl, outside parental control, to have got herself into trouble. The point is that the charge against Anna Maria is not proved.

One is all the more inclined to give Anna Maria the benefit of the doubt in the case of the Roman episode on discovering that she has almost certainly been libelled about the Neapolitan episode five years later. As Dent mentions, Alessandro owed his appointment as Maestro di Cappella to the fact that one of his sisters was the mistress of Don Giovanni de Leone, Secretary of Justice to the Viceroy. On the day of his appointment old Provenzale, the second *maestro*, who apparently expected to get the job himself, resigned, and six of the singers of the Royal Chapel left with him. Their places were taken by singers and instrumentalists who had been brought from Rome by Alessandro (*see* the documents published by Prota-Giurleo in his " Breve Storia . . . "). Even though Don Giovanni and his friends were subsequently relieved of their offices and disgraced, Alessandro retained his position. But his sister and her fellow *puttane commedianti* were ordered either to leave the city or to betake themselves to a convent. They chose the latter alternative, but this is, of course, not to say that they took the veil! It would be absurd to suppose that the nuns, even of Naples, were recruited in this fashion.

The description of these ladies as *puttane commedianti*, taken in conjunction with the fact that Anna Maria is known to have made at least one appearance on the stage, and her presumed identification with the sister of Alessandro who was in trouble in Rome in 1679, have sufficed to persuade everybody that it was she to whom he owed his Neapolitan appointment in 1684. Prota-Giurleo failed to see that the documents he discovered pointed rather towards *Melchiorra*. We have proof that Melchiorra came to Naples from Rome in September, 1682 ; Alessandro came there in the autumn of 1683 to prepare the performance of *Psiche* and other operas in that winter ; he decided to make his home there on being offered the post in the Royal Chapel through the influence of his sister. He himself states clearly that when he came to Naples he left Anna Maria in Rome " with other relatives of ours ". His appointment dates from February 17, 1684. Anna Maria, supposing that she followed him to Naples (there is no evidence for this), would have had to be a rapid worker to have installed herself in so short a space of time into a position of such influence ; whereas Melchiorra had been nearly eighteen months at Naples. In the absence of any evidence at all that Anna Maria was in the city the case against Melchiorra looks very black.

Dent really seems to have thought that the sister in question took the veil. But both Anna Maria and Melchiorra subsequently married (the former twice).

Pages 38 & 69. *Alessandro's Family*

As already mentioned, Alessandro married Antonia Anzalone in Rome in 1678. Besides the three children born at Naples, known to Dent, there were five more born in Rome, and two more born at Naples—ten in all. So Alessandro was certainly justified in speaking of his " numerosa famiglia ". The list is as follows: Pietro Filippo, *b.* Rome, January 5, 1679 ; Benedetto Bartolomeo, *b.* Rome, August 24, 1680 ; Alessandro Raimondo, *b.* Rome, December 23, 1681 ; Flaminia Anna Catarina, *b.* Rome, April 10, 1683 ; Cristina Eleonora Maddalena, *b.* Rome, April 6, 1684 ; Giuseppe Domenico, *b.* Naples, October 26, 1685 ; Giuseppe Nicola Ruperto, *b.* Naples, February 17, 1689 ; Caterina Eleonora Emilia, *b.* Naples, November 15, 1690 ; Carlo Francesco Giacomo, *b.* Naples, May 5, 1692 ; Giovan Francesco Diodato, *b.* Naples, May 7, 1695. The dates of birth of the first five were established by Fienga, except that by a slip he gave the birth of Alessandro Raimondo as December 23, 1684. This would have meant that he was born only eight months after Cristina Eleonora Maddalena. The true date, 1681, has now been confirmed. Scarlatti's wife evidently stayed in Rome until the birth of her fifth child, before joining Alessandro at Naples. Prota-Giurleo (" Breve Storia . . . " pp. 41, 43) has passages of pure fantasy, about Benedetto Bartolomeo dying at Naples " deprived of maternal care " and Alessandro going to Rome in 1685 to fetch his family, based entirely on Fienga's wrong date. Benedetto Bartolomeo did die at Naples on August 21, 1684, but his mother was surely with him.

Page 38. *Scarlatti's salary at Naples*

The statement that Alessandro apparently received no stipend after February, 1685, is based either on incomplete surviving records, or incomplete research (probably by Giacomo Leo). It conflicts with the documented information on p. 69 that Scarlatti wrote to complain in February, 1699, that his salary was four months in arrears.

Page 72. *Il Figlio delle Selve*

The opera of this title produced in Rome in 1687 and (probably) at Florence in 1688 was by Cosimo Bani. Scarlatti's setting was written for the theatre of Queen Marie Casimir of Poland and first performed in December, 1708 (according to Alfred Loewenberg in *Grove*), or on January 17, 1709 (according to Alberto Cametti).

Page 102. *Arminio*

The opera of this title produced at Pratolino in 1703 is now generally ascribed to Scarlatti.

Pages 113-114. *Alessandro Scarlatti at Urbino*

An article by B. Ligi, " La Cappella Musicale del Duomo d'Urbino ", in *Note d'Archivio* (Rome) for January–December, 1925, gives a list of the Maestri di Cappella. They include: " 1705 10 Feb.–1708 28 Oct., Pietro Scarlatti da Roma ". This is not only an addition to our scanty knowledge of the career of Pietro, Alessandro's eldest son, but it also provides a reason for Alessandro's own visit to Urbino in 1707.

Page 114. *L'Humanità nelle Fere*

" Probably a revival of an earlier work under a new title "— it was actually a revival of an earlier work under the same title. The opera was first produced at the Royal Palace, Naples, in 1691.

Pages 114-115. *Compositions of 1708*

A cantata *La Vittoria della Fede* was performed in Queen Marie Casimir's theatre on September 12, 1708. And, as mentioned above, *Il Figlio delle Selve* belongs to this year, or the very beginning of 1709.

Page 117. *Return to Naples*

There is no reason to doubt that Scarlatti was definitely reinstated as Maestro di Cappella. His office is named in all the libretti of operas produced at Naples in 1709–10. The repetition of the orders for his reinstatement by the new Viceroy, Count Daun, in 1713 was in accordance with Neapolitan custom, each new Viceroy appointing his own officials or confirming the appointments of his predecessor. Serenatas by Scarlatti were performed at Naples in 1711 and 1712.

The date of *L'Amor Volubile e Tiranno* is 1709 (not 1707).

The oratorio *S. Filippo Neri* was first performed in Rome in 1705.

Page 127. *The Intermezzo*

The date of Pergolesi's *Serva Padrona* is 1733, not 1731, and it is very far from being the first *intermezzo* recognised as an independent organism. We are inclined to think too exclusively of the *intermezzo* as a Neapolitan speciality, owing to that city having produced, in *La Serva Padrona*, the classic example and the only one at all well known today. But Taddeo Wiel records the performance of *intermezzi* between the acts of Antonio Bononcini's

La Regina creduta Re at Venice in 1706—long before the comic scenes had won their independence at Naples. After that date separate *intermezzi* were quite frequent at Venice.

Pages 127–128. *The Scarlattis and the origins of Neapolitan comic opera*

Claudio Sartori in " Gli Scarlatti a Napoli " (*Rivista musicale italiana*, September–October, 1942) has some fascinating speculations about the possibility that Alessandro Scarlatti had a good deal more to do with the early stages of Neapolitan comic opera than had been hitherto thought. The first recorded example of Neapolitan comic opera is no longer *Patrò Calienno de la Costa* (1709) but *La Cilla*. Sartori succeeds in pushing back the date of this work to 1706. Among other early works in this style are *Lo Spellachia* (1709) with music by Tommasiello de Mauro and another musician who did not wish to be named : " Lo primmo e terzo Atto l'ha fatto n'auto Vertoluso, che non vo essere conosciuto, pe n'essere nommenato . . . "; *Le Fenziune Abbentorate* (1710) with Tommaso Scarlatti among the singers ; *Li Viecchie Coffejate* (1710) also with Tommaso Scarlatti ; and *Lo Petrachio* (Aversa 1711), by Francesco Scarlatti, who signs the dedication in the libretto together with Nicola Pagano, who was the husband of Melchiorra Scarlatti, and who was apparently on this occasion the impresario. Quite a family affair. Sartori points out that the libretto of *Lo Petrachio* includes two characters who do not speak in Neapolitan dialect and that at least two of their arias have words that appear in Alessandro's opera *Gl'Inganni Felici*. He suggests that Alessandro provided the music for all the fifteen arias not in dialect, and that he was the musician who did not wish to be named in *Lo Spellachia* and also the anonymous " azzellente autore " mentioned in the libretto of *Patrò Calienno de la Costa*.

This brilliant piece of imaginative research by Sartori illustrates the need to re-examine older findings in the light of more recent discoveries. Croce, sixty years ago, noted that one Nicola Pagano was impresario of the Teatro dei Fiorentini at Naples in 1708. Prota-Giurleo, thirty years later, discovered that Melchiorra Scarlatti married Nicola Pagano, then a musician of the Royal Chapel, " professore di viola e di contrabasso ", in 1688. But until Sartori wrote his article no one had connected these two facts. In addition to Melchiorra's husband, the second husband of Anna Maria, Nicola Barbapiccola, had also tried his hand at theatrical direction. In 1703–04 he was impresario of the Teatro San Bartolomeo, and responsible for the production there of *Giustino*, an early opera by Domenico Scarlatti, and of Pollaroli's *Irene*, with additions (thirty-three arias) by Domenico. Croce also mentions Barbapiccola. In 1708 he was Royal Naval Contractor at the Naples Arsenal, and a passion play was performed several times at his house during Lent of that year and repeated elsewhere in 1709 under his direction.

Pages 139–140. *Scarlatti and the Neapolitan Conservatorii*

It is not true that Scarlatti was appointed master at the Conservatorio dei Poveri di Gesù Cristo in 1709. He had taught at the Conservatorio di Santa Maria di Loreto for one month only in 1689 and had no other connexion with these famous schools of music.

Page 164. *Griselda*

This was not quite Scarlatti's last opera, though it is the last surviving one. It was followed by *La Virtù negli Amori*, produced at the Teatro Capranica in Rome on November 16, 1721.

p. 206 *et seq.   Catalogue of Works*

I. OPERAS

Some revision of Dent's catalogue is necessary as the result of more recent research. Additional information here is drawn from the following publications :—

Alfred Lorenz, *Alessandro Scarlattis Jugendoper*, Augsburg, 1927.

Alberto Cametti, " Carlo Sigismondo Capeci, Alessandro e Domenico Scarlatti e la Regina di Polonia a Roma ", in *Musica d'Oggi*, February, 1931.

E. Zanetti and C. Sartori, " Contributo a un Catalogo delle Opere Teatrali di Alessandro Scarlatti ", in *Gli Scarlatti*, Siena, 1940.

Claudio Sartori, " Dori e Arione, due opere ignorate di Alessandro Scarlatti ", in *Note d'Archivio*, January–February, 1941.

Ulisse Prota-Giurleo, " Breve Storia del Teatro di Corte e della Musica a Napoli nei Sec. XVII–XVIII ", in *Il Teatro di Corte del Palazzo Reale di Napoli*, Naples, 1952.

Alfred Loewenberg, " Catalogue of Works ", in *Grove*, fifth edition, 1954.

Dent's abbreviations for the libraries where the manuscripts and libretti are to be found (p. 206) are used below, with the additions:—

BU.   Bologna, Biblioteca Universitaria.

FBM.   Florence, Biblioteca Marucelliana.

WLC.   Washington, Library of Congress.
VR.   Venice, Fondazione Giorgio Cini, Rolandi Collection.

Dent (p. 210) mentions five operas ascribed by Florimo and others to Scarlatti "without any apparent documentary evidence".

Ajace is accepted by Lorenz and Zanetti-Sartori, on the basis of a manuscript volume of 37 arias (*N.*) corresponding with the libretto (*BU. & N.*) of Naples, 1697. Loewenberg lists it as an adaptation by Scarlatti. However, Prota-Giurleo (p. 59) quotes from the contemporary *Avvisi di Napoli*, according to which this setting was by Gasparini.

Comodo Antonino, on the other hand, not accepted by Lorenz or Zanetti-Sartori, is definitely a revision and adaptation by Scarlatti of an earlier opera. He is named in the *Avvisi* (Prota-Giurleo, p. 58). The work was first performed at Naples, Teatro S. Bartolomeo, November 18, 1696.

Etio [*sic*] is accepted by Lorenz, Zanetti-Sartori, and Loewenberg on the strength of a single manuscript aria, attributed to Scarlatti (*MC.*) and corresponding with the libretto (*BU.*) of Naples, 1686.

Muzio Scevola remains dubious. A volume of 56 arias and a duet (*N.*), apparently corresponding with the libretto (*BU. & N.*) of Naples, 1698, is attributed to Scarlatti, but in the hand of Florimo, not of the contemporary copyist. Prota-Giurleo (p. 59) says the work was certainly adapted for Naples by Scarlatti, but gives no documentary evidence and may be guessing. The value of the work of this remarkable researcher is often diminished by flights of fancy, to say nothing of misprints.

Penelope la Casta is certainly by Scarlatti, who, in spite of what Dent writes, is mentioned in the "Avviso al Lettore" in the libretto (*BU. & N.*) of Naples, 1696. *Penelope* is there stated to be Scarlatti's sixtieth opera.

Other operas, unknown to Dent in 1905, are :—

Psiche, ovvero Amore Innamorato, Naples, Royal Palace, December 23, 1683 (Libretto *WLC.*).

Fetonte, Naples, Royal Palace, November 22, 1685 (Prota-Giurleo, p. 44, apparently from the *Avvisi di Napoli*).

Dori, Naples, 1689 (Libretto *BU. & N.*, without composer's name, but corresponding with manuscript arias attributed to Scarlatti (*N. & Mod.*).

Bassiano, ovvero Il Maggior Impossibile, Naples, Teatro S. Bartolomeo, Spring, 1694 (Libretto, *VR.*).

Nerone fatto Cesare, Naples, Royal Palace, November 6, 1695 (Libretto *BU. & N.*; two manuscript volumes of 14 arias and 43 arias and duets survive in *N.*).

Creonte Tiranno di Tebe, Naples, Teatro S. Bartolomeo, 1699, with additions by Scarlatti to Pollaroli's setting (Libretto *BL. & BU.*).

La Fede Riconosciuta, Naples, Teatro S. Bartolomeo, Autumn, 1710 (Libretto *FBM. & BU.*); Scarlatti's one-hundredth work for the stage.

Numerous scores and fragments have been located since Dent wrote. They are listed in detail by Lorenz and Zanetti-Sartori. The most important are :—

Carlo Re d'Allemagna (Score *BU.*).
La Donna ancora è fedele (Score and volumes of 48 arias and duets, and 28 arias and duets, all *N.*).
Emireno (43 arias *MC.*, and 32 arias and a duet *N.*).
Gli Inganni Felici (34 arias *N.*).

Some more large collections of arias (*N.*) may not be included in Dent's " fragments ". They are important where no full score survives :—

Didone Delirante (31 arias, also 51 arias *Vat.*).
Tito Sempronio Gracco (44 arias).
Tiberio Imperatore d'Oriente (44 arias).

The following original libretti have been located :—

Arminio, Pratolino, 1703 (*BU.*).
Didone Delirante, Naples, Teatro S. Bartolomeo, 1696 (*BU.*).
Il Figlio delle Selve, Rome, Queen of Poland's theatre, 1708 (*BL.*).
Gerone Tiranno di Siracusa, Naples, Royal Palace, 1692 (*BU.*).
L'Humanità nelle Fere, Naples, Royal Palace, 1691 (*BL. & BU.*).
Tiberio Imperatore d'Oriente, Naples, Royal Palace and Teatro S. Bartolomeo, 1702 (*BL. & BU.*).

p. 207. *Carlo Re d'Allemagna*
   The Naples libretto is of 1716, not 1718.

   Dal Male il Bene
   The original title is *Tutto il Male non vien per nuocere.*

p. 208. *Gli Equivoci nel Sembiante*
   The Ravenna libretto is of 1685.

   Il Figlio delle Selve
   As mentioned above, first performed in 1708 or 1709,
   rather than 1687.

   Flavio Cuniberto
   Performed in Rome, Teatro Capranica, in 1696, not
   1698.

   L'Humanità nelle Fere
   First performed at Naples, Teatro S. Bartolomeo,
   February 25, 1691 (Prota-Giurleo, p. 51) ; also in the
   Royal Palace, December 22, 1691 (Loewenberg).

   Odoardo
   According to Prota-Giurleo (p. 63), rehearsals were
   begun but the work was never performed, owing to
   the death of Pope Innocent XII.

p. 209. *Olimpia Vendicata*
   Libretto dated 1686, but first performed on December 23, 1685.

   Teodosio
   Scarlatti is in fact mentioned in the libretto ; " Vieni
   e godi, se non altro, in esso l'abbigliamento, che ha
   sortito dell'armoniose Note del Sig. Alessandro
   Scarlatti Maestro di questa Real Cappella . . . ."

II. ORATORIOS

La Concettione della B.V., according to Loewenberg, was first
 given at Naples in 1693 as *I Dolori di Maria Sempre Vergine,*
 which is one of the works ascribed to Scarlatti of which
 Dent (p. 211) found no trace.
San Filippo Neri was first performed in Rome in 1705.

The other works of which Dent found no trace are all accepted
 by Loewenberg. *Il Trionfo del Valore* is mentioned in the
 Avvisi di Napoli (Prota-Giurleo, pp. 87–88).

Other oratorios, unknown to Dent, are :—

Ismaele Soccorso, Florence, 1695.
Il Martirio di Santa Orsola, Lyon, c. 1705.
Cain, Venice, 1706, Rome, 1710.
La Gloriosa Gara tra la Santità e la Sapienza, Rome, 1720.

III. Serenatas and Cantatas for Festivals, etc.

Additional works, unknown to Dent, include :—
Il Trionfo del Valore, Rome, 1708.
Le Glorie della Bellezza del Corpo e dell'Anima, Naples, 1709.
Untitled Serenatas, given at Naples in 1711, 1712, and 1713
are mentioned in the *Avvisi* (Prota-Giurleo, p. 89).

INDEX

MI

DATE DUE

#47-0108 Peel Off Pressure Sensitive